The Super Easy
Mediterranean
Diet Cookbook

2000 Days of Simple and Wholesome Recipes with Tips for a Rich and Flavorful Cuisine, Including a 30-Day Meal Plan for Beginners to Manage their Body

Vincent P. Wade

Table of Contents

Chapter 5 Beef, Pork, and Lamb

Chapter 6 Fish and Seafood

Chapter 7 Snacks and Appetizers

Chapter 8 Vegetables and Sides

Chapter 9 Vegetarian Mains

Chapter 10 Desserts

Chapter 11 Salads

Chapter 12 Pizzas, Wraps, and Sandwiches

Chapter 13 Pasta

Chapter 14 Staples, Sauces, Dips, and Dressings

Appendix 1: Measurement Conversion Chart

Appendix 2: The Dirty Dozen and Clean Fifteen

INTRODUCTION

Welcome to the world of the Mediterranean diet—a culinary journey that promises not only exquisite flavors and vibrant dishes but also a path to optimal health and well-being. As the author of this cookbook, I am thrilled to take you on a gastronomic adventure through the sun-kissed lands of the Mediterranean, where the art of nourishment intertwines with a rich tapestry of cultural traditions and a deep appreciation for the simple pleasures of life.

In recent years, the Mediterranean diet has gained widespread recognition and admiration for its numerous health benefits. From reducing the risk of chronic diseases to promoting longevity, this way of eating has captured the attention of health enthusiasts, researchers, and food lovers alike. But the Mediterranean diet is more than just a passing trend—it is a lifestyle deeply rooted in centuries of wisdom, ancient traditions, and a profound understanding of the connection between food, nature, and the human body.

In this cookbook, I invite you to explore the essence of the Mediterranean diet, to unravel its secrets, and to embrace its principles in your own culinary journey. Together, we will embark on a captivating voyage through the flavors, aromas, and textures of the Mediterranean region, where each dish tells a story and every ingredient holds the key to nourishment and vitality.

But what exactly is the Mediterranean diet? At its core, it is a way of eating inspired by the traditional dietary patterns of the Mediterranean countries, including Greece, Italy, Spain, and many others. It is characterized by an abundance of fresh fruits and vegetables, whole grains, legumes, lean proteins, and healthy fats such as olive oil and nuts. It celebrates the joy of sharing meals with loved ones, savoring each bite, and embracing the diversity and beauty of seasonal produce.

Throughout this cookbook, we will delve into the fundamental principles of the Mediterranean diet, exploring its origins, health benefits, and the science behind its remarkable effects on the body and mind. We will uncover the essential ingredients that grace the Mediterranean pantry, from luscious tomatoes and fragrant herbs to succulent seafood and tangy cheeses. We will master the cooking techniques that bring out the best in Mediterranean cuisine, from grilling to braising, from simmering to baking.

But the Mediterranean diet is more than just a collection of recipes and techniques—it is a lifestyle that extends beyond the kitchen walls. It encompasses the joy of physical activity, the connection to nature, the appreciation of local and seasonal produce, and the shared moments of gathering around a table filled with love and laughter. We will delve into these aspects of the Mediterranean lifestyle, understanding how they contribute to overall well-being and a sense of fulfillment.

As you embark on this Mediterranean culinary adventure, I encourage you to approach it with an open mind and a willingness to embrace new flavors, textures, and ingredients. Whether you are a seasoned cook or a novice in the kitchen, this cookbook will provide you with the knowledge, inspiration, and practical tips to embark on your own Mediterranean journey.

So, join me as we uncover the treasures of the Mediterranean diet, savor the goodness it has to offer, and nourish our bodies and souls with every bite. Together, let us embark on a path to health, happiness, and the joy of Mediterranean living.

Chapter 1 Mediterranean Diet Essentials

The Mediterranean Diet Unveiled

Origins of the Mediterranean Diet

The origins of the Mediterranean diet can be traced back thousands of years to the countries surrounding the Mediterranean Sea, including Greece, Italy, Spain, and Morocco. These regions share a rich history of agriculture, fishing, and culinary traditions that have heavily influenced their dietary practices.

The ancient Greeks and Romans, for example, enjoyed a diet based on whole grains, legumes, vegetables, fruits, olive oil, fish, and wine. Their cuisine incorporated fresh and local ingredients, reflecting the abundance of the Mediterranean region. This way of eating was not only flavorful but also provided essential nutrients for physical well-being.

In Italy, the traditional Mediterranean diet was shaped by the country's diverse landscapes and regional culinary traditions. Italian cuisine embraces the use of fresh vegetables, pasta, olive oil, tomatoes, herbs, and a variety of cheeses. Meals are often enjoyed with family and friends, emphasizing the social and communal aspects of eating.

Spain has its own unique contributions to the Mediterranean diet. Spanish cuisine incorporates a wide range of fresh vegetables, legumes, seafood, olive oil, cured meats (such as jamón), and spices like saffron and paprika. The Spanish culture also places great importance on leisurely dining experiences, with tapas and sharing plates being a popular way of enjoying meals.

Morocco, located at the western edge of the Mediterranean, showcases North African influences in the Mediterranean diet. Moroccan cuisine features a vibrant combination of flavors, incorporating spices such as cumin, coriander, and cinnamon. Dishes often include couscous, tagines (slow-cooked stews), olives, dates, and a variety of fruits and vegetables.

The modern concept of the Mediterranean diet as a health-promoting way of eating gained recognition in the mid-20th century. In the 1940s, the Seven Countries Study conducted by Ancel Keys and his colleagues revealed that populations in Mediterranean countries had lower rates of heart disease compared to those in Western countries. The study attributed this difference to the traditional dietary patterns observed in Mediterranean regions.

Since then, numerous scientific studies have highlighted the health benefits of the Mediterranean diet, including its positive effects on cardiovascular health, weight management, cognitive function, and longevity. Today, the Mediterranean diet has gained popularity worldwide as a sustainable and enjoyable approach to eating, emphasizing whole foods, plant-based ingredients, healthy fats, and moderate consumption of seafood, poultry, and dairy.

The origins of the Mediterranean diet are deeply rooted in the cultural traditions and agricultural practices of the Mediterranean region. Its enduring appeal lies in its combination of flavorful ingredients, nutritional balance, and a lifestyle that values community, leisurely meals, and appreciation for the simple pleasures of food.

Principles of the Mediterranean Diet

The Mediterranean diet is characterized by a set of principles that guide its dietary pattern and lifestyle practices. These principles include:

♦ Abundance of Plant-Based Foods: The Mediterranean diet places a strong emphasis on consuming a variety of plant-based foods. This includes fruits, vegetables, whole grains, legumes, nuts, and seeds. These foods provide essential vitamins, minerals, fiber, and antioxidants that contribute to overall health and well-being.

♦ Healthy Fats: The Mediterranean diet incorporates healthy fats, particularly monounsaturated fats, found in olive oil, avocados, and nuts. These fats are known to have a positive impact on heart health by reducing bad cholesterol levels (LDL cholesterol) and increasing good cholesterol levels (HDL cholesterol).

♦ Lean Proteins: While the Mediterranean diet is not strictly vegetarian, it favors lean protein sources such as fish, poultry, and legumes. Fish, especially fatty fish like salmon, sardines, and mackerel, are rich in omega-3 fatty acids, which are beneficial for heart health. Legumes, including lentils, chickpeas, and beans, are excellent plant-based protein sources.

♦ Moderate Consumption of Dairy: Dairy products like Greek yogurt and cheese are consumed in moderation in the Mediterranean diet. These provide calcium, protein, and other essential nutrients. However, the diet encourages choosing low-fat or reduced-fat options.

♦ Limited Red Meat: Red meat consumption is limited in the Mediterranean diet, with a focus on leaner protein sources instead. Red meat is occasionally enjoyed in smaller portions during special occasions or as an accent to a dish.

♦ Fresh Herbs and Spices: The Mediterranean diet relies on the flavors of fresh herbs and spices, such as basil, oregano, rosemary, thyme, and garlic. These ingredients add depth and complexity to dishes, reducing the need for excessive salt or unhealthy flavorings.

♦ Enjoyment of Meals and Social Connections: The Mediterranean diet emphasizes the enjoyment of meals in a relaxed and social setting. Sharing meals with family and friends is encouraged, as it fosters a sense of community and enhances the overall dining experience.

♦ Physical Activity and Balanced Lifestyle: The Mediterranean diet is not just about food; it promotes a balanced lifestyle that includes regular physical activity. Whether it's walking, cycling, gardening, or participating in recreational sports, staying active is an integral part of the Mediterranean way of life.

By following these principles, the Mediterranean diet promotes overall health, reduces the risk of chronic diseases like heart disease and diabetes, and supports sustainable and enjoyable eating habits. It is not a restrictive diet but rather a flexible and inclusive approach to nourishing the body and embracing a balanced lifestyle.

Health Benefits

The Mediterranean diet is renowned for its numerous health benefits, backed by extensive scientific research. Here are some key health benefits associated with the Mediterranean diet:

♦ Heart Health: The Mediterranean diet has been consistently linked to a reduced risk of heart disease and lower incidence of cardiovascular events, such as heart attacks and strokes. This is attributed to the diet's emphasis on healthy fats (such as monounsaturated fats found in olive oil), omega-3 fatty acids from fish, and high intake of fruits, vegetables, whole grains, and legumes. These components contribute to improved cholesterol levels, reduced inflammation, and better blood vessel function.

♦ Weight Management: The Mediterranean diet has been found to be effective in promoting healthy weight management. The diet's focus on whole, unprocessed foods, fiber-rich plant-based ingredients, and moderate portions of lean protein helps to increase satiety and reduce overeating. Additionally, the Mediterranean diet discourages excessive consumption of sugary foods, processed snacks, and unhealthy fats, which are commonly associated with weight gain.

♦ Diabetes Prevention and Management: Following the Mediterranean diet has been shown to lower the risk of developing type 2 diabetes. The diet's emphasis on whole grains, legumes, fruits, and vegetables, which are low on the glycemic index, helps to stabilize blood sugar levels and improve insulin sensitivity. Furthermore, the diet's healthy fats and moderate protein intake contribute to better blood sugar control.

♦ Cognitive Function: Several studies suggest that the Mediterranean diet may have a protective effect on cognitive health, reducing the risk of cognitive decline and Alzheimer's disease. The high intake of antioxidant-rich fruits, vegetables, and olive oil, along with the anti-inflammatory properties of the diet, are believed to support brain health and reduce oxidative stress and inflammation, which are associated with cognitive impairment.

♦ Cancer Prevention: While no diet can guarantee the prevention of cancer, research indicates that the Mediterranean diet may help

reduce the risk of certain types of cancer, including breast, colorectal, and prostate cancer. The diet's emphasis on plant-based foods, which provide an array of beneficial compounds like antioxidants and phytochemicals, is thought to have protective effects against cancer development.

♦ Longevity: The Mediterranean diet has been associated with increased longevity and a lower risk of premature death. Its nutrient-dense, antioxidant-rich foods, coupled with a balanced lifestyle that includes physical activity and social engagement, contribute to overall health and well-being, thereby promoting a longer and healthier life.

It's important to note that the Mediterranean diet's health benefits are not solely derived from individual food components, but rather the synergistic effect of the overall dietary pattern and lifestyle. By adopting the Mediterranean diet, individuals can enjoy a wide range of delicious and nutritious foods while reaping the rewards of improved health and well-being.

Sustainability

Sustainability is an essential aspect of the Mediterranean diet, promoting a harmonious relationship with the environment and the wise use of resources. Here's a closer look at the sustainability principles associated with the Mediterranean diet:

♦ Locally Sourced and Seasonal Foods: The Mediterranean diet emphasizes the use of locally sourced ingredients that are in season. This practice supports local farmers and reduces the carbon footprint associated with long-distance transportation of food. By choosing seasonal produce, individuals can enjoy the freshest and most flavorful ingredients while minimizing the environmental impact.

♦ Plant-Based Emphasis: The Mediterranean diet's focus on plant-based foods aligns with sustainable practices. Plant-based ingredients generally have a lower environmental footprint compared to animal products. By prioritizing fruits, vegetables, legumes, and whole grains, the diet promotes biodiversity, conserves water resources, and reduces greenhouse gas emissions.

♦ Reduced Meat Consumption: While the Mediterranean diet does include moderate amounts of fish, poultry, and dairy, it encourages the reduction of red meat consumption. Livestock production, particularly industrialized meat production, has significant environmental impacts, including deforestation, water pollution, and greenhouse gas emissions. By minimizing the consumption of red meat, the diet promotes more sustainable food choices.

♦ Seafood Choices: The Mediterranean region has a rich variety of seafood, and the diet incorporates fish as a lean protein source. However, it is important to choose sustainable seafood options to protect marine ecosystems. Selecting locally sourced and sustainably caught or farmed fish helps preserve fish stocks and marine biodiversity, ensuring the long-term viability of seafood resources.

♦ Minimizing Food Waste: The Mediterranean diet encourages mindful consumption and reducing food waste. By planning meals, using leftovers creatively, and properly storing perishable items, individuals can minimize the amount of food that goes to waste. Reducing food waste not only saves money but also reduces the environmental impact associated with production, transportation, and disposal of food.

♦ Traditional Food Preservation Methods: The Mediterranean diet draws on traditional food preservation methods such as drying, pickling, and fermenting. These techniques help extend the shelf life of seasonal produce and reduce food waste. Additionally, these preservation methods often require less energy compared to industrial food processing methods.

♦ Connection to Nature and Appreciation of Food: The Mediterranean diet encourages a deep connection to nature and an appreciation for the quality and flavors of food. This fosters an understanding of the origins of food, the importance of sustainable agricultural practices, and the value of supporting local and organic food systems.

By embracing these sustainability principles, the Mediterranean diet promotes responsible and conscious food choices that not only benefit individual health but also contribute to the long-term well-being of the planet. It encourages a holistic approach to eating that considers the environmental, social, and economic aspects of food production and consumption.

Essential Ingredients of the Mediterranean Pantry

The Mediterranean pantry is filled with a wide array of essential ingredients that form the foundation of the region's vibrant and flavorful cuisine. These ingredients are not only versatile in cooking but also offer numerous health benefits. Let's delve into the essential ingredients you can find in a Mediterranean pantry:

♦ Olive Oil: At the heart of Mediterranean cooking is olive oil, often referred to as "liquid gold." It is used as the primary source of fat in the diet, providing a rich and distinctive flavor to dishes. Extra virgin olive oil, cold-pressed from olives, is highly prized for its antioxidants and healthy monounsaturated fats.

♦ Fruits and Vegetables: The Mediterranean diet encourages a plentiful consumption of fruits and vegetables, which provide an array of vitamins, minerals, and fiber. Tomatoes, eggplants, zucchini, bell peppers, leafy greens, citrus fruits, figs, and grapes are just a few examples of the diverse range of produce used in Mediterranean cuisine.

♦ Whole Grains: Whole grains such as bulgur, farro, couscous, and whole wheat pasta are staples in the Mediterranean pantry. They offer a hearty and nutritious base for many dishes while providing complex carbohydrates, fiber, and essential nutrients.

♦ Legumes: Legumes, including chickpeas, lentils, beans, and peas, are excellent sources of plant-based protein, fiber, and minerals. They are a versatile ingredient in Mediterranean cooking, used in soups, stews, salads, and spreads like hummus.

♦ Nuts and Seeds: Almonds, walnuts, pistachios, and pine nuts are commonly found in the Mediterranean pantry. These nutrient-dense ingredients provide healthy fats, protein, and a satisfying crunch. Sesame seeds, flaxseeds, and chia seeds are also used for added texture and nutritional benefits.

♦ Fresh Herbs: Fresh herbs are a hallmark of Mediterranean cuisine, adding fragrance and depth of flavor to dishes. Basil, parsley, oregano, thyme, rosemary, and mint are frequently used. They can be added to sauces, salads, marinades, and dressings, enhancing the taste and nutritional profile of meals.

♦ Spices: Mediterranean dishes are often seasoned with a variety of spices that add complexity and warmth to the flavors. Commonly used spices include cumin, coriander, cinnamon, paprika, saffron, and turmeric. These spices not only enhance taste but also offer potential health benefits due to their antioxidant and anti-inflammatory properties.

♦ Seafood: The Mediterranean region is abundant in seafood, and it plays a prominent role in the diet. Fish like salmon, sardines, anchovies, and mackerel are rich in omega-3 fatty acids, which are beneficial for heart health. Other seafood options include shrimp, calamari, octopus, and mussels.

♦ Yogurt and Cheese: Mediterranean cuisine includes moderate amounts of yogurt and cheese. Greek yogurt is a staple, providing probiotics and protein. Feta cheese, halloumi, and mozzarella are popular choices for adding tang and creaminess to salads, pastas, and sandwiches.

♦ Olives and Capers: Olives, whether green or black, are ubiquitous in Mediterranean cuisine. They add a distinctive briny flavor to dishes and are consumed as snacks or incorporated into salads, pasta sauces, and spreads. Capers, derived from the flower buds of the caper bush, provide a unique tangy taste and are commonly used in Mediterranean sauces and marinades.

♦ Wine: Wine is an integral part of Mediterranean culture and is often consumed in moderation with meals. Red wine, in particular, is associated with the Mediterranean diet and is rich in antioxidants.

By stocking your pantry with these essential Mediterranean ingredients, you'll be equipped to create a diverse range of flavorful, healthy, and satisfying dishes. They form the backbone of the Mediterranean diet, ensuring that your meals are nourishing, delicious, and true to the region's culinary heritage.

Mastering Mediterranean Cooking Techniques

Mastering the cooking techniques used in Mediterranean cuisine allows you to unlock the full potential of the ingredients and create dishes that showcase the flavors and textures unique to this culinary tradition. Here are some key techniques to help you navigate the world of Mediterranean cooking:

♦ Sautéing: Sautéing is a fundamental technique used in Mediterranean cooking. It involves quickly cooking ingredients in a small amount of oil or fat over medium-high heat. This technique is often used to cook vegetables, meats, and seafood, allowing them to retain their natural flavors and develop a desirable caramelized exterior.

♦ Grilling: Grilling is a popular cooking method in Mediterranean cuisine, especially during the warm summer months. Whether using a barbecue grill or a stovetop grill pan, this technique imparts a smoky flavor to vegetables, meats, and fish. Marinating ingredients prior to grilling can enhance their taste and tenderness.

♦ Roasting: Roasting is a versatile technique used to bring out the natural sweetness and depth of flavor in various Mediterranean ingredients. It involves cooking food in the oven at a high temperature, often with a drizzle of olive oil and a sprinkle of herbs and spices. Roasting is particularly suited for vegetables, chicken, lamb, and root crops like potatoes and beets.

♦ Braising: Braising is a slow-cooking method that involves searing ingredients in a hot pan, then simmering them in a flavorful liquid, such as broth, wine, or tomato sauce. This technique is commonly used for tougher cuts of meat, such as lamb shanks or beef stew meat, as well as for vegetables like eggplant or artichokes. Braising tenderizes the ingredients and allows them to absorb the rich flavors of the liquid.

♦ Poaching: Poaching is a gentle and moist cooking technique widely used for delicate fish and eggs. It involves simmering the ingredients in a liquid, such as water, broth, or wine, until they are cooked through and tender. Poaching helps retain moisture and enhance the natural flavors of the food.

♦ Marinating: Marinating is a technique used to infuse ingredients with flavors and tenderize them. Meats, poultry, seafood, and vegetables can be marinated in a mixture of herbs, spices, garlic, citrus juice, and olive oil. Marinating allows the ingredients to absorb the flavors and results in more flavorful and succulent dishes.

♦ Mezzes and Dips: Mezzes are small dishes or appetizers that are commonly served in Mediterranean cuisine. These can include hummus, tzatziki, baba ganoush, and various other spreads and dips. Mastering the art of making these dips involves blending ingredients like chickpeas, yogurt, eggplant, tahini, garlic, and olive oil to achieve the desired creamy texture and balanced flavors.

♦ Fresh Herb and Spice Blends: The Mediterranean pantry is full of aromatic herbs and spices. Mastering the art of blending these flavors can elevate your dishes to new heights. Experiment with combinations like oregano and basil, cumin and coriander, or thyme and rosemary to create unique and vibrant flavor profiles.

♦ Embracing Simplicity: Mediterranean cuisine often celebrates simplicity by allowing the natural flavors of the ingredients to shine. Embrace techniques that highlight the freshness and quality of your chosen produce, whether it's a simple salad dressed with olive oil and lemon juice or a grilled fish seasoned with just a sprinkle of salt and pepper.

♦ Balancing Flavors: Mediterranean cooking is all about achieving a harmonious balance of flavors. Experiment with the combination of sweet, sour, salty, and bitter elements in your dishes. Use ingredients like lemon juice, vinegar, olives, capers, and fresh herbs to add brightness and complexity to your meals.

By mastering these Mediterranean cooking techniques, you'll gain the confidence and skills necessary to create authentic and delicious dishes that reflect the vibrant and diverse flavors of the region. Allow your creativity to flourish as you explore the endless possibilities of Mediterranean cuisine.

Embracing the Mediterranean Lifestyle

Embracing the Mediterranean lifestyle extends beyond the realm of food and encompasses a holistic approach to overall well-being. By adopting the principles of the Mediterranean diet and incorporating other aspects of Mediterranean living, you can enhance your health, happiness, and quality of life. Here's a closer look at the key components of embracing the Mediterranean lifestyle:

♦ Nourishing Food Choices: The Mediterranean diet forms the foundation of a nourishing and sustainable eating pattern. By prioritizing whole, unprocessed foods such as fruits, vegetables, whole grains, legumes, fish, and healthy fats, you provide your body with a wide range of nutrients and antioxidants. This not only promotes physical health but also contributes to mental well-being.

♦ Mindful Eating Habits: In the Mediterranean culture, meals are savored and enjoyed in the company of loved ones. By adopting mindful eating habits, such as slowing down during meals, paying attention to hunger and fullness cues, and engaging in meaningful conversations while dining, you can cultivate a healthier relationship with food and derive greater satisfaction from your meals.

♦ Active Lifestyle: Physical activity is an integral part of the Mediterranean lifestyle. Engaging in regular exercise, whether it's walking, cycling, swimming, or participating in sports, promotes cardiovascular health, strengthens muscles, and improves overall fitness. Incorporating physical activity into your daily routine not only benefits your physical well-being but also enhances your mood and reduces stress.

♦ Connection with Nature: The Mediterranean lifestyle embraces a deep connection with nature. Taking time to appreciate the beauty of the outdoors, whether it's walking in nature, tending to a garden, or enjoying picnics by the beach, can provide a sense of tranquility and rejuvenation. Connecting with nature has been shown to reduce stress levels, improve mental clarity, and enhance overall well-being.

♦ Social Engagement: Strong social connections are a cornerstone of Mediterranean living. Cultivating meaningful relationships, spending time with family and friends, and participating in community activities contribute to a sense of belonging and support. Engaging in social interactions and fostering positive relationships can enhance mental and emotional well-being.

♦ Stress Management: The Mediterranean lifestyle encourages effective stress management techniques. Taking time for relaxation, engaging in activities that bring joy and fulfillment, practicing mindfulness or meditation, and prioritizing self-care are important aspects of managing stress and promoting overall balance and harmony in life.

♦ Moderation and Enjoyment: The Mediterranean lifestyle emphasizes moderation rather than deprivation. Enjoying a glass of red wine with meals in moderation, savoring occasional indulgences of sweets or desserts, and celebrating special occasions with traditional dishes are part of the Mediterranean approach. By finding a balance between nourishing foods and occasional treats, you can cultivate a sustainable and enjoyable relationship with food.

♦ Cultural Traditions: Embracing the Mediterranean lifestyle means embracing the rich cultural traditions associated with the region. Exploring Mediterranean cuisines, traditions, music, art, and customs can deepen your appreciation for the diverse and vibrant heritage of the Mediterranean and provide a sense of connection to a larger community.

By embracing the Mediterranean lifestyle, you can experience a multitude of benefits that extend beyond physical health. Nourishing your body with wholesome foods, engaging in regular physical activity, connecting with nature, fostering social connections, managing stress, and finding joy in everyday life are all essential components of a holistic approach to well-being. Embrace the Mediterranean lifestyle and discover a path to a healthier, happier, and more fulfilling life.

30 Days Mediterranean Diet Meal Plan

DAYS	BREAKFAST	LUNCH	DINNER	SNACK/DESSERT
1	Marinara Eggs with Parsley	Quinoa with Artichokes	Tabbouleh	Honeyed Roasted Apples with Walnuts
2	Cauliflower Avocado Toast	Fasolakia (Greek Green Beans)	Orange-Tarragon Chicken Salad Wrap	Fruit Compote
3	Spinach Pie	Tomato Bulgur	Quinoa with Zucchini, Mint, and Pistachios	Pomegranate-Quinoa Dark Chocolate Bark
4	Breakfast Quinoa with Figs and Walnuts	Garbanzo and Pita No-Bake Casserole	Endive with Shrimp	Vanilla-Poached Apricots
5	Enjoy-Your-Veggies Breakfast	Brown Rice with Dried Fruit	Spinach-Arugula Salad with Nectarines and Lemon Dressing	Creamy Spiced Almond Milk
6	Morning Buzz Iced Coffee	Spicy Black Beans with Root Veggies	Tomato and Pepper Salad	Crunchy Sesame Cookies
7	Strawberry Basil Honey Ricotta Toast	Creamy Thyme Polenta	Flank Steak Spinach Salad	Date and Nut Balls
8	Egg Salad with Red Pepper and Dill	White Beans with Kale	Pipirrana (Spanish Summer Salad)	Honey-Vanilla Apple Pie with Olive Oil Crust
9	Tiropita (Greek Cheese Pie)	Vegetable Barley Soup	Four-Bean Salad	Brown Betty Apple Dessert
10	Mediterranean Fruit Bulgur Breakfast Bowl	Lemon and Garlic Rice Pilaf	Roasted Cauliflower "Steak" Salad	Honey Ricotta with Espresso and Chocolate Chips
11	Greek Yogurt and Berries	Chili-Spiced Beans	Classic Tabouli	Ricotta-Lemon Cheesecake
12	Mediterranean Omelet	Quinoa Salad with Tomatoes	Mediterranean Potato Salad	Tortilla Fried Pies
13	Hearty Berry Breakfast Oats	Herbed Wild Rice Dressing	Citrus Fennel Salad	Dark Chocolate Lava Cake
14	Crunchy Vanilla Protein Bars	Slow Cooker Vegetarian Chili	Beets with Goat Cheese and Chermoula	Lemon Coconut Cake
15	Buffalo Egg Cups	Couscous with Apricots	Arugula and Artichokes	Crispy Apple Phyllo Tart
16	Veggie Hash with Eggs	Crunchy Pea and Barley Salad	Greek Potato Salad	Baklava and Honey
17	Ricotta and Fruit Bruschetta	Asparagus Fries	Israeli Salad with Nuts and Seeds	Dark Chocolate Bark with Fruit and Nuts
18	Tortilla Española (Spanish Omelet)	Coriander-Cumin Roasted Carrots	Tuna Niçoise	Spanish Cream

DAYS	BREAKFAST	LUNCH	DINNER	SNACK/DESSERT
19	Berry Baked Oatmeal	Potato Vegetable Hash	No-Mayo Florence Tuna Salad	Chocolate Turtle Hummus
20	Turkish Egg Bowl	Roasted Broccoli with Tahini Yogurt Sauce	Wild Greens Salad with Fresh Herbs	Lightened-Up Baklava Rolls
21	Homemade Pumpkin Parfait	Grits Casserole	Riviera Tuna Salad	Mascarpone and Fig Crostin
22	Power Peach Smoothie Bowl	Lightened-Up Eggplant Parmigiana	Raw Zucchini Salad	Tahini Baklava Cups
23	Peachy Green Smoothie	Caponata (Sicilian Eggplant)	Traditional Greek Salad	Figs with Mascarpone and Honey
24	Portobello Eggs Benedict	Spicy Roasted Bok Choy	Tomato-Braised Chicken Thighs with Capers	Date and Honey Almond Milk Ice Cream
25	South of the Coast Sweet Potato Toast	Sweet-and-Sour Brussels Sprouts	One-Pan Parsley Chicken and Potatoes	Blueberry Compote
26	Egg in a "Pepper Hole" with Avocado	Caramelized Root Vegetables	Roasted Pork with Apple-Dijon Sauce	Strawberry-Pomegranate Molasses Sauce
27	Quickie Honey Nut Granola	Maple-Roasted Tomatoes	Bone-in Pork Chops	Whipped Greek Yogurt with Chocolate
28	Crostini with Smoked Trout	Greek Fasolakia (Green Beans)	Parmesan Artichokes	Fresh Figs with Chocolate Sauce
29	Greek Yogurt Parfait	Puréed Cauliflower Soup	One-Pan Mushroom Pasta with Mascarpone	Light and Lemony Olive Oil Cupcakes
30	Quick Low-Carb Avocado Toasts	Corn on the Cob	Vegetable Burgers	Chocolate Lava Cakes

Spinach and Feta Frittata

Prep time: 10 minutes | Cook time: 26 minutes | Serves 4

- 1 tablespoon olive oil
- ½ medium onion, peeled and chopped
- ½ medium red bell pepper, seeded and chopped
- 2 cups chopped fresh baby spinach
- 1 cup water
- 1 cup crumbled feta cheese
- 6 large eggs, beaten
- ¼ cup low-fat plain Greek yogurt
- ½ teaspoon salt
- ½ teaspoon ground black pepper

1. Press the Sauté button on the Instant Pot® and heat oil. Add onion and bell pepper, and cook until tender, about 8 minutes. Add spinach and cook until wilted, about 3 minutes. Press the Cancel button and transfer vegetables to a medium bowl to cool. Wipe out inner pot. 2. Place the rack in the Instant Pot® and add water. Spray a 1.5-liter baking dish with nonstick cooking spray. Drain excess liquid from spinach mixture, then add to dish with cheese. 3. In a separate medium bowl, mix eggs, yogurt, salt, and black pepper until well combined. Pour over vegetable and cheese mixture. Cover dish tightly with foil, then gently lower into machine. 4. Close lid, set steam release to Sealing, press the Manual button, and set time to 15 minutes. When the timer beeps, let pressure release naturally for 10 minutes, then quick-release any remaining pressure until the float valve drops. Press the Cancel button and open lid. Let stand for 10–15 minutes before carefully removing dish from pot. 5. Run a thin knife around the edge of the frittata and turn it out onto a serving platter. Serve warm.

Per Serving:

calories: 259 | fat: 19g | protein: 16g | carbs: 6g | fiber: 1g | sodium: 766mg

Tiropita (Greek Cheese Pie)

Prep time: 15 minutes | Cook time: 45 minutes | Serves 12

- 1 tablespoon extra virgin olive oil plus 3 tablespoons for brushing
- 1 pound (454 g) crumbled feta
- 8 ounces (227g) ricotta cheese
- 2 tablespoons chopped fresh mint, or 1 tablespoon dried
- mint
- 2 tablespoons chopped fresh dill, or 1 tablespoon dried dill
- ¼ teaspoon freshly ground black pepper
- 3 eggs
- 12 phyllo sheets, defrosted
- 1 tsp white sesame seeds

1. Preheat the oven to 350°F (180 C). Brush a 9 × 13-inch (23 × 33cm) casserole dish with olive oil. 2. Combine the feta and ricotta in a large bowl, using a fork to mash the ingredients together. Add the mint, dill, and black pepper, and mix well. In a small bowl, beat the eggs and then add them to the cheese mixture along with 1 tablespoon olive oil. Mix well. 3. Carefully place 1 phyllo sheet in the bottom of the prepared dish. (Keep the rest of the dough covered with a damp towel.) Brush the sheet with olive oil, then place a second phyllo sheet on top of the first and brush with olive oil. Repeat until you have 6 layers of phyllo. 4. Spread the cheese mixture evenly over the phyllo and then fold the excess phyllo edges in and over the mixture. Cover the mixture with 6 more phyllo sheets, repeating the process by placing a single phyllo sheet in the pan and brushing it with olive oil. Roll the excess phyllo in to form an edge around the pie. 5. Brush the top phyllo layer with olive oil and then use a sharp knife to score it into 12 pieces, being careful to cut only through the first 3–4 layers of the phyllo dough. Sprinkle the sesame seeds and a bit of water over the top of the pie. 6. Place the pie on the middle rack of the oven. Bake for 40 minutes or until the phyllo turns a deep golden color. Carefully lift one side of the pie to ensure the bottom crust is baked. If it's baked, move the pan to the bottom rack and bake for an additional 5 minutes. 7. Remove the pie from the oven and set aside to cool for 15 minutes. Use a sharp knife to cut the pie into 12 pieces. Store covered in the refrigerator for up to 3 days.

Per Serving:

calories: 230 | fat: 15g | protein: 11g | carbs: 13g | fiber: 1g | sodium: 510mg

Breakfast Quinoa with Figs and Walnuts

Prep time: 10 minutes | Cook time: 12 minutes | Serves 4

- 1½ cups quinoa, rinsed and drained
- 2½ cups water
- 1 cup almond milk
- 2 tablespoons honey
- 1 teaspoon vanilla extract
- ½ teaspoon ground
- cinnamon
- ¼ teaspoon salt
- ½ cup low-fat plain Greek yogurt
- 8 fresh figs, quartered
- 1 cup chopped toasted walnuts

1. Place quinoa, water, almond milk, honey, vanilla, cinnamon, and salt in the Instant Pot®. Stir to combine. Close lid, set steam release to Sealing, press the Rice button, and set time to 12 minutes. When the timer beeps, let pressure release naturally, about 20 minutes. 2. Press the Cancel button, open lid, and fluff quinoa with a fork. Serve warm with yogurt, figs, and walnuts.

Per Serving:

calories: 413 | fat: 25g | protein: 10g | carbs: 52g | fiber: 7g | sodium: 275mg

Greek Yogurt and Berries

Prep time: 5 minutes | Cook time: 30 minutes | Serves 4

- 4 cups plain full-fat Greek yogurt
- 1 cup granola
- ½ cup blackberries
- 2 bananas, sliced and frozen
- 1 teaspoon chia seeds, for topping
- 1 teaspoon chopped fresh mint leaves, for topping
- 4 teaspoons honey, for topping (optional)

1. Evenly divide the yogurt among four bowls. Top with the granola, blackberries, bananas, chia seeds, mint, and honey (if desired), dividing evenly among the bowls. Serve.

Per Serving:

calories: 283 | fat: 9g | protein: 12g | carbs: 42g | fiber: 5g | sodium: 115mg

Buffalo Egg Cups

Prep time: 10 minutes | Cook time: 15 minutes | Serves 2

- 4 large eggs
- 2 ounces (57 g) full-fat cream cheese
- 2 tablespoons buffalo sauce
- ½ cup shredded sharp Cheddar cheese

1. Crack eggs into two ramekins. 2. In a small microwave-safe bowl, mix cream cheese, buffalo sauce, and Cheddar. Microwave for 20 seconds and then stir. Place a spoonful into each ramekin on top of the eggs. 3. Place ramekins into the air fryer basket. 4. Adjust the temperature to 320ºF (160ºC) and bake for 15 minutes. 5. Serve warm.

Per Serving:

calories: 354 | fat: 29g | protein: 21g | carbs: 3g | fiber: 0g | sodium: 343mg

Mediterranean Omelet

Prep time: 10 minutes | Cook time: 12 minutes | Serves 2

- 2 teaspoons extra-virgin olive oil, divided
- 1 garlic clove, minced
- ½ red bell pepper, thinly sliced
- ½ yellow bell pepper, thinly sliced
- ¼ cup thinly sliced red onion
- 2 tablespoons chopped fresh basil
- 2 tablespoons chopped fresh parsley, plus extra for garnish
- ½ teaspoon salt
- ½ teaspoon freshly ground black pepper
- 4 large eggs, beaten

1. In a large, heavy skillet, heat 1 teaspoon of the olive oil over medium heat. Add the garlic, peppers, and onion to the pan and sauté, stirring frequently, for 5 minutes. 2. Add the basil, parsley, salt, and pepper, increase the heat to medium-high, and sauté for 2 minutes. Slide the vegetable mixture onto a plate and return the pan to the heat. 3. Heat the remaining 1 teaspoon olive oil in the same pan and pour in the beaten eggs, tilting the pan to coat evenly. Cook the eggs just until the edges are bubbly and all but the center is dry, 3 to 5 minutes. 4. Either flip the omelet or use a spatula to turn it over. 5. Spoon the vegetable mixture onto one-half of the omelet and use a spatula to fold the empty side over the top. Slide the omelet onto a platter or cutting board. 6. To serve, cut the omelet in half and garnish with fresh parsley.

Per Serving:

calories: 218 | fat: 14g | protein: 14g | carbs: 9g | fiber: 1g | sodium: 728mg

Hearty Berry Breakfast Oats

Prep time: 5 minutes | Cook time: 0 minutes | Serves 2

- 1½ cups whole-grain rolled or quickcooking oats (not instant)
- ¾ cup fresh blueberries, raspberries, or blackberries, or a combination
- 2 teaspoons honey
- 2 tablespoons walnut pieces

1. Prepare the whole-grain oats according to the package directions and divide between 2 deep bowls. 2. In a small microwave-safe bowl, heat the berries and honey for 30 seconds. Top each bowl of oatmeal with the fruit mixture. Sprinkle the walnuts over the fruit and serve hot.

Per Serving:

calories: 556 | fat: 13g | protein: 22g | carbs: 92g | fiber: 14g | sodium: 3mg

Golden Egg Skillet

Prep time: 15 minutes | Cook time: 20 minutes | Serves 2

- 2 tablespoons extra-virgin avocado oil or ghee
- 2 medium spring onions, white and green parts separated, sliced
- 1 clove garlic, minced
- 3½ ounces (99 g) Swiss chard or collard greens, stalks and leaves separated, chopped
- 1 medium zucchini, sliced into coins
- 2 tablespoons water
- 1 teaspoon Dijon or yellow mustard
- ½ teaspoon ground turmeric
- ¼ teaspoon black pepper
- Salt, to taste
- 4 large eggs
- ¾ cup grated Manchego or Pecorino Romano cheese
- 2 tablespoons (30 ml) extra-virgin olive oil

1. Preheat the oven to 360°F (182ºC) fan assisted or 400°F (205ºC) conventional. 2. Grease a large, ovenproof skillet (with a lid) with the avocado oil. Cook the white parts of the spring onions and the garlic for about 1 minute, until just fragrant. Add the chard stalks, zucchini, and water. Stir, then cover with a lid. Cook over medium-low heat for about 10 minutes or until the zucchini is tender. Add the mustard, turmeric, pepper, and salt. Add the chard leaves and cook until just wilted. 3. Use a spatula to make 4 wells in the mixture. Crack an egg into each well and cook until the egg whites start to set while the yolks are still runny. Top with the cheese, transfer to the oven, and bake for 5 to 7 minutes. Remove from the oven and sprinkle with the reserved spring onions. Drizzle with the olive oil and serve warm.

Per Serving:

calories: 600 | fat: 49g | protein: 31g | carbs: 10g | fiber: 4g | sodium: 213mg

Crunchy Vanilla Protein Bars

Prep time: 10 minutes | Cook time: 5 minutes | Serves 8

Topping:
- ½ cup flaked coconut
- 2 tablespoons raw cacao nibs

Bars:
- 1½ cups almond flour
- 1 cup collagen powder
- 2 tablespoons ground or whole chia seeds
- 1 teaspoon vanilla powder or 1 tablespoon unsweetened vanilla extract
- ¼ cup virgin coconut oil
- ½ cup coconut milk
- 1½ teaspoons fresh lemon zest
- ⅓ cup macadamia nuts, halved
- Optional: low-carb sweetener, to taste

1. Preheat the oven to 350°F (180°C) fan assisted or 380°F (193°C) conventional. 2. Make the topping: Place the coconut flakes on a baking tray and bake for 2 to 3 minutes, until lightly golden. Set aside to cool. 3. Make the bars: In a bowl, combine all of the ingredients for the bars. Line a small baking tray with parchment paper or use a silicone baking tray. A square 8 × 8–inch (20 × 20 cm) or a rectangular tray of similar size will work best. 4. Press the dough into the pan and sprinkle with the cacao nibs, pressing them into the bars with your fingers. Add the toasted coconut and lightly press the flakes into the dough. Refrigerate until set, for about 1 hour. Slice to serve. Store in the refrigerator for up to 1 week.

Per Serving:

calories: 285 | fat: 27g | protein: 5g | carbs: 10g | fiber: 4g | sodium: 19mg

Tortilla Española (Spanish Omelet)

Prep time: 10 minutes | Cook time: 40 minutes | Serves 4

- 1½ pounds (680 g) Yukon gold potatoes, scrubbed and thinly sliced
- 3 tablespoons olive oil, divided
- 1 teaspoon kosher salt, divided
- 1 sweet white onion, thinly sliced
- 3 cloves garlic, minced
- 8 eggs
- ½ teaspoon ground black pepper

1. Preheat the oven to 350°F(180°C). Line 2 baking sheets with parchment paper. 2. In a large bowl, toss the potatoes with 1 tablespoon of the oil and ½ teaspoon of the salt until well coated. Spread over the 2 baking sheets in a single layer. Roast the potatoes, rotating the baking sheets halfway through cooking, until tender but not browned, about 15 minutes. Using a spatula, remove the potatoes from the baking sheets and let cool until warm. 3. Meanwhile, in a medium skillet over medium-low heat, cook the onion in 1 tablespoon of the oil, stirring, until soft and golden, about 10 minutes. Add the garlic and cook until fragrant, about 2 minutes. Transfer the onion and garlic to a plate and let cool until warm. 4. In a large bowl, beat the eggs, pepper, and the remaining ½ teaspoon salt vigorously until the yolks and whites are completely combined and slightly frothy. Stir in the potatoes and onion and garlic and combine well, being careful not to break too many potatoes. 5. In the same skillet over medium-high heat, warm the remaining 1 tablespoon oil until shimmering, swirling to cover the whole surface. Pour in the egg mixture and spread the contents evenly. Cook for 1 minute and reduce the heat to medium-low. Cook until the edges of the egg are set and the center is slightly wet, about 8 minutes. Using a spatula, nudge the omelet to make sure it moves freely in the skillet. 6. Place a rimless plate, the size of the skillet, over the omelet. Place one hand over the plate and, in a swift motion, flip the omelet onto the plate. Slide the omelet back into the skillet, cooked side up. Cook until completely set, a toothpick inserted into the middle comes out clean, about 6 minutes. 7. Transfer to a serving plate and let cool for 5 minutes. Serve warm or room temperature.

Per Serving:

calories: 376 | fat: 19g | protein: 15g | carbs: 37g | fiber: 5g | sodium: 724mg

Berry Baked Oatmeal

Prep time: 10 minutes | Cook time: 45 to 50 minutes | Serves 8

- 2 cups gluten-free rolled oats
- 2 cups (10-ounce / 283-g bag) frozen mixed berries (blueberries and raspberries work best)
- 2 cups plain, unsweetened almond milk
- 1 cup plain Greek yogurt
- ¼ cup maple syrup
- 2 tablespoons extra-virgin olive oil
- 2 teaspoons ground cinnamon
- 1 teaspoon baking powder
- 1 teaspoon vanilla extract
- ½ teaspoon kosher salt
- ¼ teaspoon ground nutmeg
- ⅛ teaspoon ground cloves

1. Preheat the oven to 375°F (190°C). 2. Mix all the ingredients together in a large bowl. Pour into a 9-by-13-inch baking dish. Bake for 45 to 50 minutes, or until golden brown.

Per Serving:

calories: 180 | fat: 6g | protein: 6g | carbs: 28g | fiber: 4g | sodium: 180mg

Ricotta and Fruit Bruschetta

Prep time: 5 minutes | Cook time: 0 minutes | Serves 2

- ¼ cup full-fat ricotta cheese
- 1½ teaspoons honey, divided
- 3 drops almond extract
- 2 slices whole-grain bread, toasted
- ½ medium banana, peeled
- and cut into ¼-inch slices
- ½ medium pear (any variety), thinly sliced
- 2 teaspoons chopped walnuts
- 2 pinches of ground cinnamon

1. In a small bowl, combine the ricotta, ¼ teaspoon honey, and the almond extract. Stir well. 2. Spread 1½ tablespoons of the ricotta mixture over each slice of toast. 3. Divide the pear slices and banana slices equally on top of each slice of toast. 4. Drizzle equal amounts of the remaining honey over each slice, and sprinkle 1 teaspoon of the walnuts over each slice. Top each serving with a pinch of cinnamon.

Per Serving:

calories: 207 | fat: 7g | protein: 8g | carbs: 30g | fiber: 4g | sodium: 162mg

Turkish Egg Bowl

- 2 tablespoons ghee
- ½–1 teaspoon red chile flakes
- 2 tablespoons extra-virgin olive oil
- 1 cup full-fat goat's or sheep's milk yogurt
- 1 clove garlic, minced
- 1 tablespoon fresh lemon

- juice
- Salt and black pepper, to taste
- Dash of vinegar
- 4 large eggs
- Optional: pinch of sumac
- 2 tablespoons chopped fresh cilantro or parsley

1. In a skillet, melt the ghee over low heat. Add the chile flakes and let it infuse while you prepare the eggs. Remove from the heat and mix with the extra-virgin olive oil. Set aside. Combine the yogurt, garlic, lemon juice, salt, and pepper. 2. Poach the eggs. Fill a medium saucepan with water and a dash of vinegar. Bring to a boil over high heat. Crack each egg individually into a ramekin or a cup. Using a spoon, create a gentle whirlpool in the water; this will help the egg white wrap around the egg yolk. Slowly lower the egg into the water in the center of the whirlpool. Turn off the heat and cook for 3 to 4 minutes. Use a slotted spoon to remove the egg from the water and place it on a plate. Repeat for all remaining eggs. 3. To assemble, place the yogurt mixture in a bowl and add the poached eggs. Drizzle with the infused oil, and garnish with cilantro. Add a pinch of sumac, if using. Eat warm.

Per Serving:

calories: 576 | fat: 46g | protein: 27g | carbs: 17g | fiber: 4g | sodium: 150mg

Mediterranean Fruit Bulgur Breakfast Bowl

- 1½ cups uncooked bulgur
- 2 cups 2% milk
- 1 cup water
- ½ teaspoon ground cinnamon
- 2 cups frozen (or fresh, pitted) dark sweet cherries

- 8 dried (or fresh) figs, chopped
- ½ cup chopped almonds
- ¼ cup loosely packed fresh mint, chopped
- Warm 2% milk, for serving (optional)

1. In a medium saucepan, combine the bulgur, milk, water, and cinnamon. Stir once, then bring just to a boil. Cover, reduce the heat to medium-low, and simmer for 10 minutes or until the liquid is absorbed. 2. Turn off the heat, but keep the pan on the stove, and stir in the frozen cherries (no need to thaw), figs, and almonds. Stir well, cover for 1 minute, and let the hot bulgur thaw the cherries and partially hydrate the figs. Stir in the mint. 3. Scoop into serving bowls. Serve with warm milk, if desired. You can also serve it chilled.

Per Serving:

calories: 273 | fat: 7g | protein: 10g | carbs: 48g | fiber: 8g | sodium: 46mg

Marinara Eggs with Parsley

- 1 tablespoon extra-virgin olive oil
- 1 cup chopped onion (about ½ medium onion)
- 2 garlic cloves, minced (about 1 teaspoon)
- 2 (14½-ounce / 411-g) cans Italian diced tomatoes,

- undrained, no salt added
- 6 large eggs
- ½ cup chopped fresh flat-leaf (Italian) parsley
- Crusty Italian bread and grated Parmesan or Romano cheese, for serving (optional)

1. In a large skillet over medium-high heat, heat the oil. Add the onion and cook for 5 minutes, stirring occasionally. Add the garlic and cook for 1 minute. 2. Pour the tomatoes with their juices over the onion mixture and cook until bubbling, 2 to 3 minutes. While waiting for the tomato mixture to bubble, crack one egg into a small custard cup or coffee mug. 3. When the tomato mixture bubbles, lower the heat to medium. Then use a large spoon to make six indentations in the tomato mixture. Gently pour the first cracked egg into one indentation and repeat, cracking the remaining eggs, one at a time, into the custard cup and pouring one into each indentation. Cover the skillet and cook for 6 to 7 minutes, or until the eggs are done to your liking (about 6 minutes for soft-cooked, 7 minutes for harder cooked). 4. Top with the parsley, and serve with the bread and grated cheese, if desired.

Per Serving:

calories: 127 | fat: 7g | protein: 8g | carbs: 8g | fiber: 2g | sodium: 82mg

Veggie Hash with Eggs

- Nonstick cooking spray
- 1 onion, chopped
- 2 garlic cloves, minced
- 1 red bell pepper, chopped
- 1 yellow summer squash, chopped
- 2 carrots, chopped
- 2 Yukon Gold potatoes, peeled and chopped
- 2 large tomatoes, seeded and

- chopped
- ¼ cup vegetable broth
- ½ teaspoon salt
- ⅛ teaspoon freshly ground black pepper
- ½ teaspoon dried thyme leaves
- 3 or 4 eggs
- ½ teaspoon ground sweet paprika

1. Spray the slow cooker with the nonstick cooking spray. 2. In the slow cooker, combine all the ingredients except the eggs and paprika, and stir. 3. Cover and cook on low for 6 hours. 4. Uncover and make 1 indentation in the vegetable mixture for each egg. Break 1 egg into a small cup and slip the egg into an indentation. Repeat with the remaining eggs. Sprinkle with the paprika. 5. Cover and cook on low for 10 to 15 minutes, or until the eggs are just set, and serve.

Per Serving:

calories: 381 | fat: 8g | protein: 17g | carbs: 64g | fiber: 12g | sodium: 747mg

Strawberry Basil Honey Ricotta Toast

Prep time: 10 minutes | Cook time: 0 minutes | Serves 2

- 4 slices of whole-grain bread
- ½ cup ricotta cheese (whole milk or low-fat)
- 1 tablespoon honey
- Sea salt
- 1 cup fresh strawberries, sliced
- 4 large fresh basil leaves, sliced into thin shreds

1. Toast the bread. 2. In a small bowl, combine the ricotta, honey, and a pinch or two of sea salt. Taste and add additional honey or salt if desired. 3. Spread the mixture evenly over each slice of bread (about 2 tablespoons per slice). 4. Top each piece with sliced strawberries and a few pieces of shredded basil.

Per Serving:

calories: 275 | fat: 8g | protein: 15g | carbs: 41g | fiber: 5g | sodium: 323mg

Morning Buzz Iced Coffee

Prep time: 10 minutes | Cook time: 0 minutes | Serves 1

- 1 cup freshly brewed strong black coffee, cooled slightly
- 1 tablespoon extra-virgin olive oil
- 1 tablespoon half-and-half or heavy cream (optional)
- 1 teaspoon MCT oil (optional)
- ⅛ teaspoon almond extract
- ⅛ teaspoon ground cinnamon

1. Pour the slightly cooled coffee into a blender or large glass (if using an immersion blender). 2. Add the olive oil, half-and-half (if using), MCT oil (if using), almond extract, and cinnamon. 3. Blend well until smooth and creamy. Drink warm and enjoy.

Per Serving:

calories: 124 | fat: 14g | protein: 0g | carbs: 0g | fiber: 0g | sodium: 5mg

Egg Salad with Red Pepper and Dill

Prep time: 5 minutes | Cook time: 10 minutes | Serves 6

- 6 large eggs
- 1 cup water
- 1 tablespoon olive oil
- 1 medium red bell pepper, seeded and chopped
- ¼ teaspoon salt
- ¼ teaspoon ground black pepper
- ½ cup low-fat plain Greek yogurt
- 2 tablespoons chopped fresh dill

1. Have ready a large bowl of ice water. Place rack or egg holder into bottom of the Instant Pot®. 2. Arrange eggs on rack or holder and add water to the Instant Pot®. Close lid, set steam release to Sealing, press the Manual button, and set time to 5 minutes. 3. When the timer beeps, let pressure release naturally for 5 minutes, then quick-release the remaining pressure until the float valve drops. Press the Cancel button and open lid. Carefully transfer eggs to the bowl of ice water. Let stand in ice water for 10 minutes, then peel, chop, and add eggs to a medium bowl. 4. Clean out pot, dry well, and return to machine. Press the Sauté button and heat oil.

Add bell pepper, salt, and black pepper. Cook, stirring often, until bell pepper is tender, about 5 minutes. Transfer to bowl with eggs. 5. Add yogurt and dill to bowl, and fold to combine. Cover and chill for 1 hour before serving.

Per Serving:

calories: 111 | fat: 8g | protein: 8g | carbs: 3g | fiber: 0g | sodium: 178mg

Homemade Pumpkin Parfait

Prep time: 5 minutes | Cook time: 0 minutes | Serves 4

- 1 (15-ounce / 425-g) can pure pumpkin purée
- 4 teaspoons honey, additional to taste
- 1 teaspoon pumpkin pie spice
- ¼ teaspoon ground cinnamon
- 2 cups plain, unsweetened, full-fat Greek yogurt
- 1 cup honey granola

1. In a large bowl, mix the pumpkin purée, honey, pumpkin pie spice, and cinnamon. Cover and refrigerate for at least 2 hours. 2. To make the parfaits, in each cup, pour ¼ cup pumpkin mix, ¼ cup yogurt and ¼ cup granola. Repeat Greek yogurt and pumpkin layers and top with honey granola.

Per Serving:

calories: 264 | fat: 9g | protein: 15g | carbs: 35g | fiber: 6g | sodium: 90mg

Enjoy-Your-Veggies Breakfast

Prep time: 20 minutes | Cook time: 10 minutes | Serves 4

- 1 tablespoon olive oil
- 1 small sweet onion, peeled and diced
- 2 large carrots, peeled and diced
- 2 medium potatoes, peeled and diced
- 1 stalk celery, diced
- 1 large red bell pepper, seeded and diced
- 1 tablespoon low-sodium soy sauce
- ¼ cup water
- 1 cup diced peeled zucchini or summer squash
- 2 medium tomatoes, peeled and diced
- 2 cups cooked brown rice
- ½ teaspoon ground black pepper

1. Press the Sauté button on the Instant Pot® and heat oil. Add onion and cook until just tender, about 2 minutes. 2. Stir in carrots, potatoes, celery, and bell pepper and cook until just tender, about 2 minutes. Add soy sauce and water. Press the Cancel button. 3. Close lid, set steam release to Sealing, press the Manual button, and set time to 2 minutes. When the timer beeps, quick-release the pressure until the float valve drops. Press the Cancel button. 4. Open lid and add squash and tomatoes, and stir. Close lid, set steam release to Sealing, press the Manual button, and set time to 1 minute. When the timer beeps, quick-release the pressure until the float valve drops. Press the Cancel button and open lid. 5. Serve over rice and sprinkle with black pepper.

Per Serving:

calories: 224 | fat: 5g | protein: 6g | carbs: 41g | fiber: 5g | sodium: 159mg

Cauliflower Avocado Toast

- 1 (12-ounce / 340-g) steamer bag cauliflower
- 1 large egg
- ½ cup shredded Mozzarella cheese
- 1 ripe medium avocado
- ½ teaspoon garlic powder
- ¼ teaspoon ground black pepper

1. Cook cauliflower according to package instructions. Remove from bag and place into cheesecloth or clean towel to remove excess moisture. 2. Place cauliflower into a large bowl and mix in egg and Mozzarella. Cut a piece of parchment to fit your air fryer basket. Separate the cauliflower mixture into two, and place it on the parchment in two mounds. Press out the cauliflower mounds into a ¼-inch-thick rectangle. Place the parchment into the air fryer basket. 3. Adjust the temperature to 400°F (204°C) and set the timer for 8 minutes. 4. Flip the cauliflower halfway through the cooking time. 5. When the timer beeps, remove the parchment and allow the cauliflower to cool 5 minutes. 6. Cut open the avocado and remove the pit. Scoop out the inside, place it in a medium bowl, and mash it with garlic powder and pepper. Spread onto the cauliflower. Serve immediately.

Per Serving:

calories: 321 | fat: 22g | protein: 16g | carbs: 19g | fiber: 10g | sodium: 99mg

Spinach Pie

- Nonstick cooking spray
- 2 tablespoons extra-virgin olive oil
- 1 onion, chopped
- 1 pound (454 g) frozen spinach, thawed
- ¼ teaspoon garlic salt
- ¼ teaspoon freshly ground black pepper
- ¼ teaspoon ground nutmeg
- 4 large eggs, divided
- 1 cup grated Parmesan cheese, divided
- 2 puff pastry doughs, (organic, if available), at room temperature
- 4 hard-boiled eggs, halved

1. Preheat the oven to 350°F(180°C). Spray a baking sheet with nonstick cooking spray and set aside. 2. Heat a large sauté pan or skillet over medium-high heat. Put in the oil and onion and cook for about 5 minutes, until translucent. 3. Squeeze the excess water from the spinach, then add to the pan and cook, uncovered, so that any excess water from the spinach can evaporate. Add the garlic salt, pepper, and nutmeg. Remove from heat and set aside to cool. 4. In a small bowl, crack 3 eggs and mix well. Add the eggs and ½ cup Parmesan cheese to the cooled spinach mix. 5. On the prepared baking sheet, roll out the pastry dough. Layer the spinach mix on top of dough, leaving 2 inches around each edge. 6. Once the spinach is spread onto the pastry dough, place hard-boiled egg halves evenly throughout the pie, then cover with the second pastry dough. Pinch the edges closed. 7. Crack the remaining egg in a small bowl and mix well. Brush the egg wash over the pastry dough. 8. Bake for 15 to 20 minutes, until golden brown and warmed through.

Per Serving:

calories: 417 | fat: 28g | protein: 17g | carbs: 25g | fiber: 3g | sodium: 490mg

Egg in a "Pepper Hole" with Avocado

- 4 bell peppers, any color
- 1 tablespoon extra-virgin olive oil
- 8 large eggs
- ¾ teaspoon kosher salt, divided
- ¼ teaspoon freshly ground
- black pepper, divided
- 1 avocado, peeled, pitted, and diced
- ¼ cup red onion, diced
- ¼ cup fresh basil, chopped
- Juice of ½ lime

1. Stem and seed the bell peppers. Cut 2 (2-inch-thick) rings from each pepper. Chop the remaining bell pepper into small dice, and set aside. 2. Heat the olive oil in a large skillet over medium heat. Add 4 bell pepper rings, then crack 1 egg in the middle of each ring. Season with ¼ teaspoon of the salt and ⅛ teaspoon of the black pepper. Cook until the egg whites are mostly set but the yolks are still runny, 2 to 3 minutes. Gently flip and cook 1 additional minute for over easy. Move the egg-bell pepper rings to a platter or onto plates, and repeat with the remaining 4 bell pepper rings. 3. In a medium bowl, combine the avocado, onion, basil, lime juice, reserved diced bell pepper, the remaining ¼ teaspoon kosher salt, and the remaining ⅛ teaspoon black pepper. Divide among the 4 plates.

Per Serving:

2 egg-pepper rings: calories: 270 | fat: 19g | protein: 15g | carbs: 12g | fiber: 5g | sodium: 360mg

Quickie Honey Nut Granola

- 2½ cups regular rolled oats
- ⅓ cup coarsely chopped almonds
- ⅛ teaspoon kosher or sea salt
- ½ teaspoon ground cinnamon
- ½ cup chopped dried apricots
- 2 tablespoons ground flaxseed
- ¼ cup honey
- ¼ cup extra-virgin olive oil
- 2 teaspoons vanilla extract

1. Preheat the oven to 325°F(165°C). Line a large, rimmed baking sheet with parchment paper. 2. In a large skillet, combine the oats, almonds, salt, and cinnamon. Turn the heat to medium-high and cook, stirring often, to toast, about 6 minutes. 3. While the oat mixture is toasting, in a microwave-safe bowl, combine the apricots, flaxseed, honey, and oil. Microwave on high for about 1 minute, or until very hot and just beginning to bubble. (Or heat these ingredients in a small saucepan over medium heat for about 3 minutes.) 4. Stir the vanilla into the honey mixture, then pour it over the oat mixture in the skillet. Stir well. 5. Spread out the granola on the prepared baking sheet. Bake for 15 minutes, until lightly browned. Remove from the oven and cool completely. 6. Break the granola into small pieces, and store in an airtight container in the refrigerator for up to 2 weeks (if it lasts that long!).

Per Serving:

calories: 449 | fat: 17g | protein: 13g | carbs: 64g | fiber: 9g | sodium: 56mg

Portobello Eggs Benedict

Prep time: 10 minutes | Cook time: 10 to 14 minutes | Serves 2

- 1 tablespoon olive oil
- 2 cloves garlic, minced
- ¼ teaspoon dried thyme
- 2 portobello mushrooms, stems removed and gills scraped out
- 2 Roma tomatoes, halved lengthwise
- Salt and freshly ground black pepper, to taste
- 2 large eggs
- 2 tablespoons grated Pecorino Romano cheese
- 1 tablespoon chopped fresh parsley, for garnish
- 1 teaspoon truffle oil (optional)

1. Preheat the air fryer to 400°F (204°C). 2. In a small bowl, combine the olive oil, garlic, and thyme. Brush the mixture over the mushrooms and tomatoes until thoroughly coated. Season to taste with salt and freshly ground black pepper. 3. Arrange the vegetables, cut side up, in the air fryer basket. Crack an egg into the center of each mushroom and sprinkle with cheese. Air fry for 10 to 14 minutes until the vegetables are tender and the whites are firm. When cool enough to handle, coarsely chop the tomatoes and place on top of the eggs. Scatter parsley on top and drizzle with truffle oil, if desired, just before serving.

Per Serving:

calories: 189 | fat: 13g | protein: 11g | carbs: 7g | fiber: 2g | sodium: 87mg

South of the Coast Sweet Potato Toast

Prep time: 5 minutes | Cook time: 15 minutes | Serves 4

- 2 plum tomatoes, halved
- 6 tablespoons extra-virgin olive oil, divided
- Salt
- Freshly ground black pepper
- 2 large sweet potatoes, sliced lengthwise
- 1 cup fresh spinach
- 8 medium asparagus,
- trimmed
- 4 large cooked eggs or egg substitute (poached, scrambled, or fried)
- 1 cup arugula
- 4 tablespoons pesto
- 4 tablespoons shredded Asiago cheese

1. Preheat the oven to 450°F(235°C). 2. On a baking sheet, brush the plum tomato halves with 2 tablespoons of olive oil and season with salt and pepper. Roast the tomatoes in the oven for approximately 15 minutes, then remove from the oven and allow to rest. 3. Put the sweet potato slices on a separate baking sheet and brush about 2 tablespoons of oil on each side and season with salt and pepper. Bake the sweet potato slices for about 15 minutes, flipping once after 5 to 7 minutes, until just tender. Remove from the oven and set aside. 4. In a sauté pan or skillet, heat the remaining 2 tablespoons of olive oil over medium heat and sauté the fresh spinach until just wilted. Remove from the pan and rest on a paper-towel-lined dish. In the same pan, add the asparagus and sauté, turning throughout. Transfer to a paper towel-lined dish. 5. Place the slices of grilled sweet potato on serving plates and divide the spinach and asparagus evenly among the slices. Place a prepared egg on top of the spinach and asparagus. Top this with ¼ cup of arugula. 6. Finish by drizzling with 1 tablespoon of pesto and sprinkle with 1 tablespoon of cheese. Serve with 1 roasted plum tomato.

Per Serving:

calories: 441 | fat: 35g | protein: 13g | carbs: 23g | fiber: 4g | sodium: 481mg

Power Peach Smoothie Bowl

Prep time: 15 minutes | Cook time: 0 minutes | Serves 2

- 2 cups packed partially thawed frozen peaches
- ½ cup plain or vanilla Greek yogurt
- ½ ripe avocado
- 2 tablespoons flax meal
- 1 teaspoon vanilla extract
- 1 teaspoon orange extract
- 1 tablespoon honey (optional)

1. Combine all of the ingredients in a blender and blend until smooth. 2. Pour the mixture into two bowls, and, if desired, sprinkle with additional toppings.

Per Serving:

calories: 213 | fat: 13g | protein: 6g | carbs: 23g | fiber: 7g | sodium: 41mg

Red Pepper and Feta Egg Bites

Prep time: 5 minutes | Cook time: 8 minutes | Serves 6

- 1 tablespoon olive oil
- ½ cup crumbled feta cheese
- ¼ cup chopped roasted red peppers
- 6 large eggs, beaten
- ¼ teaspoon ground black pepper
- 1 cup water

1. Brush silicone muffin or poaching cups with oil. Divide feta and roasted red peppers among prepared cups. In a bowl with a pour spout, beat eggs with black pepper. 2. Place rack in the Instant Pot® and add water. Place cups on rack. Pour egg mixture into cups. Close lid, set steam release to Sealing, press the Manual button, and set time to 8 minutes. 3. When the timer beeps, quick-release the pressure until the float valve drops and open lid. Remove silicone cups carefully and slide eggs from cups onto plates. Serve warm.

Per Serving:

calories: 145 | fat: 11g | protein: 10g | carbs: 3g | fiber: 1g | sodium: 294mg

Peachy Green Smoothie

Prep time: 10 minutes | Cook time: 0 minutes | Serves 2

- 1 cup almond milk
- 3 cups kale or spinach
- 1 banana, peeled
- 1 orange, peeled
- 1 small green apple
- 1 cup frozen peaches
- ¼ cup vanilla Greek yogurt

1. Put the ingredients in a blender in the order listed and blend on high until smooth. 2. Serve and enjoy.

Per Serving:

calories: 257 | fat: 5g | protein: 9g | carbs: 50g | fiber: 7g | sodium: 87mg

Chapter 3 Poultry

Grilled Chicken and Vegetables with Lemon-Walnut Sauce

Prep time: 20 minutes | Cook time: 16 minutes | Serves 4

- 1 cup chopped walnuts, toasted
- 1 small shallot, very finely chopped
- ½ cup olive oil, plus more for brushing
- Juice and zest of 1 lemon
- 4 boneless, skinless chicken breasts
- Sea salt and freshly ground pepper, to taste
- 2 zucchini, sliced diagonally ¼-inch thick
- ½ pound (227 g) asparagus
- 1 red onion, sliced ⅓-inch thick
- 1 teaspoon Italian seasoning

1. Preheat a grill to medium-high. 2. Put the walnuts, shallots, olive oil, lemon juice, and zest in a food processor and process until smooth and creamy. 3. Season the chicken with sea salt and freshly ground pepper, and grill on an oiled grate until cooked through, about 7–8 minutes a side or until an instant-read thermometer reaches 180°F (82°C) in the thickest part. 4. When the chicken is halfway done, put the vegetables on the grill. Sprinkle Italian seasoning over the chicken and vegetables to taste. 5. To serve, lay the grilled veggies on a plate, place the chicken breast on the grilled vegetables, and spoon the lemon-walnut sauce over the chicken and vegetables.

Per Serving:
calories: 800 | fat: 54g | protein: 68g | carbs: 13g | fiber: 5g | sodium: 134mg

Tomato-Braised Chicken Thighs with Capers

Prep time: 10 minutes | Cook time: 45 minutes | Serves 4

- 1 tablespoon olive oil
- 8 boneless, skinless chicken thighs, trimmed
- ¼ teaspoon kosher salt
- ¼ teaspoon ground black pepper
- 1 onion, sliced
- 4 tablespoons drained capers, divided
- 1 clove garlic, minced
- ½ cup dry red wine or chicken broth
- 1 (28-ounce / 794-g) can diced tomatoes
- 1 sprig fresh oregano or 1 teaspoon dried
- 2 tablespoons sliced fresh basil

1. In a Dutch oven or large wide-bottom pot over medium-high heat, warm the oil. Season the chicken with the salt and pepper. Add it to the pot, in batches, and cook until browned on both sides and it releases easily from the pot, 8 to 10 minutes total. Remove to a plate. 2. Reduce the heat to medium. Add the onion, 3 tablespoons of the capers, and the garlic. Cook, stirring frequently, until the onion is tender, 2 to 3 minutes. 3. Add the wine or broth and scrape up the browned bits from the bottom of the pot. Cook until the liquid is nearly cooked away, 4 to 5 minutes. Add the tomatoes and oregano and bring to a simmer. 4. Nestle the chicken into the tomato mixture and add the collected juices from the plate. Reduce the heat to maintain a bare simmer, cover, and cook until the chicken reaches 165°F(74°C) in the thickest portion, about 15 minutes. Chop the remaining 1 tablespoon capers and sprinkle with the basil over the chicken before serving.

Per Serving:
calories: 567 | fat: 20g | protein: 78g | carbs: 11g | fiber: 5g | sodium: 735mg

Chicken Piccata with Mushrooms

Prep time: 25 minutes | Cook time: 25 minutes | Serves 4

- 1 pound (454 g) thinly sliced chicken breasts
- 1½ teaspoons salt, divided
- ½ teaspoon freshly ground black pepper
- ¼ cup ground flaxseed
- 2 tablespoons almond flour
- 8 tablespoons extra-virgin olive oil, divided
- 4 tablespoons butter, divided
- 2 cups sliced mushrooms
- ½ cup dry white wine or chicken stock
- ¼ cup freshly squeezed lemon juice
- ¼ cup roughly chopped capers
- Zucchini noodles, for serving
- ¼ cup chopped fresh flat-leaf Italian parsley, for garnish

1. Season the chicken with 1 teaspoon salt and the pepper. On a plate, combine the ground flaxseed and almond flour and dredge each chicken breast in the mixture. Set aside. 2. In a large skillet, heat 4 tablespoons olive oil and 1 tablespoon butter over medium-high heat. Working in batches if necessary, brown the chicken, 3 to 4 minutes per side. Remove from the skillet and keep warm. 3. Add the remaining 4 tablespoons olive oil and 1 tablespoon butter to the skillet along with mushrooms and sauté over medium heat until just tender, 6 to 8 minutes. 4. Add the white wine, lemon juice, capers, and remaining ½ teaspoon salt to the skillet and bring to a boil, whisking to incorporate any little browned bits that have stuck to the bottom of the skillet. Reduce the heat to low and whisk in the final 2 tablespoons butter. 5. Return the browned chicken to skillet, cover, and simmer over low heat until the chicken is cooked through and the sauce has thickened, 5 to 6 more minutes. 6. Serve chicken and mushrooms warm over zucchini noodles, spooning the mushroom sauce over top and garnishing with chopped parsley.

Per Serving:
calories: 596 | fat: 48g | protein: 30g | carbs: 8g | fiber: 4g | sodium: 862mg

Easy Turkey Tenderloin

Prep time: 20 minutes | Cook time: 30 minutes | Serves 4

- Olive oil
- ½ teaspoon paprika
- ½ teaspoon garlic powder
- ½ teaspoon salt
- ½ teaspoon freshly ground
- black pepper
- Pinch cayenne pepper
- 1½ pounds (680 g) turkey breast tenderloin

1. Spray the air fryer basket lightly with olive oil. 2. In a small bowl, combine the paprika, garlic powder, salt, black pepper, and cayenne pepper. Rub the mixture all over the turkey. 3. Place the turkey in the air fryer basket and lightly spray with olive oil. 4. Air fry at 370ºF (188ºC) for 15 minutes. Flip the turkey over and lightly spray with olive oil. Air fry until the internal temperature reaches at least 170ºF (77ºC) for an additional 10 to 15 minutes. 5. Let the turkey rest for 10 minutes before slicing and serving.

Per Serving:

calories: 196 | fat: 3g | protein: 40g | carbs: 1g | fiber: 0g | sodium: 483mg

Citrus Chicken with Pecan Wild Rice

Prep time: 15 minutes | Cook time: 10 minutes | Serves 4

- 4 boneless, skinless chicken breasts
- Sea salt and freshly ground pepper, to taste
- 2 tablespoons olive oil
- Juice and zest of 1 orange
- 2 cups wild rice, cooked
- 2 green onions, sliced
- 1 cup pecans, toasted and chopped

1. Season chicken breasts with sea salt and freshly ground pepper. 2. Heat a large skillet over medium heat. Add the oil and sear the chicken until browned on 1 side. 3. Flip the chicken and brown other side. 4. Add the orange juice to the skillet and let cook down. 5. In a large bowl, combine the rice, onions, pecans, and orange zest. Season with sea salt and freshly ground pepper to taste. 6. Serve the chicken alongside the rice and a green salad for a complete meal.

Per Serving:

calories: 870 | fat: 34g | protein: 76g | carbs: 66g | fiber: 8g | sodium: 128mg

Sheet Pan Lemon Chicken and Roasted Artichokes

Prep time: 10 minutes |Cook time: 20 minutes| Serves: 4

- 2 large lemons
- 3 tablespoons extra-virgin olive oil, divided
- ½ teaspoon kosher or sea
- salt
- 2 large artichokes
- 4 (6-ounce / 170-g) bone-in, skin-on chicken thighs

1. Put a large, rimmed baking sheet in the oven. Preheat the oven to 450ºF (235ºC) with the pan inside. Tear off four sheets of aluminum foil about 8-by-10 inches each; set aside. 2. Using a Microplane or citrus zester, zest 1 lemon into a large bowl. Halve both lemons and squeeze all the juice into the bowl with the zest. Whisk in 2

tablespoons of oil and the salt. Set aside. 3. Rinse the artichokes with cool water, and dry with a clean towel. Using a sharp knife, cut about 1½ inches off the tip of each artichoke. Cut about ¼ inch off each stem. Halve each artichoke lengthwise so each piece has equal amounts of stem. Immediately plunge the artichoke halves into the lemon juice and oil mixture (to prevent browning) and turn to coat on all sides. Lay one artichoke half flat-side down in the center of a sheet of aluminum foil, and close up loosely to make a foil packet. Repeat the process with the remaining three artichoke halves. Set the packets aside. 4. Put the chicken in the remaining lemon juice mixture and turn to coat. 5. Using oven mitts, carefully remove the hot baking sheet from the oven and pour on the remaining tablespoon of oil; tilt the pan to coat. Carefully arrange the chicken, skin-side down, on the hot baking sheet. Place the artichoke packets, flat-side down, on the baking sheet as well. (Arrange the artichoke packets and chicken with space between them so air can circulate around them.) 6. Roast for 20 minutes, or until the internal temperature of the chicken measures 165ºF (74ºC) on a meat thermometer and any juices run clear. Before serving, check the artichokes for doneness by pulling on a leaf. If it comes out easily, the artichoke is ready.

Per Serving:

calories: 566 | fat: 42g | protein: 35g | carbs: 13g | fiber: 6g | sodium: 524mg

Harissa-Rubbed Cornish Game Hens

Prep time: 30 minutes | Cook time: 21 minutes | Serves 4

Harissa:
- ½ cup olive oil
- 6 cloves garlic, minced
- 2 tablespoons smoked paprika
- 1 tablespoon ground coriander

- 1 tablespoon ground cumin
- 1 teaspoon ground caraway
- 1 teaspoon kosher salt
- ½ to 1 teaspoon cayenne pepper

Hens:
- ½ cup yogurt
- 2 Cornish game hens, any

giblets removed, split in half lengthwise

1. For the harissa: In a medium microwave-safe bowl, combine the oil, garlic, paprika, coriander, cumin, caraway, salt, and cayenne. Microwave on high for 1 minute, stirring halfway through the cooking time. (You can also heat this on the stovetop until the oil is hot and bubbling. Or, if you must use your air fryer for everything, cook it in the air fryer at 350ºF (177ºC) for 5 to 6 minutes, or until the paste is heated through.) 2. For the hens: In a small bowl, combine 1 to 2 tablespoons harissa and the yogurt. Whisk until well combined. Place the hen halves in a resealable plastic bag and pour the marinade over. Seal the bag and massage until all of the pieces are thoroughly coated. Marinate at room temperature for 30 minutes or in the refrigerator for up to 24 hours. 3. Arrange the hen halves in a single layer in the air fryer basket. (If you have a smaller air fryer, you may have to cook this in two batches.) Set the air fryer to 400ºF (204ºC) for 20 minutes. Use a meat thermometer to ensure the game hens have reached an internal temperature of 165ºF (74ºC).

Per Serving:

calories: 421 | fat: 33g | protein: 26g | carbs: 6g | fiber: 2g | sodium: 683mg

Greek Turkey Burger

Prep time: 10 minutes | Cook time: 10 minutes | Serves 4

- 1 pound (454 g) ground turkey
- 1 medium zucchini, grated
- ¼ cup whole-wheat bread crumbs
- ¼ cup red onion, minced
- ¼ cup crumbled feta cheese
- 1 large egg, beaten
- 1 garlic clove, minced
- 1 tablespoon fresh oregano, chopped
- 1 teaspoon kosher salt
- ¼ teaspoon freshly ground black pepper
- 1 tablespoon extra-virgin olive oil

1. In a large bowl, combine the turkey, zucchini, bread crumbs, onion, feta cheese, egg, garlic, oregano, salt, and black pepper, and mix well. Shape into 4 equal patties. 2. Heat the olive oil in a large nonstick grill pan or skillet over medium-high heat. Add the burgers to the pan and reduce the heat to medium. Cook on one side for 5 minutes, then flip and cook the other side for 5 minutes more.

Per Serving:

calories: 285 | fat: 16g | protein: 26g | carbs: 9g | fiber: 2g | sodium: 465mg

One-Pan Parsley Chicken and Potatoes

Prep time: 5 minutes |Cook time: 25 minutes| Serves: 6

- 1½ pounds (680 g) boneless, skinless chicken thighs, cut into 1-inch cubes
- 1 tablespoon extra-virgin olive oil
- 1½ pounds (680 g) Yukon Gold potatoes, unpeeled, cut into ½-inch cubes (about 6 small potatoes)
- 2 garlic cloves, minced (about 1 teaspoon)
- ¼ cup dry white wine or apple cider vinegar
- 1 cup low-sodium or no-salt-added chicken broth
- 1 tablespoon Dijon mustard
- ¼ teaspoon kosher or sea salt
- ¼ teaspoon freshly ground black pepper
- 1 cup chopped fresh flat-leaf (Italian) parsley, including stems
- 1 tablespoon freshly squeezed lemon juice (½ small lemon)

1. Pat the chicken dry with a few paper towels. In a large skillet over medium-high heat, heat the oil. Add the chicken and cook for 5 minutes, stirring only after the chicken has browned on one side. Remove the chicken from the pan with a slotted spoon, and put it on a plate; it will not yet be fully cooked. Leave the skillet on the stove. 2. Add the potatoes to the skillet and cook for 5 minutes, stirring only after the potatoes have become golden and crispy on one side. Push the potatoes to the side of the skillet, add the garlic, and cook, stirring constantly, for 1 minute. Add the wine and cook for 1 minute, until nearly evaporated. Add the chicken broth, mustard, salt, pepper, and reserved chicken pieces. Turn the heat up to high, and bring to a boil. 3. Once boiling, cover the skillet, reduce the heat to medium-low, and cook for 10 to 12 minutes, until the potatoes are tender and the internal temperature of the chicken measures 165°F (74°C) on a meat thermometer and any juices run clear. 4. During the last minute of cooking, stir in the parsley.

Remove from the heat, stir in the lemon juice, and serve.

Per Serving:

calories: 266 | fat: 7g | protein: 26g | carbs: 22g | fiber: 3g | sodium 258mg

Rosemary Baked Chicken Thighs

Prep time: 20 minutes | Cook time: 20 minutes | Serves 4 to 6

- 5 tablespoons extra-virgin olive oil, divided
- 3 medium shallots, diced
- 4 garlic cloves, peeled and crushed
- 1 rosemary sprig
- 2 to 2½ pounds (907 g to 1.1 kg) bone-in, skin-on
- chicken thighs (about 6 pieces)
- 2 teaspoons kosher salt
- ¼ teaspoon freshly ground black pepper
- 1 lemon, juiced and zested
- ⅓ cup low-sodium chicken broth

1. In a large sauté pan or skillet, heat 3 tablespoons of olive oil over medium heat. Add the shallots and garlic and cook for about a minute, until fragrant. Add the rosemary sprig. 2. Season the chicken with salt and pepper. Place it in the skillet, skin-side down, and brown for 3 to 5 minutes. 3. Once it's cooked halfway through, turn the chicken over and add lemon juice and zest. 4. Add the chicken broth, cover the pan, and continue to cook for 10 to 15 more minutes, until cooked through and juices run clear. Serve.

Per Serving:

calories: 294 | fat: 18g | protein: 30g | carbs: 3g | fiber: 1g | sodium: 780mg

Jerk Chicken Thighs

Prep time: 30 minutes | Cook time: 15 to 20 minutes | Serves 6

- 2 teaspoons ground coriander
- 1 teaspoon ground allspice
- 1 teaspoon cayenne pepper
- 1 teaspoon ground ginger
- 1 teaspoon salt
- 1 teaspoon dried thyme
- ½ teaspoon ground cinnamon
- ½ teaspoon ground nutmeg
- 2 pounds (907 g) boneless chicken thighs, skin on
- 2 tablespoons olive oil

1. In a small bowl, combine the coriander, allspice, cayenne, ginger, salt, thyme, cinnamon, and nutmeg. Stir until thoroughly combined. 2. Place the chicken in a baking dish and use paper towels to pat dry. Thoroughly coat both sides of the chicken with the spice mixture. Cover and refrigerate for at least 2 hours, preferably overnight. 3. Preheat the air fryer to 360ºF (182ºC). 4. Working in batches if necessary, arrange the chicken in a single layer in the air fryer basket and lightly coat with the olive oil. Pausing halfway through the cooking time to flip the chicken, air fry for 15 to 20 minutes, until a thermometer inserted into the thickest part registers 165ºF (74ºC).

Per Serving:

calories: 227 | fat: 11g | protein: 30g | carbs: 1g | fiber: 0g | sodium: 532mg

Whole-Roasted Spanish Chicken

Prep time: 1 hour | Cook time: 55 minutes | Serves 4

- 4 tablespoons (½ stick) unsalted butter, softened
- 2 tablespoons lemon zest
- 2 tablespoons smoked paprika
- 2 tablespoons garlic, minced
- 1½ teaspoons salt
- 1 teaspoon freshly ground black pepper
- 1 (5-pound / 2.3-kg) whole chicken

1. In a small bowl, combine the butter with the lemon zest, paprika, garlic, salt, and pepper. 2. Pat the chicken dry using a paper towel. Using your hands, rub the seasoned butter all over the chicken. Refrigerate the chicken for 30 minutes. 3. Preheat the oven to 425°F(220ºC). Take the chicken out of the fridge and let it sit out for 20 minutes. 4. Put the chicken in a baking dish in the oven and let it cook for 20 minutes. Turn the temperature down to 350°F (180ºC) and let the chicken cook for another 35 minutes. 5. Take the chicken out of the oven and let it stand for 10 minutes before serving.

Per Serving:
calories: 705 | fat: 17g | protein: 126g | carbs: 4g | fiber: 1g | sodium: 880mg

Chicken and Shrimp Paella

Prep time: 20 minutes | Cook time: 40 minutes | Serves 6

- 3 tablespoons olive oil
- 1 onion, chopped (about 2 cups)
- 5 garlic cloves, minced
- 1 pound (454 g) chicken breasts, cut into 1-inch pieces
- 1 cup Arborio rice
- 1 teaspoon ground cumin
- 1 teaspoon smoked paprika
- ½ teaspoon ground turmeric
- 1½ cups low-sodium chicken broth
- 1 (14½-ounce / 411-g) can diced tomatoes, with their juices
- Zest and juice of 1 lemon
- ½ teaspoon salt
- 1 cup thawed frozen peas
- 1 medium zucchini, cut into cubes (about 2 cups)
- 8 ounces (227 g) uncooked shrimp, thawed, peeled, and deveined
- 2 tablespoons chopped fresh parsley

1. In a large saucepan, heat 2 tablespoons of the olive oil over medium heat. Add the onion and cook, occasionally stirring, for 5 minutes, or until softened. Add the garlic, chicken, rice, and remaining 1 tablespoon olive oil. Stir until the rice is coated with the oil. 2. Add the cumin, smoked paprika, turmeric, broth, tomatoes with their juices, lemon zest, lemon juice, and salt. Spread the rice mixture evenly in the pan. Bring to a boil. Reduce the heat to medium-low, cover, and cook for 25 minutes—do not stir. 3. Remove the lid and stir in the peas and zucchini. Add the shrimp, nestling them into the rice. Cover and cook for 8 to 10 minutes. Remove from the heat and let stand for 10 minutes. 4. Top with the parsley and serve.

Per Serving:
calories: 310 | fat: 18g | protein: 26g | carbs: 18g | fiber: 7g | sodium: 314mg

Cashew Chicken and Snap Peas

Prep time: 15 minutes | Cook time: 6 hours | Serves 2

- 16 ounces (454 g) boneless, skinless chicken breasts, cut into 2-inch pieces
- 2 cups sugar snap peas, strings removed
- 1 teaspoon grated fresh ginger
- 1 teaspoon minced garlic
- 2 tablespoons low-sodium
- soy sauce
- 1 tablespoon ketchup
- 1 tablespoon rice vinegar
- 1 teaspoon honey
- Pinch red pepper flakes
- ¼ cup toasted cashews
- 1 scallion, white and green parts, sliced thin

1. Put the chicken and sugar snap peas into the slow cooker. 2. In a measuring cup or small bowl, whisk together the ginger, garlic, soy sauce, ketchup, vinegar, honey, and red pepper flakes. Pour the mixture over the chicken and snap peas. 3. Cover and cook on low for 6 hours. The chicken should be cooked through, and the snap peas should be tender, but not mushy. 4. Just before serving, stir in the cashews and scallions.

Per Serving:
calories: 463 | fat: 14g | protein: 59g | carbs: 23g | fiber: 5g | sodium: 699mg

Chicken with Lemon Asparagus

Prep time: 10 minutes | Cook time: 13 minutes | Serves 4

- 2 tablespoons olive oil
- 4 (6-ounce / 170-g) boneless, skinless chicken breasts
- ½ teaspoon ground black pepper
- ¼ teaspoon salt
- ¼ teaspoon smoked paprika
- 2 cloves garlic, peeled and minced
- 2 sprigs thyme
- 2 sprigs oregano
- 1 tablespoon grated lemon zest
- ¼ cup lemon juice
- ¼ cup low-sodium chicken broth
- 1 bunch asparagus, trimmed
- ¼ cup chopped fresh parsley
- 4 lemon wedges

1. Press Sauté on the Instant Pot® and heat oil. Season chicken with pepper, salt, and smoked paprika. Brown chicken on both sides, about 4 minutes per side. Add garlic, thyme, oregano, lemon zest, lemon juice, and chicken broth. Press the Cancel button. 2. Close lid, set steam release to Sealing, press the Manual button, and set time to 5 minutes. 3. When the timer beeps, quick-release the pressure until the float valve drops. Press the Cancel button and open lid. Transfer chicken breasts to a serving platter. Tent with foil to keep warm. 4. Add asparagus to the Instant Pot®. Close lid, set steam release to Sealing, press the Manual button, and set time to 0. When the timer beeps, quick-release the pressure until the float valve drops. Open lid and remove asparagus. Arrange asparagus around chicken and garnish with parsley and lemon wedges. Serve immediately.

Per Serving:
calories: 227 | fat: 11g | protein: 35g | carbs: 0g | fiber: 0g | sodium: 426mg

Chicken and Olives with Couscous

Prep time: 15 minutes | Cook time: 1 hour | Serves 6

- 2 tablespoons olive oil, divided
- 8 bone-in, skin-on chicken thighs
- ½ teaspoon kosher salt
- ¼ teaspoon ground black pepper
- 2 cloves garlic, chopped
- 1 small red onion, chopped
- 1 red bell pepper, seeded and chopped
- 1 green bell pepper, seeded and chopped
- 1 tablespoon fresh thyme
- leaves
- 2 teaspoons fresh oregano leaves
- 1 (28-ounce / 794-g) can no-salt-added diced tomatoes
- 1 cup low-sodium chicken broth
- 1 cup pitted green olives, coarsely chopped
- 2 cups whole wheat couscous
- Chopped flat-leaf parsley, for garnish

1. Preheat the oven to 350°F(180°C). 2. In a large ovenproof or cast-iron skillet over medium heat, warm 1 tablespoon of the oil. Pat the chicken thighs dry with a paper towel, season with the salt and black pepper, and cook, turning once, until golden and crisp, 8 to 10 minutes per side. Remove the chicken from the skillet and set aside. 3. Add the remaining 1 tablespoon oil to the skillet. Cook the garlic, onion, bell peppers, thyme, and oregano until softened, about 5 minutes. Add the tomatoes and broth and bring to a boil. Return the chicken to the skillet, add the olives, cover, and place the skillet in the oven. Roast until the chicken is tender and a thermometer inserted in the thickest part registers 165°F(74°C), 40 to 50 minutes. 4. While the chicken is cooking, prepare the couscous according to package directions. 5. To serve, pile the couscous on a serving platter and nestle the chicken on top. Pour the vegetables and any pan juices over the chicken and couscous. Sprinkle with the parsley and serve.

Per Serving:

calories: 481 | fat: 15g | protein: 29g | carbs: 61g | fiber: 11g | sodium: 893mg

Hot Goan-Style Coconut Chicken

Prep time: 20 minutes | Cook time: 4 to 6 hours | Serves 6

Spice Paste:
- 8 dried Kashmiri chiles, broken into pieces
- 2 tablespoons coriander seeds
- 2-inch piece cassia bark, broken into pieces
- 1 teaspoon black peppercorns
- 1 teaspoon cumin seeds
Chicken:
- 12 chicken thigh and drumstick pieces, on the bone, skinless
- 1 teaspoon salt (or to taste)
- 1 teaspoon turmeric
- 1 teaspoon fennel seeds
- 4 cloves
- 2 star anise
- 1 tablespoon poppy seeds
- 1 cup freshly grated coconut, or desiccated coconut shreds
- 6 garlic cloves
- ⅓ cup water
- 2 tablespoons coconut oil
- 2 medium onions, finely sliced
- ⅓ cup water
- ½ teaspoon ground nutmeg

- 2 teaspoons tamarind paste
- Handful fresh coriander leaves, chopped for garnish
- 1 or 2 fresh red chiles, for garnish

Make the Spice Paste: 1. In a dry frying pan, roast the Kashmiri chiles, coriander seeds, cassia bark, peppercorns, cumin seeds, fennel seeds, cloves, and star anise until fragrant, about 1 minute. Add the poppy seeds and continue roasting for a few minutes. Then remove from the heat and leave to cool. 2. Once cooled, grind the toasted spices in your spice grinder and set aside. 3. In the same pan, add the dried coconut and toast it for 5 to 7 minutes, until it just starts to turn golden. 4. Transfer to a blender with the garlic and add the water. Blend to make a thick, wet paste. 5. Add the ground spices and blend again to mix together. Make the Chicken: 6. In a large bowl, toss the chicken with the salt and turmeric. Marinate for 15 to 20 minutes. In the meantime, heat the slow cooker to high. 7. Heat the oil in a frying pan (or in the slow cooker if you have a sear setting). Cook the sliced onions for 10 minutes and then add the spice and coconut paste. Cook until it becomes fragrant. 8. Transfer everything to the slow cooker. Add the chicken, then the water. Cover and cook on low for 6 hours, or on high for 4 hours. 9. Sprinkle in the nutmeg and stir in the tamarind paste. Cover and cook for another 5 minutes. 10. Garnish with fresh coriander leaves and whole red chiles to serve.

Per Serving:

calories: 583 | fat: 26g | protein: 77g | carbs: 7g | fiber: 3g | sodium: 762mg

Greek Chicken Souvlaki

Prep time: 30 minutes | Cook time: 15 minutes | Serves 3 to 4

Chicken:
- Grated zest and juice of 1 lemon
- 2 tablespoons extra-virgin olive oil
- 1 tablespoon Greek souvlaki
For Serving:
- Warm pita bread or hot cooked rice
- Sliced ripe tomatoes
- Sliced cucumbers
- seasoning
- 1 pound (454 g) boneless, skinless chicken breast, cut into 2-inch chunks
- Vegetable oil spray
- Thinly sliced red onion
- Kalamata olives
- Tzatziki

1. For the chicken: In a small bowl, combine the lemon zest, lemon juice, olive oil, and souvlaki seasoning. Place the chicken in a gallon-size resealable plastic bag. Pour the marinade over chicken. Seal bag and massage to coat. Place the bag in a large bowl and marinate for 30 minutes, or cover and refrigerate up to 24 hours, turning the bag occasionally. 2. Place the chicken a single layer in the air fryer basket. Set the air fryer to 350°F (177°C) for 10 minutes, turning the chicken and spraying with a little vegetable oil spray halfway through the cooking time. Increase the air fryer temperature to 400°F (204°C) for 5 minutes to allow the chicken to crisp and brown a little. 3. Transfer the chicken to a serving platter and serve with pita bread or rice, tomatoes, cucumbers, onion, olives and tzatziki.

Per Serving:

calories: 198 | fat: 10g | protein: 26g | carbs: 1g | fiber: 0g | sodium: 51mg

Chicken Marinara and Zucchini

Prep time: 10 minutes | Cook time: 15 minutes | Serves 4

- 2 large zucchini, trimmed and chopped
- 4 (6-ounce / 170-g) chicken breast halves
- 3 cups marinara sauce
- 1 tablespoon Italian seasoning
- ½ teaspoon salt
- 1 cup shredded mozzarella cheese

1. Place zucchini on the bottom of the Instant Pot®. Place chicken on zucchini. Pour marinara sauce over chicken. Sprinkle with Italian seasoning and salt. 2. Close lid, set steam release to Sealing, press the Poultry button, and cook for the default time of 15 minutes. When the timer beeps, let pressure release naturally for 10 minutes. Quick-release any remaining pressure until the float valve drops and then open lid. Check chicken using a meat thermometer to ensure the internal temperature is at least 165°F (74°C). 3. Sprinkle chicken with cheese. Close lid and let stand on the Keep Warm setting for 5 minutes to allow the cheese to melt. 4. Transfer chicken and zucchini to a serving platter. Serve hot.

Per Serving:

calories: 21 | fat: 13g | protein: 51g | carbs: 21g | fiber: 5g | sodium: 442mg

Grape Chicken Panzanella

Prep time: 10 minutes |Cook time: 5 minutes| Serves: 6

- 3 cups day-old bread (like a baguette, crusty Italian bread, or whole-grain bread), cut into 1-inch cubes
- 5 tablespoons extra-virgin olive oil, divided
- 2 cups chopped cooked chicken breast (about 1 pound / 454 g)
- 1 cup red seedless grapes, halved
- ½ pint grape or cherry tomatoes, halved (about ¾ cup)
- ½ cup Gorgonzola cheese
- crumbles (about 2 ounces / 57 g)
- ⅓ cup chopped walnuts
- ¼ cup diced red onion (about ⅛ onion)
- 3 tablespoons chopped fresh mint leaves
- ¼ teaspoon freshly ground black pepper
- 1 tablespoon balsamic vinegar
- Zest and juice of 1 small lemon
- 1 teaspoon honey

1. Line a large, rimmed baking sheet with aluminum foil. Set aside. Set one oven rack about 4 inches below the broiler element. Preheat the broiler to high. 2. In a large serving bowl, drizzle the cubed bread with 2 tablespoons of oil, and mix gently with your hands to coat. Spread the mixture over the prepared baking sheet. Place the baking sheet under the broiler for 2 minutes. Stir the bread, then broil for another 30 to 60 seconds, watching carefully so the bread pieces are toasted and not burned. Remove from the oven and set aside. 3. In the same (now empty) large serving bowl, mix together the chicken, grapes, tomatoes, Gorgonzola, walnuts, onion, mint, and pepper. Add the toasted bread pieces, and gently mix together. 4. In a small bowl, whisk together the remaining 3 tablespoons of oil, vinegar, zest and juice from the lemon, and honey. Drizzle the dressing over the salad, toss gently to mix, and serve.

Per Serving:

calories: 334 | fat: 21g | protein: 19g | carbs: 19g | fiber: 2g | sodium: 248mg

Classic Whole Chicken

Prep time: 5 minutes | Cook time: 50 minutes | Serves 4

- Oil, for spraying
- 1 (4-pound / 1.8-kg) whole chicken, giblets removed
- 1 tablespoon olive oil
- 1 teaspoon paprika
- ½ teaspoon granulated garlic
- ½ teaspoon salt
- ½ teaspoon freshly ground black pepper
- ¼ teaspoon finely chopped fresh parsley, for garnish

1. Line the air fryer basket with parchment and spray lightly with oil. 2. Pat the chicken dry with paper towels. Rub it with the olive oil until evenly coated. 3. In a small bowl, mix together the paprika, garlic, salt, and black pepper and sprinkle it evenly over the chicken. 4. Place the chicken in the prepared basket, breast-side down. 5. Air fry at 360°F (182°C) for 30 minutes, flip, and cook for another 20 minutes, or until the internal temperature reaches 165°F (74°C) and the juices run clear. 6. Sprinkle with the parsley before serving.

Per Serving:

calories: 549 | fat: 11g | protein: 105g | carbs: 0g | fiber: 0g | sodium: 523mg

Mediterranean Roasted Turkey Breast

Prep time: 15 minutes | Cook time: 6 to 8 hours | Serves 4

- 3 garlic cloves, minced
- 1 teaspoon sea salt
- 1 teaspoon dried oregano
- ½ teaspoon freshly ground black pepper
- ½ teaspoon dried basil
- ½ teaspoon dried parsley
- ½ teaspoon dried rosemary
- ½ teaspoon dried thyme
- ¼ teaspoon dried dill
- ¼ teaspoon ground nutmeg
- 2 tablespoons extra-virgin olive oil
- 2 tablespoons freshly squeezed lemon juice
- 1 (4- to 6-pound / 1.8- to 2.7-kg) boneless or bone-in turkey breast
- 1 onion, chopped
- ½ cup low-sodium chicken broth
- 4 ounces (113 g) whole Kalamata olives, pitted
- 1 cup sun-dried tomatoes (packaged, not packed in oil), chopped

1. In a small bowl, stir together the garlic, salt, oregano, pepper, basil, parsley, rosemary, thyme, dill, and nutmeg. 2. Drizzle the olive oil and lemon juice all over the turkey breast and generously season it with the garlic-spice mix. 3. In a slow cooker, combine the onion and chicken broth. Place the seasoned turkey breast on top of the onion. Top the turkey with the olives and sun-dried tomatoes. 4. Cover the cooker and cook for 6 to 8 hours on Low heat. 5. Slice or shred the turkey for serving.

Per Serving:

calories: 676 | fat: 19g | protein: 111g | carbs: 14g | fiber: 3g | sodium: 626mg

Citrus and Spice Chicken

Prep time: 15 minutes | Cook time: 17 minutes | Serves 8

- 2 tablespoons olive oil
- 3 pounds (1.4 kg) boneless, skinless chicken thighs
- 1 teaspoon smoked paprika
- ½ teaspoon salt
- ⅛ teaspoon ground cinnamon
- ⅛ teaspoon ground ginger
- ⅛ teaspoon ground nutmeg
- ½ cup golden raisins
- ½ cup slivered almonds
- 1 cup orange juice
- ⅛ cup lemon juice
- ⅛ cup lime juice
- 1 pound (454 g) carrots, peeled and chopped
- 2 tablespoons water
- 1 tablespoon arrowroot powder

1. Press the Sauté button on the Instant Pot® and heat oil. Fry chicken thighs for 2 minutes on each side until browned. 2. Add paprika, salt, cinnamon, ginger, nutmeg, raisins, almonds, orange juice, lemon juice, lime juice, and carrots. Press the Cancel button. 3. Close lid, set steam release to Sealing, press the Manual button, and set time to 10 minutes. When the timer beeps, let pressure release naturally for 5 minutes. Quick-release any remaining pressure until the float valve drops and then open lid. Check chicken using a meat thermometer to make sure the internal temperature is at least 165°F (74°C). 4. Use a slotted spoon to remove chicken, carrots, and raisins, and transfer to a serving platter. Press the Cancel button. 5. In a small bowl, whisk together water and arrowroot to create a slurry. Add to liquid in the Instant Pot® and stir to combine. Press the Sauté button, press the Adjust button to change the temperature to Less, and simmer uncovered for 3 minutes until sauce is thickened. Pour sauce over chicken and serve.

Per Serving:

calories: 332 | fat: 14g | protein: 36g | carbs: 14g | fiber: 3g | sodium: 337mg

Turkey Breast Romano

Prep time: 15 minutes | Cook time: 20 minutes | Serves 8

- ½ cup all-purpose flour
- ½ teaspoon salt
- ½ teaspoon ground black pepper
- 2 pounds (907 g) boneless, skinless turkey breast, cut into bite-sized pieces
- 2 tablespoons olive oil
- 1 large sweet onion, peeled and diced
- 4 cloves garlic, peeled and minced
- 1 tablespoon dried oregano
- 1 teaspoon dried basil
- 2 tablespoons tomato paste
- ½ cup low-sodium chicken broth
- 1 (8-ounce / 227-g) can tomato sauce
- 1 teaspoon balsamic vinegar
- 2 (4-ounce / 113-g) cans sliced mushrooms, drained
- 1 tablespoon sugar
- 1 pound (454 g) spaghetti, cooked
- 8 ounces (227 g) Romano cheese, grated

1. Place flour, salt, and pepper in a large zip-top plastic bag. Seal and shake to mix. Add turkey to the bag, seal, and shake to coat turkey in flour mixture. 2. Press the Sauté button on the Instant Pot® and heat oil. Add turkey and onion, and cook until turkey begins to brown and onion is translucent, about 5 minutes. 3. Stir in garlic, oregano, basil, and tomato paste, and cook for 2 minutes. Stir in broth, tomato sauce, vinegar, mushrooms, and sugar. Press the Cancel button. 4. Close lid, set steam release to Sealing, press the Manual button, and set time to 12 minutes. When the timer beeps, let pressure release naturally for 10 minutes. 5. Quick release any remaining pressure until the float valve drops. Open lid and stir turkey and sauce, pour over pasta, and top with grated Romano cheese.

Per Serving:

calories: 498 | fat: 11g | protein: 47g | carbs: 53g | fiber: 4g | sodium: 734mg

Baked Chicken Caprese

Prep time: 5minutes |Cook time: 25 minutes| Serves: 4

- Nonstick cooking spray
- 1 pound (454 g) boneless, skinless chicken breasts
- 2 tablespoons extra-virgin olive oil
- ¼ teaspoon freshly ground black pepper
- ¼ teaspoon kosher or sea salt
- 1 large tomato, sliced thinly
- 1 cup shredded mozzarella or 4 ounces (113 g) fresh mozzarella cheese, diced
- 1 (14½-ounce / 411-g) can low-sodium or no-salt-added crushed tomatoes
- 2 tablespoons fresh torn basil leaves
- 4 teaspoons balsamic vinegar

1. Set one oven rack about 4 inches below the broiler element. Preheat the oven to 450°F(235°C). Line a large, rimmed baking sheet with aluminum foil. Place a wire cooling rack on the aluminum foil, and spray the rack with nonstick cooking spray. Set aside. 2. Cut the chicken into 4 pieces (if they aren't already). Put the chicken breasts in a large zip-top plastic bag. With a rolling pin or meat mallet, pound the chicken so it is evenly flattened, about ¼-inch thick. Add the oil, pepper, and salt to the bag. Reseal the bag, and massage the ingredients into the chicken. Take the chicken out of the bag and place it on the prepared wire rack. 3. Cook the chicken for 15 to 18 minutes, or until the internal temperature of the chicken is 165°F(74°C) on a meat thermometer and the juices run clear. Turn the oven to the high broiler setting. Layer the tomato slices on each chicken breast, and top with the mozzarella. Broil the chicken for another 2 to 3 minutes, or until the cheese is melted (don't let the chicken burn on the edges). Remove the chicken from the oven. 4. While the chicken is cooking, pour the crushed tomatoes into a small, microwave-safe bowl. Cover the bowl with a paper towel, and microwave for about 1 minute on high, until hot. When you're ready to serve, divide the tomatoes among four dinner plates. Place each chicken breast on top of the tomatoes. Top with the basil and a drizzle of balsamic vinegar.

Per Serving:

calories: 304 | fat: 15g | protein: 34g | carbs: 7g | fiber: 3g | sodium: 215mg

Chapter 4 Beans and Grains

Tomato Bulgur

Prep time: 10 minutes | Cook time: 25 minutes | Serves 4

◄ 3 tablespoons olive oil
◄ 1 onion, diced
◄ 1 garlic clove, minced
◄ 1 tablespoon tomato paste
◄ ½ teaspoon paprika
◄ 3 Roma (plum) tomatoes, finely chopped, or 1 cup canned crushed tomatoes
with their juices
◄ Juice of ½ lemon
◄ ¼ teaspoon sea salt, plus more as needed
◄ 1 cup dried bulgur
◄ 2 cups vegetable broth, chicken broth, or water

1. In a large saucepan, heat the olive oil over medium-high heat. Add the onion and garlic and sauté for 4 to 5 minutes, until the onion is soft. Add the tomato paste and paprika and stir for about 30 seconds. 2. Add the chopped tomatoes, lemon juice, and salt and cook for 1 to 2 minutes more. 3. Add the bulgur and stir for about 30 seconds. Add the broth, bring to a simmer, reduce the heat to low, cover, and simmer for 13 to 15 minutes, until the liquid has been absorbed. Uncover and stir, then remove from the heat, cover, and let stand for 5 minutes. 4. Taste and adjust the seasoning, then serve.

Per Serving:
calories: 243 | fat: 11g | protein: 6g | carbs: 34g | fiber: 6g | sodium: 92mg

Spicy Black Beans with Root Veggies

Prep time: 20 minutes | Cook time: 8 hours | Serves 2

◄ 1 onion, chopped
◄ 1 leek, white part only, sliced
◄ 3 garlic cloves, minced
◄ 1 jalapeño pepper, minced
◄ 2 Yukon Gold potatoes, peeled and cubed
◄ 1 parsnip, peeled and cubed
◄ 1 carrot, sliced
◄ 1 cup dried black beans,
sorted and rinsed
◄ 2 cups vegetable broth
◄ 2 teaspoons chili powder
◄ ½ teaspoon dried marjoram leaves
◄ ½ teaspoon salt
◄ ⅛ teaspoon freshly ground black pepper
◄ ⅛ teaspoon crushed red pepper flakes

1. In the slow cooker, combine all the ingredients. 2. Cover and cook on low for 7 to 8 hours, or until the beans and vegetables are tender, and serve.

Per Serving:
calories: 597 | fat: 2g | protein: 27g | carbs: 124g | fiber: 25g | sodium: 699mg

Garbanzo and Pita No-Bake Casserole

Prep time: 10 minutes | Cook time: 10 minutes | Serves 4

◄ 4 cups Greek yogurt
◄ 3 cloves garlic, minced
◄ 1 teaspoon salt
◄ 2 (16-ounce/ 454-g) cans garbanzo beans, rinsed and
drained
◄ 2 cups water
◄ 4 cups pita chips
◄ 5 tablespoons unsalted butter

1. In a large bowl, whisk together the yogurt, garlic, and salt. Set aside. 2. Put the garbanzo beans and water in a medium pot. Bring to a boil; let beans boil for about 5 minutes. 3. Pour the garbanzo beans and the liquid into a large casserole dish. 4. Top the beans with pita chips. Pour the yogurt sauce over the pita chip layer. 5. In a small saucepan, melt and brown the butter, about 3 minutes. Pour the brown butter over the yogurt sauce.

Per Serving:
calories: 772 | fat: 36g | protein: 39g | carbs: 73g | fiber: 13g | sodium: 1,003mg

Brown Rice with Dried Fruit

Prep time: 15 minutes | Cook time: 20 minutes | Serves 6

◄ 2 tablespoons olive oil
◄ 2 stalks celery, thinly sliced
◄ 2 large carrots, peeled and diced
◄ 1 large sweet potato, peeled and diced
◄ 1½ cups brown rice
◄ ⅓ cup chopped prunes
◄ ⅓ cup chopped dried
apricots
◄ ½ teaspoon ground cinnamon
◄ 2 teaspoons grated orange zest
◄ 3 cups water
◄ 1 bay leaf
◄ ½ teaspoon salt

1. Press the Sauté button on the Instant Pot® and heat oil. Add celery, carrots, sweet potato, and rice. Cook until vegetables are just tender, about 3 minutes. Stir in prunes, apricots, cinnamon, and orange zest. Cook until cinnamon is fragrant, about 30 seconds. Add water, bay leaf, and salt. 2. Press the Cancel button, close lid, set steam release to Sealing, press the Manual button, and set time to 16 minutes. When the timer beeps, let pressure release naturally for 10 minutes. Quick-release any remaining pressure until the float valve drops and open the lid. Fluff rice with a fork. 3. Remove and discard bay leaf. Transfer to a serving bowl. Serve hot.

Per Serving:
calories: 192 | fat: 5g | protein: 3g | carbs: 34g | fiber: 4g | sodium: 272mg

Creamy Thyme Polenta

Prep time: 5 minutes | Cook time: 10 minutes | Serves 6

- 3½ cups water
- ½ cup coarse polenta
- ½ cup fine cornmeal
- 1 cup corn kernels
- 1 teaspoon dried thyme
- 1 teaspoon salt

1. Add all ingredients to the Instant Pot® and stir. 2. Close lid, set steam release to Sealing, press the Manual button, and set time to 10 minutes. When the timer beeps, quick-release the pressure until the float valve drops and open lid. Serve immediately.

Per Serving:

calories: 74 | fat: 1g | protein: 2g | carbs: 14g | fiber: 2g | sodium: 401mg

White Beans with Kale

Prep time: 15 minutes | Cook time: 7½ hours | Serves 2

- 1 onion, chopped
- 1 leek, white part only, sliced
- 2 celery stalks, sliced
- 2 garlic cloves, minced
- 1 cup dried white lima beans or cannellini beans, sorted and rinsed
- 2 cups vegetable broth
- ½ teaspoon salt
- ½ teaspoon dried thyme leaves
- ⅛ teaspoon freshly ground black pepper
- 3 cups torn kale

1. In the slow cooker, combine all the ingredients except the kale. 2. Cover and cook on low for 7 hours, or until the beans are tender. 3. Add the kale and stir. 4. Cover and cook on high for 30 minutes, or until the kale is tender but still firm, and serve.

Per Serving:

calories: 176 | fat: 1g | protein: 9g | carbs: 36g | fiber: 9g | sodium: 616mg

Lebanese Rice and Broken Noodles with Cabbage

Prep time: 5 minutes |Cook time: 25 minutes| Serves: 6

- 1 tablespoon extra-virgin olive oil
- 1 cup (about 3 ounces / 85 g) uncooked vermicelli or thin spaghetti, broken into 1- to 1½-inch pieces
- 3 cups shredded cabbage (about half a 14-ounce package of coleslaw mix or half a small head of cabbage)
- 3 cups low-sodium or no-
- salt-added vegetable broth
- ½ cup water
- 1 cup instant brown rice
- 2 garlic cloves
- ¼ teaspoon kosher or sea salt
- ⅛ to ¼ teaspoon crushed red pepper
- ½ cup loosely packed, coarsely chopped cilantro
- Fresh lemon slices, for serving (optional)

1. In a large saucepan over medium-high heat, heat the oil. Add the pasta and cook for 3 minutes to toast, stirring often. Add the cabbage and cook for 4 minutes, stirring often. Add the broth, water, rice, garlic, salt, and crushed red pepper, and bring to a boil over high heat. Stir, cover, and reduce the heat to medium-low. Simmer for 10 minutes. 2. Remove the pan from the heat, but do not lift the lid. Let sit for 5 minutes. Fish out the garlic cloves, mash them with a fork, then stir the garlic back into the rice. Stir in the cilantro. Serve with the lemon slices (if using).

Per Serving:

calories: 150 | fat: 4g | protein: 3g | carbs: 27g | fiber: 3g | sodium: 664mg

Za'atar Chickpeas and Chicken

Prep time: 10 minutes | Cook time: 4 to 6 hours | Serves 4

- 2 pounds (907 g) bone-in chicken thighs or legs
- 1 (15-ounce/ 425-g) can reduced-sodium chickpeas, drained and rinsed
- ½ cup low-sodium chicken broth
- Juice of 1 lemon
- 1 tablespoon extra-virgin olive oil
- 2 teaspoons white vinegar
- 2 tablespoons za'atar
- 1 garlic clove, minced
- ½ teaspoon sea salt
- ¼ teaspoon freshly ground black pepper

1. In a slow cooker, combine the chicken and chickpeas. Stir to mix well. 2. In a small bowl, whisk together the chicken broth, lemon juice, olive oil, vinegar, za'atar, garlic, salt, and pepper until combined. Pour the mixture over the chicken and chickpeas. 3. Cover the cooker and cook for 4 to 6 hours on Low heat.

Per Serving:

calories: 647 | fat: 41g | protein: 46g | carbs: 23g | fiber: 7g | sodium: 590mg

Quinoa with Artichokes

Prep time: 10 minutes | Cook time: 26 minutes | Serves 4

- 2 tablespoons light olive oil
- 1 medium yellow onion, peeled and diced
- 2 cloves garlic, peeled and minced
- ½ teaspoon salt
- ½ teaspoon ground black pepper
- 1 cup quinoa, rinsed and
- drained
- 2 cups vegetable broth
- 1 cup roughly chopped marinated artichoke hearts
- ½ cup sliced green olives
- ½ cup minced fresh flat-leaf parsley
- 2 tablespoons lemon juice

1. Press the Sauté button on the Instant Pot® and heat oil. Add onion and cook until tender, about 5 minutes. Add garlic, salt, and pepper, and cook until fragrant, about 30 seconds. Press the Cancel button. 2. Stir in quinoa and broth. Close lid, set steam release to Sealing, press the Manual button, and set time to 20 minutes. When the timer beeps, let pressure release naturally, about 20 minutes, then open lid. Fluff quinoa with a fork, then stir in remaining ingredients. Serve immediately.

Per Serving:

calories: 270 | fat: 13g | protein: 6g | carbs: 33g | fiber: 4g | sodium: 718mg

Vegetable Barley Soup

Prep time: 30 minutes | Cook time: 26 minutes | Serves 8

- 2 tablespoons olive oil
- ½ medium yellow onion, peeled and chopped
- 1 medium carrot, peeled and chopped
- 1 stalk celery, chopped
- 2 cups sliced button mushrooms
- 2 cloves garlic, peeled and minced
- ½ teaspoon dried thyme
- ½ teaspoon ground black pepper
- 1 large russet potato, peeled and cut into ½" pieces
- 1(14½-ounce / 411-g) can fire-roasted diced tomatoes, undrained
- ½ cup medium pearl barley, rinsed and drained
- 4 cups vegetable broth
- 2 cups water
- 1 (15-ounce / 425-g) can corn, drained
- 1 (15-ounce / 425-g) can cut green beans, drained
- 1 (15-ounce / 425-g) can Great Northern beans, drained and rinsed
- ½ teaspoon salt

1. Press the Sauté button on the Instant Pot® and heat oil. Add onion, carrot, celery, and mushrooms. Cook until just tender, about 5 minutes. Add garlic, thyme, and pepper. Cook 30 seconds. Press the Cancel button. 2. Add potato, tomatoes, barley, broth, and water to pot. Close lid, set steam release to Sealing, press the Soup button, and cook for the default time of 20 minutes. 3. When the timer beeps, let pressure release naturally, about 15 minutes. Open lid and stir soup, then add corn, green beans, and Great Northern beans. Close lid and let stand on the Keep Warm setting for 10 minutes. Stir in salt. Serve hot.

Per Serving:

calories: 190 | fat: 4g | protein: 7g | carbs: 34g | fiber: 8g | sodium: 548mg

Lemon and Garlic Rice Pilaf

Prep time: 10 minutes | Cook time: 34 minutes | Serves 8

- 2 tablespoons olive oil
- 1 medium yellow onion, peeled and chopped
- 4 cloves garlic, peeled and minced
- 1 tablespoon grated lemon zest
- ½ teaspoon ground black
- pepper
- 1 teaspoon dried thyme
- 1 teaspoon dried oregano
- ¼ teaspoon salt
- 2 tablespoons white wine
- 2 tablespoons lemon juice
- 2 cups brown rice
- 2 cups vegetable broth

1. Press the Sauté button on the Instant Pot® and heat oil. Add onion and cook until soft, about 6 minutes. Add garlic and cook until fragrant, about 30 seconds. Add lemon zest, pepper, thyme, oregano, and salt. Cook until fragrant, about 1 minute. 2. Add wine and lemon juice and cook, stirring well, until liquid has almost evaporated, about 1 minute. Add rice and cook, stirring constantly, until coated and starting to toast, about 3 minutes. Press the Cancel button. 3. Stir in broth. Close lid, set steam release to Sealing, press the Manual button, and set time to 22 minutes. 4. When the timer beeps, let pressure release naturally for 10 minutes, then quick-release the remaining pressure until the float valve drops. Open lid

and fluff rice with a fork. Serve warm.

Per Serving:

calories: 202 | fat: 5g | protein: 4g | carbs: 37g | fiber: 1g | sodium: 274mg

Chili-Spiced Beans

Prep time: 10 minutes | Cook time: 30 minutes | Serves 8

- 1 pound (454 g) dried pinto beans, soaked overnight and drained
- 1 medium onion, peeled and chopped
- ¼ cup chopped fresh cilantro
- 1 (15-ounce / 425-g) can tomato sauce
- ¼ cup chili powder
- 2 tablespoons smoked paprika
- 1 teaspoon ground cumin
- 1 teaspoon ground coriander
- ½ teaspoon ground black pepper
- 2 cups vegetable broth
- 1 cup water

1. Place all ingredients in the Instant Pot® and stir to combine. 2. Close lid, set steam release to Sealing, press the Chili button, and cook for the default time of 30 minutes. When the timer beeps, quick-release the pressure until the float valve drops, open lid, and stir well. If beans are too thin, press the Cancel button, then press the Sauté button and let beans simmer, uncovered, until desired thickness is reached. Serve warm.

Per Serving:

calories: 86 | fat: 0g | protein: 5g | carbs: 17g | fiber: 4g | sodium: 323mg

Fasolakia (Greek Green Beans)

Prep time: 5 minutes | Cook time: 45 minutes | Serves 2

- ⅓ cup olive oil (any variety)
- 1 medium onion (red or white), chopped
- 1 medium russet or white potato, sliced into ¼-inch (.5cm) thick slices
- 1 pound (454 g) green beans (fresh or frozen)
- 3 medium tomatoes, grated, or 1 (15-ounce / 425-g) can crushed tomatoes
- ¼ cup chopped fresh parsley
- 1 teaspoon granulated sugar
- ½ teaspoon salt
- ¼ teaspoon freshly ground black pepper

1. Add the olive oil a medium pot over medium-low heat. When the oil begins to shimmer, add the onions and sauté until soft, about 5 minutes. 2. Add the potatoes to the pot, and sauté for an additional 2–3 minutes. 3. Add the green beans and stir until the beans are thoroughly coated with the olive oil. Add the tomatoes, parsley, sugar, salt, and black pepper. Stir to combine. 4. Add just enough hot water to the pot to cover half the beans. Cover and simmer for 40 minutes or until there is no water left in the pot and the beans are soft. (Do not allow the beans to boil.) 5. Allow the beans to cool until they're warm or until they reach room temperature, but do not serve hot. Store in refrigerator for up to 3 days.

Per Serving:

calories: 536 | fat: 37g | protein: 9g | carbs: 50g | fiber: 11g | sodium: 617mg

Buckwheat and Halloumi Bowl with Mint Dressing

Prep time: 20 minutes | Cook time: 12 minutes | Serves 4

- 1 cup raw buckwheat groats, rinsed and drained
- 1¼ cups water
- ¼ teaspoon salt
- 2 tablespoons light olive oil, divided
- 8 ounces (227 g) Halloumi, cut into ¼" slices
- 4 cups chopped kale or spinach
- ½ medium red onion, peeled and diced
- ½ large English cucumber, chopped
- 1 cup halved cherry tomatoes
- ½ cup pitted Kalamata olives
- ¼ cup lemon juice
- ¼ cup extra-virgin olive oil
- ¼ cup fresh mint leaves
- 1 teaspoon honey
- 1 teaspoon Dijon mustard
- ¼ teaspoon ground black pepper

1. Place buckwheat, water, salt, and 1 tablespoon light olive oil in the Instant Pot® and stir well. Close lid and set steam release to Sealing. Press the Manual button and set time to 6 minutes. 2. When the timer beeps, let pressure release naturally, about 20 minutes, then open lid and transfer buckwheat to a separate medium bowl. Clean and dry pot. Press the Cancel button. 3. Press the Sauté button and heat remaining 1 tablespoon light olive oil. Add Halloumi slices and brown for 3 minutes per side. 4. To assemble, place a layer of greens in four bowls. Top with buckwheat, Halloumi slices, onion, cucumber, tomatoes, and olives. 5. Place lemon juice, extra-virgin olive oil, mint, honey, Dijon mustard, and pepper in a blender. Blend until completely combined, about 30 seconds. Pour dressing over bowls and serve immediately.

Per Serving:

calories: 453 | fat: 25g | protein: 12g | carbs: 46g | fiber: 8g | sodium: 246mg

Herbed Wild Rice Dressing

Prep time: 15 minutes | Cook time: 32 minutes | Serves 8

- 2 tablespoons extra-virgin olive oil
- 2 stalks celery, chopped
- 1 medium white onion, peeled and chopped
- 1 medium carrot, peeled and chopped
- 2 cups sliced baby bella mushrooms
- 2 cloves garlic, peeled and minced
- 1 tablespoon chopped fresh
- rosemary
- 1 tablespoon chopped fresh sage
- ¼ teaspoon salt
- ½ teaspoon ground black pepper
- 2 cups wild rice
- 2½ cups vegetable broth
- ½ cup dried cranberries
- ½ cup chopped toasted pecans

1. Press the Sauté button on the Instant Pot® and heat oil. Add celery, onion, carrot, and mushrooms. Cook until soft, about 10 minutes. Add garlic, rosemary, sage, salt, and pepper. Cook until fragrant, about 1 minute. Add rice and mix well. Press the Cancel button. 2. Stir in broth. Close lid, set steam release to Sealing, press the Manual button, and set time to 20 minutes. When the timer

beeps, let pressure release naturally for 10 minutes, then quick release the remaining pressure. Open lid and fold in cranberries and pecans. Serve warm.

Per Serving:

calories: 356 | fat: 13g | protein: 9g | carbs: 50g | fiber: 5g | sodium: 147mg

Quinoa with Kale, Carrots, and Walnuts

Prep time: 10 minutes | Cook time: 20 minutes | Serves 4

- 1 cup quinoa, rinsed and drained
- 2 cups water
- ¼ cup olive oil
- 2 tablespoons apple cider vinegar
- 1 clove garlic, peeled and minced
- ½ teaspoon ground black pepper
- ½ teaspoon salt
- 2 cups chopped kale
- 1 cup shredded carrot
- 1 cup toasted walnut pieces
- ½ cup crumbled feta cheese

1. Add quinoa and water to the Instant Pot® and stir well. Close lid, set steam release to Sealing, press the Manual button, and set time to 20 minutes. When the timer beeps, let pressure release naturally, about 20 minutes, then open lid. Fluff quinoa with a fork, then transfer to a medium bowl and set aside to cool to room temperature, about 40 minutes. 2. Add oil, vinegar, garlic, pepper, salt, kale, carrot, walnuts, and feta to quinoa and toss well. Refrigerate for 4 hours before serving.

Per Serving:

calories: 625 | fat: 39g | protein: 19g | carbs: 47g | fiber: 10g | sodium: 738mg

Quinoa Salad with Tomatoes

Prep time: 10 minutes | Cook time: 22 minutes | Serves 4

- 2 tablespoons olive oil
- 2 cloves garlic, peeled and minced
- 1 cup diced fresh tomatoes
- ¼ cup chopped fresh Italian flat-leaf parsley
- 1 tablespoon lemon juice
- 1 cup quinoa, rinsed and drained
- 2 cups water
- 1 teaspoon salt

1. Press the Sauté button on the Instant Pot® and heat oil. Add garlic and cook 30 seconds, then add tomatoes, parsley, and lemon juice. Cook an additional 1 minute. Transfer mixture to a small bowl and set aside. Press the Cancel button. 2. Add quinoa and water to the Instant Pot®. Close lid, set steam release to Sealing, press the Multigrain button, and set time to 20 minutes. 3. When timer beeps, let pressure release naturally, about 20 minutes, then open lid. Fluff with a fork and stir in tomato mixture and salt. Serve immediately.

Per Serving:

calories: 223 | fat: 10g | protein: 6g | carbs: 29g | fiber: 3g | sodium: 586mg

Brown Rice Vegetable Bowl with Roasted Red Pepper Dressing

Prep time: 10 minutes | Cook time: 22 minutes | Serves 2

- ¼ cup chopped roasted red bell pepper
- 2 tablespoons extra-virgin olive oil
- 1 tablespoon red wine vinegar
- 1 teaspoon honey
- 2 tablespoons light olive oil
- 2 cloves garlic, peeled and minced
- ½ teaspoon ground black pepper
- ¼ teaspoon salt
- 1 cup brown rice
- 1 cup vegetable broth
- ¼ cup chopped fresh flat-leaf parsley
- 2 tablespoons chopped fresh chives
- 2 tablespoons chopped fresh dill
- ½ cup diced tomato
- ½ cup chopped red onion
- ½ cup diced cucumber
- ½ cup chopped green bell pepper

1. Place roasted red pepper, extra-virgin olive oil, red wine vinegar, and honey in a blender. Purée until smooth, about 1 minute. Refrigerate until ready to serve. 2. Press the Sauté button on the Instant Pot® and heat light olive oil. Add garlic and cook until fragrant, about 30 seconds. Add black pepper, salt, and rice and stir well. Press the Cancel button. 3. Stir in broth. Close lid, set steam release to Sealing, press the Manual button, and set time to 22 minutes.

Per Serving:

calories: 561 | fat: 23g | protein: 10g | carbs: 86g | fiber: 5g | sodium: 505mg

Slow Cooker Vegetarian Chili

Prep time: 20 minutes | Cook time: 4 to 6 hours | Serves 4

- 1 (28-ounce/ 794-g) can chopped whole tomatoes, with the juice
- 1 medium green bell pepper, chopped
- 1 (15-ounce / 425-g) can red beans, drained and rinsed
- 1 (15-ounce / 425-g) can black beans, drained and rinsed
- 1 yellow onion, chopped
- 1 tablespoon olive oil
- 1 tablespoon onion powder
- 1 teaspoon garlic powder
- 1 teaspoon cayenne pepper
- 1 teaspoon paprika
- ½ teaspoon sea salt
- ½ teaspoon black pepper
- 1 large hass avocado, pitted, peeled, and chopped, for garnish

1. Combine the tomatoes, bell pepper, red beans, black beans, and onion in the slow cooker. Sprinkle with the onion powder, garlic powder, cayenne pepper, paprika, ½ teaspoon salt, and ½ teaspoon black pepper. 2. Cover and cook on high for 4 to 6 hours or on low for 8 hours, or until thick. 3. Season with salt and black pepper if needed. Served hot, garnished with some of the avocado.

Per Serving:

calories:446 | fat: 15g | protein: 21g | carbs: 61g | fiber: 22g | sodium: 599mg

Couscous with Apricots

Prep time: 10 minutes | Cook time: 15 minutes | Serves 4

- 2 tablespoons olive oil
- 1 small onion, diced
- 1 cup whole-wheat couscous
- 2 cups water or broth
- ½ cup dried apricots, soaked
- in water overnight
- ½ cup slivered almonds or pistachios
- ½ teaspoon dried mint
- ½ teaspoon dried thyme

1. Heat the olive oil in a large skillet over medium-high heat. Add the onion and cook until translucent and soft. 2. Stir in the couscous and cook for 2–3 minutes. 3. Add the water or broth, cover, and cook for 8–10 minutes until the water is mostly absorbed. 4. Remove from the heat and let stand for a few minutes. 5. Fluff with a fork and fold in the apricots, nuts, mint, and thyme.

Per Serving:

calories: 294 | fat: 15g | protein: 8g | carbs: 38g | fiber: 6g | sodium: 6mg

Vegetable Risotto with Beet Greens

Prep time: 30 minutes | Cook time: 10 minutes | Serves 6

- ¼ cup light olive oil
- 1 clove garlic, peeled and minced
- 1 small Asian eggplant, sliced
- 1 small zucchini, trimmed and sliced
- 1 large red bell pepper, seeded and cut in quarters
- 1 large portobello mushroom, gills and stem removed, cap sliced
- 1 medium onion, peeled and
- thickly sliced
- ½ teaspoon salt
- ½ teaspoon ground black pepper
- 1 cup Arborio rice
- ½ cup dry white wine
- 2 cups low-sodium chicken broth
- 2 cups sliced young beet greens
- ¼ cup sliced fresh basil
- ½ cup grated Parmesan cheese

1. Combine oil and garlic in a small bowl. Stir to mix and set aside 10 minutes to infuse. 2. Preheat a grill or a grill pan over medium-high heat. 3. Brush all sides of eggplant slices, zucchini slices, bell pepper quarters, mushroom slices, and onion slices with garlic-infused oil, making sure to reserve 1 tablespoon of the oil. 4. Place vegetables on the grill rack or in the grill pan. Sprinkle with salt and black pepper. 5. Grill vegetables for several minutes on each side or until softened and slightly charred, about 1 minute per side. Set aside to cool, and then coarsely chop. 6. Press the Sauté button on the Instant Pot® and heat reserved 1 tablespoon garlic-infused oil. Add rice and stir it to coat it in oil. Stir in wine and broth. Press the Cancel button. 7. Close lid, set steam release to Sealing, press the Manual button, and set time to 7 minutes. When the timer beeps, quick-release the pressure until the float valve drops and open the lid. 8. Add chopped grilled vegetables, beet greens, and basil. Cover the Instant Pot® (but do not lock the lid into place). Set aside for 5 minutes or until greens are wilted. Stir in cheese and serve hot.

Per Serving:

calories: 261 | fat: 12g | protein: 9g | carbs: 30g | fiber: 5g | sodium: 544mg

Crunchy Pea and Barley Salad

Prep time: 10 minutes | Cook time: 15 minutes | Serves 4

- 2 cups water
- 1 cup quick-cooking barley
- 2 cups sugar snap pea pods
- Small bunch flat-leaf parsley, chopped
- ½ small red onion, diced
- 2 tablespoons olive oil
- Juice of 1 lemon
- Sea salt and freshly ground pepper, to taste

1. Bring water to boil in a saucepan. Stir in the barley and cover. 2. Simmer for 10 minutes until all water is absorbed, and then let stand about 5 minutes covered. 3. Rinse the barley under cold water and combine it with the peas, parsley, onion, olive oil, and lemon juice. 4. Season with sea salt and freshly ground pepper to taste.

Per Serving:

calories: 277 | fat: 8g | protein: 8g | carbs: 47g | fiber: 11g | sodium: 19mg

South Indian Split Yellow Pigeon Peas with Mixed Vegetables

Prep time: 20 minutes | Cook time: 4½ to 6½ minutes | Serves 6

Sambar Masala:
- 1 teaspoon rapeseed oil
- 3 tablespoons coriander seeds
- 2 tablespoons split gram
- 1 teaspoon black

Sambar:
- 1½ cups split yellow pigeon peas, washed
- 2 fresh green chiles, sliced lengthwise
- 2 garlic cloves, chopped
- 6 pearl onions
- 4 to 5 tablespoons sambar masala
- 2 teaspoons salt
- 1 to 2 carrots, peeled and chopped
- 1 red potato, peeled and diced
- 1 white radish (mooli), peeled and chopped into

- peppercorns
- ½ teaspoon fenugreek seeds
- ½ teaspoon mustard seeds
- ¼ teaspoon cumin seeds
- 12 whole dried red chiles

- 2¾-inch sticks
- 1 tomato, roughly chopped
- 4 cups water
- 2 to 3 moringa seed pods, or ⅓ pound (151 g) green beans or asparagus, chopped into 2¾-inch lengths
- 2 tablespoons tamarind paste
- ½ teaspoon asafetida
- 2 teaspoons coconut oil
- 1 teaspoon mustard seeds
- 20 curry leaves
- 2 dried red chilies
- Handful fresh coriander leaves, chopped (optional)

Make the Sambar Masala: 1. Add the oil to a medium nonstick skillet. Add all of the remaining ingredients and roast for a few minutes until fragrant. The spices will brown a little, but don't let them burn. 2. Remove from the heat and pour onto a plate to cool. Once cooled, place into your spice grinder or mortar and pestle and grind to a powder. Set aside. Make the Sambar: 3. Heat the slow cooker to high and add the pigeon peas, green chiles, garlic, pearl onions, sambar masala, salt, carrots, potatoes, radish, tomato, and water. 4. Cover and cook for 4 hours on high, or for 6 hours on low. 5. Add the moringa (or green beans or asparagus), tamarind paste, and asafetida. Cover and cook for another 30 minutes. 6. When you're ready to serve, heat the coconut oil in a frying pan and pop the mustard seeds with the curry leaves and dried chiles. Pour over the sambar. Top with coriander leaves (if using) and serve.

Per Serving:

calories: 312 | fat: 7g | protein: 12g | carbs: 59g | fiber: 16g | sodium: 852mg

Wheat Berry Salad

Prep time: 20 minutes | Cook time: 50 minutes | Serves 12

- 1½ tablespoons vegetable oil
- 6¾ cups water
- 1½ cups wheat berries
- 1½ teaspoons Dijon mustard
- 1 teaspoon sugar
- 1 teaspoon salt
- ½ teaspoon ground black pepper
- ¼ cup white wine vinegar
- ½ cup extra-virgin olive oil
- ½ small red onion, peeled and diced
- 1⅓ cups frozen corn, thawed
- 1 medium zucchini, trimmed, grated, and drained
- 2 stalks celery, finely diced
- 1 medium red bell pepper, seeded and diced
- 4 scallions, diced
- ¼ cup diced sun-dried tomatoes
- ¼ cup chopped fresh parsley

1. Add vegetable oil, water, and wheat berries to the Instant Pot®. Close lid, set steam release to Sealing, press the Manual button, and set time to 50 minutes. When the timer beeps, quick-release the pressure until the float valve drops and open lid. Fluff wheat berries with a fork. Drain any excess liquid, transfer to a large bowl, and set aside to cool. 2. Purée mustard, sugar, salt, black pepper, vinegar, olive oil, and onion in a blender. Stir dressing into wheat berries. Stir in rest of ingredients. Serve.

Per Serving:

calories: 158 | fat: 10g | protein: 2g | carbs: 16g | fiber: 2g | sodium: 268mg

Rice and Lentils

Prep time: 10 minutes | Cook time: 55 minutes | Serves 4

- 2 cups green or brown lentils
- 1 cup brown rice
- 5 cups water or chicken stock
- ½ teaspoon sea salt
- ½ teaspoon freshly ground pepper
- ½ teaspoon dried thyme
- ¼ cup olive oil
- 3 onions, peeled and sliced

1. Place the lentils and rice in a large saucepan with water or chicken stock. Bring to a boil, cover, and simmer for 20–25 minutes, or until almost tender. 2. Add the seasonings and cook an additional 20–30 minutes, or until the rice is tender and the water is absorbed. 3. In another saucepan, heat the olive oil over medium heat. Add the onions and cook very slowly, stirring frequently, until the onions become browned and caramelized, about 20 minutes. 4. To serve, ladle the lentils and rice into bowls and top with the caramelized onions.

Per Serving:

calories: 661 | fat: 16g | protein: 28g | carbs: 104g | fiber: 13g | sodium: 303mg

Chapter 5 Beef, Pork, and Lamb

Roasted Pork with Apple-Dijon Sauce

Prep time: 15 minutes | Cook time: 40 minutes | Serves 8

- 1½ tablespoons extra-virgin olive oil
- 1 (12-ounce/ 340-g) pork tenderloin
- ¼ teaspoon kosher salt
- ¼ teaspoon freshly ground black pepper
- ¼ cup apple jelly
- ¼ cup apple juice
- 2 to 3 tablespoons Dijon mustard
- ½ tablespoon cornstarch
- ½ tablespoon cream

1. Preheat the oven to 325°F(165ºC). 2. In a large sauté pan or skillet, heat the olive oil over medium heat. 3. Add the pork to the skillet, using tongs to turn and sear the pork on all sides. Once seared, sprinkle pork with salt and pepper, and set it on a small baking sheet. 4. In the same skillet, with the juices from the pork, mix the apple jelly, juice, and mustard into the pan juices. Heat thoroughly over low heat, stirring consistently for 5 minutes. Spoon over the pork. 5. Put the pork in the oven and roast for 15 to 17 minutes, or 20 minutes per pound. Every 10 to 15 minutes, baste the pork with the apple-mustard sauce. 6. Once the pork tenderloin is done, remove it from the oven and let it rest for 15 minutes. Then, cut it into 1-inch slices. 7. In a small pot, blend the cornstarch with cream. Heat over low heat. Add the pan juices into the pot, stirring for 2 minutes, until thickened. Serve the sauce over the pork.

Per Serving:
calories: 146 | fat: 7g | protein: 13g | carbs: 8g | fiber: 0g | sodium: 192mg

Lamb Chops with Shaved Zucchini Salad

Prep time: 20 minutes | Cook time: 40 minutes | Serves 4

- 4 (8- to 12-ounce/ 227- to 340-g) lamb shoulder chops (blade or round bone), about ¾ inch thick, trimmed
- ¾ teaspoon table salt, divided
- ¾ teaspoon pepper, divided
- 2 tablespoons extra-virgin olive oil, divided
- 1 onion, chopped
- 5 garlic cloves, minced
- ½ cup chicken broth
- 1 bay leaf
- 4 zucchini (6 ounces / 170 g each), sliced lengthwise into ribbons
- 1 teaspoon grated lemon zest plus 1 tablespoon juice
- 2 ounces (57 g) goat cheese, crumbled (½ cup)
- ¼ cup chopped fresh mint
- 2 tablespoons raisins

1. Pat lamb chops dry with paper towels and sprinkle with ½ teaspoon salt and ½ teaspoon pepper. Using highest sauté function, heat 1½ teaspoons oil in Instant Pot for 5 minutes (or until just smoking). Brown half of chops on both sides, 6 to 8 minutes;

transfer to plate. Repeat with 1½ teaspoons oil and remaining chops; transfer to plate. 2. Add onion to fat left in pot and cook, using highest sauté function, until softened, about 5 minutes. Stir in garlic and cook until fragrant, about 30 seconds. Stir in broth and bay leaf, scraping up any browned bits. Return chops to pot along with any accumulated juices (chops will overlap). Lock lid in place and close pressure release valve. Select high pressure cook function and cook for 20 minutes. 3. Turn off Instant Pot and let pressure release naturally for 15 minutes. Quick-release any remaining pressure, then carefully remove lid, allowing steam to escape away from you. Transfer chops to serving dish. Gently toss zucchini with lemon zest and juice, remaining 1 tablespoon oil, remaining ¼ teaspoon salt, and remaining ¼ teaspoon pepper in bowl. Arrange zucchini on serving dish with lamb, and sprinkle with goat cheese, mint, and raisins. Serve.

Per Serving:
calories: 390 | fat: 20g | protein: 38g | carbs: 14g | fiber: 2g | sodium: 720mg

Spanish Meatballs

Prep time: 10 minutes | Cook time: 5 hours 10 minutes | Serves 8

- 2 pounds (907 g) ground pork
- 1 medium yellow onion, finely chopped
- 1½ teaspoons ground cumin
- 1½ teaspoons hot smoked paprika
- 5 tablespoons plain dried bread crumbs
- 2 large eggs, lightly beaten
- 3 tablespoons chopped fresh
- parsley
- Coarse sea salt
- Black pepper
- 3 tablespoons extra-virgin olive oil
- 1 (28-ounce / 794-g) can diced tomatoes, with the juice
- Rustic bread, for serving (optional)

1. In a large bowl, combine the pork, ¼ cup of the onion, cumin, ½ teaspoon of the paprika, bread crumbs, eggs, and parsley. Season with the salt and pepper. Mix thoroughly to combine. 2. Roll the meat mixture into 25 meatballs (each about 1½ inches), and put on a plate. 3. In a large nonstick skillet, heat 1½ tablespoons of the olive oil over medium-high heat. In two batches, brown the meatballs on all sides, 8 minutes per batch. Transfer the browned meatballs to the slow cooker. 4. Add the remaining onion to the skillet, and cook until fragrant, stirring often, about 2 minutes. Transfer the onion to the slow cooker, sprinkle in the remaining 1 teaspoon paprika, and add the tomatoes. Season with salt and pepper. 5. Cover and cook on low until the meatballs are tender, 5 hours. Serve with slices of rustic bread, if desired.

Per Serving:
calories: 241 | fat: 11g | protein: 27g | carbs: 9g | fiber: 3g | sodium: 137mg

Smoked Paprika and Lemon Marinated Pork Kabobs

Prep time: 10 minutes | Cook time: 10 minutes | Serves 4

- ◁ ⅓ cup finely chopped flat-leaf parsley
- ◁ ¼ cup olive oil
- ◁ 2 tablespoons minced red onion
- ◁ 1 tablespoon lemon juice
- ◁ 1 tablespoon smoked paprika
- ◁ 2 teaspoons ground cumin
- ◁ 1 clove garlic, minced
- ◁ ¼ teaspoon cayenne pepper
- ◁ ½ teaspoon salt
- ◁ 2 pork tenderloins, each about 1 pound (454 g), trimmed of silver skin and any excess fat, cut into 1¼-inch cubes
- ◁ 1 lemon, cut into wedges, for serving

1. In a large bowl, whisk together the parsley, olive oil, onion, lemon juice, smoked paprika, cumin, garlic, cayenne, and salt. Add the pork and toss to coat well. Cover and refrigerate, stirring occasionally, for at least 4 hours (or as long as overnight). 2. Soak bamboo skewers in water for 30 minutes. 3. Preheat the grill to high heat. 4. Remove the meat from the marinade, discarding the marinade. Thread the meat onto the soaked skewers and place the skewers on the grill. Cook, with the lid closed, turning occasionally, until the pork is cooked through and browned on all sides, about 8 to 10 minutes total. 5. Transfer the skewers to a serving platter and serve immediately with the lemon wedges.

Per Serving:

calories: 447 | fat: 21g | protein: 60g | carbs: 3g | fiber: 1g | sodium: 426mg

Fajita Meatball Lettuce Wraps

Prep time: 10 minutes | Cook time: 10 minutes | Serves 4

- ◁ 1 pound (454 g) ground beef (85% lean)
- ◁ ½ cup salsa, plus more for serving if desired
- ◁ ¼ cup chopped onions
- ◁ ¼ cup diced green or red bell peppers
- ◁ 1 large egg, beaten
- ◁ 1 teaspoon fine sea salt
- ◁ ½ teaspoon chili powder
- ◁ ½ teaspoon ground cumin
- ◁ 1 clove garlic, minced
- ◁ For Serving (Optional):
- ◁ 8 leaves Boston lettuce
- ◁ Pico de gallo or salsa
- ◁ Lime slices

1. Spray the air fryer basket with avocado oil. Preheat the air fryer to 350°F (177°C). 2. In a large bowl, mix together all the ingredients until well combined. 3. Shape the meat mixture into eight 1-inch balls. Place the meatballs in the air fryer basket, leaving a little space between them. Air fry for 10 minutes, or until cooked through and no longer pink inside and the internal temperature reaches 145°F (63°C). 4. Serve each meatball on a lettuce leaf, topped with pico de gallo or salsa, if desired. Serve with lime slices if desired. 5. Store leftovers in an airtight container in the fridge for 3 days or in the freezer for up to a month. Reheat in a preheated 350°F (177°C) air fryer for 4 minutes, or until heated through.

Per Serving:

calories: 289 | fat: 20g | protein: 24g | carbs: 4g | fiber: 1g | sodium: 815mg

Short Ribs with Chimichurri

Prep time: 30 minutes | Cook time: 13 minutes | Serves 4

- ◁ 1 pound (454 g) boneless short ribs
- ◁ 1½ teaspoons sea salt, divided
- ◁ ½ teaspoon freshly ground black pepper, divided
- ◁ ½ cup fresh parsley leaves
- ◁ ½ cup fresh cilantro leaves
- ◁ 1 teaspoon minced garlic
- ◁ 1 tablespoon freshly squeezed lemon juice
- ◁ ½ teaspoon ground cumin
- ◁ ¼ teaspoon red pepper flakes
- ◁ 2 tablespoons extra-virgin olive oil
- ◁ Avocado oil spray

1. Pat the short ribs dry with paper towels. Sprinkle the ribs all over with 1 teaspoon salt and ¼ teaspoon black pepper. Let sit at room temperature for 45 minutes. 2. Meanwhile, place the parsley, cilantro, garlic, lemon juice, cumin, red pepper flakes, the remaining ½ teaspoon salt, and the remaining ¼ teaspoon black pepper in a blender or food processor. With the blender running, slowly drizzle in the olive oil. Blend for about 1 minute, until the mixture is smooth and well combined. 3. Set the air fryer to 400°F (204°C). Spray both sides of the ribs with oil. Place in the basket and air fry for 8 minutes. Flip and cook for another 5 minutes, until an instant-read thermometer reads 125°F (52°C) for medium-rare (or to your desired doneness). 4. Allow the meat to rest for 5 to 10 minutes, then slice. Serve warm with the chimichurri sauce.

Per Serving:

calories: 251 | fat: 17g | protein: 25g | carbs: 1g | fiber: 1g | sodium: 651mg

Beef Bourguignon with Egg Noodles

Prep time: 15 minutes | Cook time: 8 hours | Serves 8

- ◁ 2 pounds (907 g) lean beef stew meat
- ◁ 6 tablespoons all-purpose flour
- ◁ 2 large carrots, cut into 1-inch slices
- ◁ 16 ounces (454 g) pearl onions, peeled fresh or frozen, thawed
- ◁ 8 ounces (227 g) mushrooms, stems removed
- ◁ 2 garlic cloves, minced
- ◁ ¾ cup beef stock
- ◁ ½ cup dry red wine
- ◁ ¼ cup tomato paste
- ◁ 1½ teaspoons sea salt
- ◁ ½ teaspoon dried rosemary
- ◁ ¼ teaspoon dried thyme
- ◁ ½ teaspoon black pepper
- ◁ 8 ounces (227 g) uncooked egg noodles
- ◁ ¼ cup chopped fresh thyme leaves

1. Place the beef in a medium bowl, sprinkle with the flour, and toss well to coat. 2. Place the beef mixture, carrots, onions, mushrooms, and garlic in the slow cooker. 3. Combine the stock, wine, tomato paste, salt, rosemary, thyme, and black pepper in a small bowl. Stir into the beef mixture. 4. Cover and cook on low for 8 hours. 5. Cook the noodles according to package directions, omitting any salt. 6. Serve the beef mixture over the noodles, sprinkled with the thyme.

Per Serving:

calories: 397 | fat: 6g | protein: 34g | carbs: 53g | fiber: 6g | sodium: 592mg

Herb-Marinated Grilled Lamb Loin Chops

Prep time: 5 minutes | Cook time: 10 to 12 minutes | Serves 4 to 6

- ◀ 3 tablespoons olive oil
- ◀ Zest and juice of 1 lemon
- ◀ 2 tablespoons pomegranate molasses
- ◀ 1 cup finely chopped fresh mint
- ◀ ½ cup finely chopped fresh

- cilantro or parsley
- ◀ 2 scallions (green onions), finely chopped
- ◀ 6 lamb loin chops
- ◀ Freshly ground black pepper, to taste

1. In a small bowl, whisk together the olive oil, lemon zest, lemon juice, pomegranate molasses, mint, parsley, and scallions until well combined. Put the lamb in a large zip-top plastic bag. Add the marinade, seal the bag, and massage the marinade onto all sides of the chops. Refrigerate for at least 1 hour or up to overnight. 2. When ready to cook, heat a grill to medium. 3. Remove the chops from the marinade; discard the marinade. Season with pepper, if desired. Grill the chops for 10 to 12 minutes, turning once, for medium. Let rest for 10 minutes before serving.

Per Serving:

1 cup: calories: 182 | fat: 11g | protein: 10g | carbs: 10g | fiber: 0g | sodium: 46mg

Lamb and Onion Tagine

Prep time: 10 minutes | Cook time: 2 hours 15 minutes | Serves 4

- ◀ 2 tablespoons finely chopped fresh flat-leaf parsley
- ◀ 2 tablespoons finely chopped fresh cilantro
- ◀ 2 cloves garlic, minced
- ◀ ½ teaspoon ground turmeric
- ◀ ½ teaspoon ground ginger
- ◀ 1 teaspoon ground cinnamon, divided
- ◀ 1 teaspoon plus a pinch kosher salt
- ◀ ½ teaspoon ground black pepper
- ◀ 2 tablespoons plus ⅓ cup water

- ◀ 3 tablespoons extra-virgin olive oil
- ◀ 4 bone-in leg of lamb steaks, ½' thick (about 2½ pounds / 1.1 kg)
- ◀ 1 can (28 ounces / 794-g) whole peeled plum tomatoes, drained
- ◀ 2 large red onions, 1 finely chopped, the other sliced in ⅛' rounds
- ◀ 2 teaspoons honey, divided
- ◀ 1 tablespoon toasted sesame seeds

1. In a large bowl, combine the parsley, cilantro, garlic, turmeric, ginger, ¼ teaspoon of the cinnamon, 1 teaspoon of the salt, and the pepper. Add 2 tablespoons of the water and the oil and mix. Add the lamb steaks and turn to coat each one. Cover and refrigerate, turning the steaks occasionally, for at least 1 hour. 2. Make a small cut into each tomato and squeeze out the seeds and excess juices. 3. In a 12' tagine or a deep heavy-bottom skillet, scatter the chopped onion. Arrange the lamb steaks snugly in a single layer. Drizzle the remaining marinade over the top. Add the tomatoes around the lamb. Drizzle 1 teaspoon of the honey and ¼ teaspoon of the cinnamon over the top. 4. Lay the onion rounds on top of the lamb. Drizzle the remaining 1 teaspoon honey. Sprinkle the remaining ½ teaspoon cinnamon and the pinch of salt. Turn the heat on to medium (medium-low if using a pot) and cook, uncovered, nudging the lamb occasionally, until the chopped onion below is translucent, about 15 minutes. 5. Pour in the ⅓ cup water around the outer edges of the food. Cover with a lid, slightly askew to keep air flowing in and out of the tagine or skillet. Reduce the heat to low and simmer gently, nudging the lamb occasionally to prevent sticking. Cook until the lamb is very tender, adding water as needed to keep the sauce moist, about 2 hours. 6. Sprinkle with the sesame seeds and serve.

Per Serving:

calories: 537 | fat: 25g | protein: 63g | carbs: 19g | fiber: 6g | sodium: 791mg

Meatballs in Creamy Almond Sauce

Prep time: 15 minutes | Cook time: 35 minutes | Serves 4 to 6

- ◀ 8 ounces (227 g) ground veal or pork
- ◀ 8 ounces (227 g) ground beef
- ◀ ½ cup finely minced onion, divided
- ◀ 1 large egg, beaten
- ◀ ¼ cup almond flour
- ◀ 1½ teaspoons salt, divided
- ◀ 1 teaspoon garlic powder
- ◀ ½ teaspoon freshly ground black pepper

- ◀ ½ teaspoon ground nutmeg
- ◀ 2 teaspoons chopped fresh flat-leaf Italian parsley, plus ¼ cup, divided
- ◀ ½ cup extra-virgin olive oil, divided
- ◀ ¼ cup slivered almonds
- ◀ 1 cup dry white wine or chicken broth
- ◀ ¼ cup unsweetened almond butter

1. In a large bowl, combine the veal, beef, ¼ cup onion, and the egg and mix well with a fork. In a small bowl, whisk together the almond flour, 1 teaspoon salt, garlic powder, pepper, and nutmeg. Add to the meat mixture along with 2 teaspoons chopped parsley and incorporate well. Form the mixture into small meatballs, about 1 inch in diameter, and place on a plate. Let sit for 10 minutes at room temperature. 2. In a large skillet, heat ¼ cup oil over medium-high heat. Add the meatballs to the hot oil and brown on all sides, cooking in batches if necessary, 2 to 3 minutes per side. Remove from skillet and keep warm. 3. In the hot skillet, sauté the remaining ¼ cup minced onion in the remaining ¼ cup olive oil for 5 minutes. Reduce the heat to medium-low and add the slivered almonds. Sauté until the almonds are golden, another 3 to 5 minutes. 4. In a small bowl, whisk together the white wine, almond butter, and remaining ½ teaspoon salt. Add to the skillet and bring to a boil, stirring constantly. Reduce the heat to low, return the meatballs to skillet, and cover. Cook until the meatballs are cooked through, another 8 to 10 minutes. 5. Remove from the heat, stir in the remaining ¼ cup chopped parsley, and serve the meatballs warm and drizzled with almond sauce.

Per Serving:

calories: 447 | fat: 36g | protein: 20g | carbs: 7g | fiber: 2g | sodium: 659mg

Cube Steak Roll-Ups

Prep time: 30 minutes | Cook time: 8 to 10 minutes | Serves 4

- 4 cube steaks (6 ounces / 170 g each)
- 1 (16-ounce / 454-g) bottle Italian dressing
- 1 teaspoon salt
- ½ teaspoon freshly ground black pepper
- ½ cup finely chopped yellow onion
- ½ cup finely chopped green bell pepper
- ½ cup finely chopped mushrooms
- 1 to 2 tablespoons oil

1. In a large resealable bag or airtight storage container, combine the steaks and Italian dressing. Seal the bag and refrigerate to marinate for 2 hours. 2. Remove the steaks from the marinade and place them on a cutting board. Discard the marinade. Evenly season the steaks with salt and pepper. 3. In a small bowl, stir together the onion, bell pepper, and mushrooms. Sprinkle the onion mixture evenly over the steaks. Roll up the steaks, jelly roll-style, and secure with toothpicks. 4. Preheat the air fryer to 400°F (204°C). 5. Place the steaks in the air fryer basket. 6. Cook for 4 minutes. Flip the steaks and spritz them with oil. Cook for 4 to 6 minutes more until the internal temperature reaches 145°F (63°C). Let rest for 5 minutes before serving.

Per Serving:

calories: 364 | fat: 20g | protein: 37g | carbs: 7g | fiber: 1g | sodium: 715mg

Lamb and Vegetable Bake

Prep time: 20 minutes | Cook time: 1 hour 20 minutes | Serves 8

- ¼ cup olive oil
- 1 pound (454 g) boneless, lean lamb, cut into ½-inch pieces
- 2 large red potatoes, scrubbed and diced
- 1 large onion, coarsely chopped
- 2 cloves garlic, minced
- 1 (28-ounce) can diced tomatoes with liquid (no salt added)
- 2 medium zucchini, cut into
- ½-inch slices
- 1 red bell pepper, seeded and cut into 1-inch cubes
- 2 tablespoons flat-leaf parsley, chopped
- 1 teaspoon dried thyme
- 1 tablespoon paprika
- ½ teaspoon ground cinnamon
- ½ cup red wine
- Sea salt and freshly ground pepper, to taste

1. Preheat the oven to 325°F (165°C) degrees. 2. Heat the olive oil in a large stew pot or cast-iron skillet over medium-high heat. 3. Add the lamb and brown the meat, stirring frequently. Transfer the lamb to an ovenproof baking dish. 4. Cook the potatoes, onion, and garlic in the skillet until tender, then transfer them to the baking dish. 5. Pour the tomatoes, zucchini, and pepper into the pan along with the herbs and spices, and simmer for 10 minutes. 6. Cover the lamb, onions, and potatoes with the tomato and pepper sauce and wine. 7. Cover with aluminum foil and bake for 1 hour. Uncover during the last 15 minutes of baking. 8. Season to taste, and serve with a green salad.

Per Serving:

calories: 264 | fat: 12g | protein: 15g | carbs: 24g | fiber: 5g | sodium: 75mg

Indian Mint and Chile Kebabs

Prep time: 30 minutes | Cook time: 15 minutes | Serves 4

- 1 pound (454 g) ground lamb
- ½ cup finely minced onion
- ¼ cup chopped fresh mint
- ¼ cup chopped fresh cilantro
- 1 tablespoon minced garlic
- ½ teaspoon ground turmeric
- ½ teaspoon cayenne pepper
- ¼ teaspoon ground cardamom
- ¼ teaspoon ground cinnamon
- 1 teaspoon kosher salt

1. In the bowl of a stand mixer fitted with the paddle attachment, combine the lamb, onion, mint, cilantro, garlic, turmeric, cayenne, cardamom, cinnamon, and salt. Mix on low speed until you have a sticky mess of spiced meat. If you have time, let the mixture stand at room temperature for 30 minutes (or cover and refrigerate for up to a day or two, until you're ready to make the kebabs). 2. Divide the meat into eight equal portions. Form each into a long sausage shape. Place the kebabs in a single layer in the air fryer basket. Set the air fryer to 350°F (177°C) for 10 minutes. Increase the air fryer temperature to 400°F (204°C) and cook for 3 to 4 minutes more to brown the kebabs. Use a meat thermometer to ensure the kebabs have reached an internal temperature of 160°F / 71°C (medium).

Per Serving:

calories: 231 | fat: 14g | protein: 23g | carbs: 3g | fiber: 1g | sodium: 648mg

Rosemary Pork Shoulder with Apples

Prep time: 15 minutes | Cook time: 52 minutes | Serves 8

- 1 (3½-pound / 1.6-kg) pork shoulder roast
- 3 tablespoons Dijon mustard
- 1 tablespoon olive oil
- ½ cup dry white wine
- 2 medium tart apples, peeled, cored, and quartered
- 3 cloves garlic, peeled and minced
- ½ teaspoon salt
- ½ teaspoon ground black pepper
- 1 teaspoon dried rosemary

1. Coat all sides of roast with mustard. Press the Sauté button on the Instant Pot® and heat oil. Add pork roast and brown on all sides, about 3 minutes per side. 2. Add wine and scrape up any browned bits sticking to the bottom of the pot. Add apples, garlic, salt, pepper, and rosemary. Press the Cancel button. 3. Close lid, set steam release to Sealing, press the Manual button, and set time to 45 minutes. When the timer beeps, let pressure release naturally, about 25 minutes. 4. Open the lid. Transfer roast to a serving platter. Tent and keep warm while you use an immersion blender to purée sauce in pot. Slice roast and pour the puréed juices over the slices. Serve.

Per Serving:

calories: 394 | fat: 25g | protein: 33g | carbs: 5g | fiber: 1g | sodium: 393mg

Braised Short Ribs with Red Wine

- 1½ pounds (680 g) boneless beef short ribs (if using bone-in, use 3½ pounds)
- 1 teaspoon salt
- ½ teaspoon freshly ground black pepper
- ½ teaspoon garlic powder
- ¼ cup extra-virgin olive oil
- 1 cup dry red wine (such as cabernet sauvignon or merlot)
- 2 to 3 cups beef broth, divided
- 4 sprigs rosemary

1. Preheat the oven to 350°F(180°C). 2. Season the short ribs with salt, pepper, and garlic powder. Let sit for 10 minutes. 3. In a Dutch oven or oven-safe deep skillet, heat the olive oil over medium-high heat. 4. When the oil is very hot, add the short ribs and brown until dark in color, 2 to 3 minutes per side. Remove the meat from the oil and keep warm. 5. Add the red wine and 2 cups beef broth to the Dutch oven, whisk together, and bring to a boil. Reduce the heat to low and simmer until the liquid is reduced to about 2 cups, about 10 minutes. 6. Return the short ribs to the liquid, which should come about halfway up the meat, adding up to 1 cup of remaining broth if needed. Cover and braise until the meat is very tender, about 1½ to 2 hours. 7. Remove from the oven and let sit, covered, for 10 minutes before serving. Serve warm, drizzled with cooking liquid.

Per Serving:

calories: 525 | fat: 37g | protein: 34g | carbs: 5g | fiber: 1g | sodium: 720mg

Poblano Pepper Cheeseburgers

Prep time: 5 minutes | Cook time: 30 minutes | Serves 4

- 2 poblano chile peppers
- 1½ pounds (680 g) 85% lean ground beef
- 1 clove garlic, minced
- 1 teaspoon salt
- ½ teaspoon freshly ground black pepper
- 4 slices Cheddar cheese (about 3 ounces / 85 g)
- 4 large lettuce leaves

1. Preheat the air fryer to 400°F (204°C). 2. Arrange the poblano peppers in the basket of the air fryer. Pausing halfway through the cooking time to turn the peppers, air fry for 20 minutes, or until they are softened and beginning to char. Transfer the peppers to a large bowl and cover with a plate. When cool enough to handle, peel off the skin, remove the seeds and stems, and slice into strips. Set aside. 3. Meanwhile, in a large bowl, combine the ground beef with the garlic, salt, and pepper. Shape the beef into 4 patties. 4. Lower the heat on the air fryer to 360ºF (182°C). Arrange the burgers in a single layer in the basket of the air fryer. Pausing halfway through the cooking time to turn the burgers, air fry for 10 minutes, or until a thermometer inserted into the thickest part registers 160ºF (71°C). 5. Top the burgers with the cheese slices and continue baking for a minute or two, just until the cheese has melted. Serve the burgers on a lettuce leaf topped with the roasted poblano peppers.

Per Serving:

calories: 489 | fat: 35g | protein: 39g | carbs: 3g | fiber: 1g | sodium: 703mg

Greek-Style Ground Beef Pita Sandwiches

For the beef
- 1 tablespoon olive oil
- ½ medium onion, minced
- 2 garlic cloves, minced
For the yogurt sauce
- ⅓ cup plain Greek yogurt
- 1 ounce (28 g) crumbled feta cheese (about 3 tablespoons)
- 1 tablespoon minced fresh parsley
- 1 tablespoon minced scallion
- 1 tablespoon freshly squeezed lemon juice
- 6 ounces (170 g) lean ground beef
- 1 teaspoon dried oregano
- Pinch salt
- For the sandwiches
- 2 large Greek-style pitas
- ½ cup cherry tomatoes, halved
- 1 cup diced cucumber
- Salt
- Freshly ground black pepper

Make the beef: 1. Heat the olive oil in a sauté pan over medium high-heat. 2. Add the onion, garlic, and ground beef and sauté for 7 minutes, breaking up the meat well. 3. When the meat is no longer pink, drain off any fat and stir in the oregano. 4. Turn off the heat. Make the yogurt sauce: 1. In a small bowl, combine the yogurt, feta, parsley, scallion, lemon juice, and salt. 2. To assemble the sandwiches 3. Warm the pitas in the microwave for 20 seconds each. 4. To serve, spread some of the yogurt sauce over each warm pita. 5. Top with the ground beef, cherry tomatoes, and diced cucumber. 6. Season with salt and pepper. Add additional yogurt sauce if desired.

Per Serving:

calories: 541 | fat: 21g | protein: 29g | carbs: 57g | fiber: 4g | sodium: 694mg

Bone-in Pork Chops

Prep time: 5 minutes | Cook time: 10 to 12 minutes | Serves 2

- 1 pound (454 g) bone-in pork chops
- 1 tablespoon avocado oil
- 1 teaspoon smoked paprika
- ½ teaspoon onion powder
- ¼ teaspoon cayenne pepper
- Sea salt and freshly ground black pepper, to taste

1. Brush the pork chops with the avocado oil. In a small dish, mix together the smoked paprika, onion powder, cayenne pepper, and salt and black pepper to taste. Sprinkle the seasonings over both sides of the pork chops. 2. Set the air fryer to 400ºF (204°C). Place the chops in the air fryer basket in a single layer, working in batches if necessary. Air fry for 10 to 12 minutes, until an instant-read thermometer reads 145ºF (63°C) at the chops' thickest point. 3. Remove the chops from the air fryer and allow them to rest for 5 minutes before serving.

Per Serving:

calories: 356 | fat: 16g | protein: 50g | carbs: 1g | fiber: 1g | sodium: 133mg

Pork Stew with Leeks

Prep time: 15 minutes | Cook time: 55 minutes | Serves 4

- ◀ 2 tablespoons olive oil
- ◀ 2 leeks, white parts only, chopped and rinsed well
- ◀ 1 onion, chopped
- ◀ 2 garlic cloves, minced
- ◀ 1 carrot, chopped
- ◀ 1 celery stalk, chopped
- ◀ 2 pounds (907 g) boneless pork loin chops, cut into
- 2-inch pieces
- ◀ 4 cups beef broth
- ◀ 2 cups water
- ◀ 3 potatoes, peeled and chopped
- ◀ 1 tablespoon tomato paste
- ◀ Sea salt
- ◀ Freshly ground black pepper

1. In a large skillet, heat the olive oil over medium-high heat. Add the leeks, onion, and garlic and sauté for 5 minutes, or until softened. Add the carrot and celery and cook for 3 minutes. Add the pork, broth, water, potatoes, and tomato paste and bring to a boil. 2. Reduce the heat to low, cover, and simmer for 45 minutes, or until the pork is cooked through. Season to taste with salt and pepper and serve.

Per Serving:

calories: 623 | fat: 16g | protein: 57g | carbs: 60g | fiber: 8g | sodium: 193mg

Asian Glazed Meatballs

Prep time: 15 minutes | Cook time: 10 minutes per batch | Serves 4 to 6

- ◀ 1 large shallot, finely chopped
- ◀ 2 cloves garlic, minced
- ◀ 1 tablespoon grated fresh ginger
- ◀ 2 teaspoons fresh thyme, finely chopped
- ◀ 1½ cups brown mushrooms, very finely chopped (a food processor works well here)
- ◀ 2 tablespoons soy sauce
- ◀ Freshly ground black pepper, to taste
- ◀ 1 pound (454 g) ground beef
- ◀ ½ pound (227 g) ground pork
- ◀ 3 egg yolks
- ◀ 1 cup Thai sweet chili sauce (spring roll sauce)
- ◀ ¼ cup toasted sesame seeds
- ◀ 2 scallions, sliced

1. Combine the shallot, garlic, ginger, thyme, mushrooms, soy sauce, freshly ground black pepper, ground beef and pork, and egg yolks in a bowl and mix the ingredients together. Gently shape the mixture into 24 balls, about the size of a golf ball. 2. Preheat the air fryer to 380ºF (193ºC). 3. Working in batches, air fry the meatballs for 8 minutes, turning the meatballs over halfway through the cooking time. Drizzle some of the Thai sweet chili sauce on top of each meatball and return the basket to the air fryer, air frying for another 2 minutes. Reserve the remaining Thai sweet chili sauce for serving. 4. As soon as the meatballs are done, sprinkle with toasted sesame seeds and transfer them to a serving platter. Scatter the scallions around and serve warm.

Per Serving:

calories: 274 | fat: 11g | protein: 29g | carbs: 14g | fiber: 4g | sodium: 802mg

Lamb Tagine

Prep time: 15 minutes | Cook time: 7 hours | Serves 6

- ◀ 1 navel orange
- ◀ 2 tablespoons all-purpose flour
- ◀ 2 pounds (907 g) boneless leg of lamb, trimmed and cut into 1½-inch cubes
- ◀ ½ cup chicken stock
- ◀ 2 large white onions, chopped
- ◀ 1 teaspoon pumpkin pie spice
- ◀ 1 teaspoon ground cumin
- ◀ ½ teaspoon sea salt
- ◀ ¼ teaspoon saffron threads, crushed in your palm
- ◀ ¼ teaspoon ground red pepper
- ◀ 1 cup pitted dates
- ◀ 2 tablespoons honey
- ◀ 3 cups hot cooked couscous, for serving
- ◀ 2 tablespoons toasted slivered almonds, for serving

1. Grate 2 teaspoons of zest from the orange into a small bowl. Squeeze ¼ cup juice from the orange into another small bowl. 2. Add the flour to the orange juice, stirring with a whisk until smooth. Stir in the orange zest. 3. Heat a large nonstick skillet over medium-high heat. Add the lamb and sauté 7 minutes or until browned. Stir in the stock, scraping the bottom of the pan with a wooden spoon to loosen the flavorful brown bits. Stir in the orange juice mixture. 4. Stir the onions into the lamb mixture. Add the pumpkin pie spice, cumin, salt, saffron, and ground red pepper. 5. Pour the lamb mixture into the slow cooker. Cover and cook on low for 6 hours or until the lamb is tender. 6. Stir the dates and honey into the lamb mixture. Cover and cook on low for 1 hour or until thoroughly heated. 7. Serve the lamb tagine over the couscous and sprinkle with the almonds.

Per Serving:

calories: 451 | fat: 11g | protein: 37g | carbs: 53g | fiber: 5g | sodium: 329mg

Greek Lamb Burgers

Prep time: 10 minutes | Cook time: 10 minutes | Serves 4

- ◀ 1 pound (454 g) ground lamb
- ◀ ½ teaspoon salt
- ◀ ½ teaspoon freshly ground black pepper
- ◀ 4 tablespoons feta cheese, crumbled
- ◀ Buns, toppings, and tzatziki, for serving (optional)

1. Preheat a grill, grill pan, or lightly oiled skillet to high heat. 2. In a large bowl, using your hands, combine the lamb with the salt and pepper. 3. Divide the meat into 4 portions. Divide each portion in half to make a top and a bottom. Flatten each half into a 3-inch circle. Make a dent in the center of one of the halves and place 1 tablespoon of the feta cheese in the center. Place the second half of the patty on top of the feta cheese and press down to close the 2 halves together, making it resemble a round burger. 4. Cook the stuffed patty for 3 minutes on each side, for medium-well. Serve on a bun with your favorite toppings and tzatziki sauce, if desired.

Per Serving:

calories: 345 | fat: 29g | protein: 20g | carbs: 1g | fiber: 0g | sodium: 462mg

Greek Lamb Chops

Prep time: 10 minutes | Cook time: 6 to 8 hours | Serves 6

◁ 3 pounds (1.4 kg) lamb chops
◁ ½ cup low-sodium beef broth
◁ Juice of 1 lemon
◁ 1 tablespoon extra-virgin olive oil
◁ 2 garlic cloves, minced
◁ 1 teaspoon dried oregano
◁ 1 teaspoon sea salt
◁ ½ teaspoon freshly ground black pepper

1. Put the lamb chops in a slow cooker. 2. In a small bowl, whisk together the beef broth, lemon juice, olive oil, garlic, oregano, salt, and pepper until blended. Pour the sauce over the lamb chops. 3. Cover the cooker and cook for 6 to 8 hours on Low heat.

Per Serving:
calories: 325 | fat: 13g | protein: 47g | carbs: 1g | fiber: 0g | sodium: 551mg

Nigerian Peanut-Crusted Flank Steak

Prep time: 30 minutes | Cook time: 8 minutes | Serves 4

Suya Spice Mix:
◁ ¼ cup dry-roasted peanuts
◁ 1 teaspoon cumin seeds
◁ 1 teaspoon garlic powder
◁ 1 teaspoon smoked paprika
◁ ½ teaspoon ground ginger
◁ 1 teaspoon kosher salt
◁ ½ teaspoon cayenne pepper
Steak:
◁ 1 pound (454 g) flank steak
◁ 2 tablespoons vegetable oil

1. For the spice mix: In a clean coffee grinder or spice mill, combine the peanuts and cumin seeds. Process until you get a coarse powder. (Do not overprocess or you will wind up with peanut butter! Alternatively, you can grind the cumin with ⅓ cup ready-made peanut powder, such as PB2, instead of the peanuts.) 2. Pour the peanut mixture into a small bowl, add the garlic powder, paprika, ginger, salt, and cayenne, and stir to combine. This recipe makes about ½ cup suya spice mix. Store leftovers in an airtight container in a cool, dry place for up to 1 month. 3. For the steak: Cut the flank steak into ½-inch-thick slices, cutting against the grain and at a slight angle. Place the beef strips in a resealable plastic bag and add the oil and 2½ to 3 tablespoons of the spice mixture. Seal the bag and massage to coat all of the meat with the oil and spice mixture. Marinate at room temperature for 30 minutes or in the refrigerator for up to 24 hours. 4. Place the beef strips in the air fryer basket. Set the air fryer to 400°F (204°C) for 8 minutes, turning the strips halfway through the cooking time. 5. Transfer the meat to a serving platter. Sprinkle with additional spice mix, if desired.

Per Serving:
calories: 275 | fat: 17g | protein: 27g | carbs: 3g | fiber: 1g | sodium: 644mg

Lebanese Malfouf (Stuffed Cabbage Rolls)

Prep time: 15 minutes | Cook time: 33 minutes | Serves 4

◁ 1 head green cabbage
◁ 1 pound (454 g) lean ground beef
◁ ½ cup long-grain brown rice
◁ 4 garlic cloves, minced
◁ 1 teaspoon salt
◁ ½ teaspoon black pepper
◁ 1 teaspoon ground cinnamon
◁ 2 tablespoons chopped fresh mint
◁ Juice of 1 lemon
◁ Olive oil cooking spray
◁ ½ cup beef broth
◁ 1 tablespoon olive oil

1. Cut the cabbage in half and remove the core. Remove 12 of the larger leaves to use for the cabbage rolls. 2. Bring a large pot of salted water to a boil, then drop the cabbage leaves into the water, boiling them for 3 minutes. Remove from the water and set aside. 3. In a large bowl, combine the ground beef, rice, garlic, salt, pepper, cinnamon, mint, and lemon juice, and mix together until combined. Divide this mixture into 12 equal portions. 4. Preheat the air fryer to 360°F (182°C). Lightly coat a small casserole dish with olive oil cooking spray. 5. Place a cabbage leaf on a clean work surface. Place a spoonful of the beef mixture on one side of the leaf, leaving space on all other sides. Fold the two perpendicular sides inward and then roll forward, tucking tightly as rolled (similar to a burrito roll). Place the finished rolls into the baking dish, stacking them on top of each other if needed. 6. Pour the beef broth over the top of the cabbage rolls so that it soaks down between them, and then brush the tops with the olive oil. 7. Place the casserole dish into the air fryer basket and bake for 30 minutes.

Per Serving:
calories: 329 | fat: 10g | protein: 29g | carbs: 33g | fiber: 7g | sodium: 700mg

Chapter 6 Fish and Seafood

Chili Tilapia

Prep time: 5 minutes | Cook time: 20 minutes | Serves 4

- ◀ 4 tilapia fillets, boneless
- ◀ 1 teaspoon chili flakes
- ◀ 1 teaspoon dried oregano
- ◀ 1 tablespoon avocado oil
- ◀ 1 teaspoon mustard

1. Rub the tilapia fillets with chili flakes, dried oregano, avocado oil, and mustard and put in the air fryer. 2. Cook it for 10 minutes per side at 360°F (182°C).

Per Serving:

calories: 146 | fat: 6g | protein: 23g | carbs: 1g | fiber: 0g | sodium: 94mg

Greek Fish Pitas

Prep time: 10 minutes | Cook time: 15 minutes | Serves 4

- ◀ 1 pound (454 g) pollock, cut into 1-inch pieces
- ◀ ¼ cup olive oil
- ◀ 1 teaspoon salt
- ◀ ½ teaspoon dried oregano
- ◀ ½ teaspoon dried thyme
- ◀ ½ teaspoon garlic powder
- ◀ ¼ teaspoon cayenne
- ◀ 4 whole wheat pitas
- ◀ 1 cup shredded lettuce
- ◀ 2 Roma tomatoes, diced
- ◀ Nonfat plain Greek yogurt
- ◀ Lemon, quartered

1. Preheat the air fryer to 380°F(193°C). 2. In a medium bowl, combine the pollock with olive oil, salt, oregano, thyme, garlic powder, and cayenne. 3. Put the pollock into the air fryer basket and roast for 15 minutes. 4. Serve inside pitas with lettuce, tomato, and Greek yogurt with a lemon wedge on the side.

Per Serving:

calories: 267 | fat: 15g | protein: 17g | carbs: 17g | fiber: 3g | sodium: 709mg

Tuna Nuggets in Hoisin Sauce

Prep time: 15 minutes | Cook time: 5 to 7 minutes | Serves 4

- ½ cup hoisin sauce
- ◀ 2 tablespoons rice wine vinegar
- ◀ 2 teaspoons sesame oil
- ◀ 1 teaspoon garlic powder
- ◀ 2 teaspoons dried lemongrass
- ◀ ¼ teaspoon red pepper flakes
- ◀ ½ small onion, quartered and thinly sliced
- ◀ 8 ounces (227 g) fresh tuna, cut into 1-inch cubes
- ◀ Cooking spray
- ◀ 3 cups cooked jasmine rice

1. Mix the hoisin sauce, vinegar, sesame oil, and seasonings together. 2. Stir in the onions and tuna nuggets. 3. Spray a baking pan with nonstick spray and pour in tuna mixture. 4. Roast at 390°F (199°C) for 3 minutes. Stir gently. 5. Cook 2 minutes and stir again, checking for doneness. Tuna should be barely cooked through, just beginning to flake and still very moist. If necessary, continue cooking and stirring in 1-minute intervals until done. 6. Serve warm over hot jasmine rice.

Per Serving:

calories: 342 | fat: 7g | protein: 18g | carbs: 49g | fiber: 4g | sodium: 548mg

Stuffed Shrimp

Prep time: 20 minutes | Cook time: 12 minutes per batch | Serves 4

- ◀ 16 tail-on shrimp, peeled and deveined (last tail section intact)
- ◀ ¾ cup crushed panko bread crumbs
- ◀ Oil for misting or cooking spray
- ◀ Stuffing:
- ◀ 2 (6-ounce / 170-g) cans lump crab meat
- ◀ 2 tablespoons chopped shallots
- ◀ 2 tablespoons chopped green onions
- ◀ 2 tablespoons chopped celery
- ◀ 2 tablespoons chopped green bell pepper
- ◀ ½ cup crushed saltine crackers
- ◀ 1 teaspoon Old Bay Seasoning
- ◀ 1 teaspoon garlic powder
- ◀ ¼ teaspoon ground thyme
- ◀ 2 teaspoons dried parsley flakes
- ◀ 2 teaspoons fresh lemon juice
- ◀ 2 teaspoons Worcestershire sauce
- ◀ 1 egg, beaten

1. Rinse shrimp. Remove tail section (shell) from 4 shrimp, discard, and chop the meat finely. 2. To prepare the remaining 12 shrimp, cut a deep slit down the back side so that the meat lies open flat. Do not cut all the way through. 3. Preheat the air fryer to 360°F (182°C). 4. Place chopped shrimp in a large bowl with all of the stuffing ingredients and stir to combine. 5. Divide stuffing into 12 portions, about 2 tablespoons each. 6. Place one stuffing portion onto the back of each shrimp and form into a ball or oblong shape. Press firmly so that stuffing sticks together and adheres to shrimp. 7. Gently roll each stuffed shrimp in panko crumbs and mist with oil or cooking spray. 8. Place 6 shrimp in air fryer basket and air fry at 360°F (182°C) for 10 minutes. Mist with oil or spray and cook 2 minutes longer or until stuffing cooks through inside and is crispy outside. 9. Repeat step 8 to cook remaining shrimp.

Per Serving:

calories: 223 | fat: 4g | protein: 24g | carbs: 24g | fiber: 2g | sodium: 758mg

Trout in Parsley Sauce

Prep time: 10 minutes | Cook time: 3 minutes | Serves 4

- 4 (½-pound / 227-g) river trout, rinsed and patted dry
- ¾ teaspoon salt, divided
- 4 cups torn lettuce leaves, divided
- 1 teaspoon white wine vinegar
- ½ cup water
- ½ cup minced fresh flat-leaf parsley
- 1 small shallot, peeled and minced
- 2 tablespoons olive oil mayonnaise
- ½ teaspoon lemon juice
- ¼ teaspoon sugar
- 2 tablespoons toasted sliced almonds

1. Season trout with ½ teaspoon salt inside and out. Put 3 cups lettuce leaves in the bottom of the Instant Pot®. Arrange trout over lettuce and top trout with remaining 1 cup lettuce. Stir vinegar into water and pour into pot. 2. Close lid, set steam release to Sealing, press the Manual button, and set time to 3 minutes. When the timer beeps, quick-release the pressure until the float valve drops and open lid. 3. Use a spatula to move fish to a serving plate. Peel and discard skin from fish. Remove and discard fish heads if desired. 4. In a small bowl, mix together parsley, shallot, mayonnaise, lemon juice, sugar, and remaining ¼ teaspoon salt. Evenly divide among the fish, spreading it over them. Sprinkle toasted almonds over the sauce. Serve immediately.

Per Serving:
calories: 159 | fat: 9g | protein: 15g | carbs: 4g | fiber: 1g | sodium: 860mg

Black Cod with Grapes and Kale

Prep time: 10 minutes | Cook time: 15 minutes | Serves 2

- 2 (6- to 8-ounce / 170- to 227-g) fillets of black cod
- Salt and freshly ground black pepper, to taste
- Olive oil
- 1 cup grapes, halved
- 1 small bulb fennel, sliced ¼-inch thick
- ½ cup pecans
- 3 cups shredded kale
- 2 teaspoons white balsamic vinegar or white wine vinegar
- 2 tablespoons extra-virgin olive oil

1. Preheat the air fryer to 400°F (204°C). 2. Season the cod fillets with salt and pepper and drizzle, brush or spray a little olive oil on top. Place the fish, presentation side up (skin side down), into the air fryer basket. Air fry for 10 minutes. 3. When the fish has finished cooking, remove the fillets to a side plate and loosely tent with foil to rest. 4. Toss the grapes, fennel and pecans in a bowl with a drizzle of olive oil and season with salt and pepper. Add the grapes, fennel and pecans to the air fryer basket and air fry for 5 minutes at 400°F (204°C), shaking the basket once during the cooking time. 5. Transfer the grapes, fennel and pecans to a bowl with the kale. Dress the kale with the balsamic vinegar and olive oil, season to taste with salt and pepper and serve along side the cooked fish.

Per Serving:
calories: 509 | fat: 33g | protein: 31g | carbs: 28g | fiber: 8g | sodium: 587mg

Mussels with Fennel and Leeks

Prep time: 20 minutes | Cook time: 6 minutes | Serves 4

- 1 tablespoon extra-virgin olive oil, plus extra for drizzling
- 1 fennel bulb, 1 tablespoon fronds minced, stalks discarded, bulb halved, cored, and sliced thin
- 1 leek, ends trimmed, leek halved lengthwise, sliced
- 1 inch thick, and washed thoroughly
- 4 garlic cloves, minced
- 3 sprigs fresh thyme
- ¼ teaspoon red pepper flakes
- ½ cup dry white wine
- 3 pounds (1.4 kg) mussels, scrubbed and debearded

1. Using highest sauté function, heat oil in Instant Pot until shimmering. Add fennel and leek and cook until softened, about 5 minutes. Stir in garlic, thyme sprigs, and pepper flakes and cook until fragrant, about 30 seconds. Stir in wine, then add mussels. 2. Lock lid in place and close pressure release valve. Select high pressure cook function and set cook time for 0 minutes. Once Instant Pot has reached pressure, immediately turn off pot and quick-release pressure. Carefully remove lid, allowing steam to escape away from you. 3. Discard thyme sprigs and any mussels that have not opened. Transfer mussels to individual serving bowls, sprinkle with fennel fronds, and drizzle with extra oil. Serve.

Per Serving:
calories: 384 | fat: 11g | protein: 42g | carbs: 23g | fiber: 2g | sodium: 778mg

Mediterranean Cod Stew

Prep time: 10 minutes |Cook time: 20 minutes| Serves: 6

- 2 tablespoons extra-virgin olive oil
- 2 cups chopped onion (about 1 medium onion)
- 2 garlic cloves, minced (about 1 teaspoon)
- ¾ teaspoon smoked paprika
- 1 (14½-ounce / 411-g) can diced tomatoes, undrained
- 1 (12-ounce / 340-g) jar roasted red peppers, drained and chopped
- 1 cup sliced olives, green or black
- ⅓ cup dry red wine
- ¼ teaspoon freshly ground black pepper
- ¼ teaspoon kosher or sea salt
- 1½ pounds (680 g) cod fillets, cut into 1-inch pieces
- 3 cups sliced mushrooms (about 8 ounces / 227 g)

1. In a large stockpot over medium heat, heat the oil. Add the onion and cook for 4 minutes, stirring occasionally. Add the garlic and smoked paprika and cook for 1 minute, stirring often. 2. Mix in the tomatoes with their juices, roasted peppers, olives, wine, pepper, and salt, and turn the heat up to medium-high. Bring to a boil. Add the cod and mushrooms, and reduce the heat to medium. 3. Cover and cook for about 10 minutes, stirring a few times, until the cod is cooked through and flakes easily, and serve.

Per Serving:
calories: 209 | fat: 8g | protein: 23g | carbs: 12g | fiber: 4g | sodium: 334mg

Quick Shrimp Skewers

Prep time: 10 minutes | Cook time: 5 minutes | Serves 5

◄ 4 pounds (1.8 kg) shrimp, peeled
◄ 1 tablespoon dried rosemary
◄ 1 tablespoon avocado oil
◄ 1 teaspoon apple cider vinegar

1. Mix the shrimps with dried rosemary, avocado oil, and apple cider vinegar. 2. Then sting the shrimps into skewers and put in the air fryer. 3. Cook the shrimps at 400°F (204°C) for 5 minutes.

Per Serving:

calories: 336 | fat: 5g | protein: 73g | carbs: 0g | fiber: 0g | sodium: 432mg

Coconut Cream Mackerel

Prep time: 10 minutes | Cook time: 6 minutes | Serves 4

◄ 2 pounds (907 g) mackerel fillet
◄ 1 cup coconut cream
◄ 1 teaspoon ground coriander
◄ 1 teaspoon cumin seeds
◄ 1 garlic clove, peeled, chopped

1. Chop the mackerel roughly and sprinkle it with coconut cream, ground coriander, cumin seeds, and garlic. 2. Then put the fish in the air fryer and cook at 400°F (204°C) for 6 minutes.

Per Serving:

calories: 439 | fat: 25g | protein: 48g | carbs: 4g | fiber: 1g | sodium: 362mg

Steamed Cod with Garlic and Swiss Chard

Prep time: 5 minutes | Cook time: 12 minutes | Serves 4

◄ 1 teaspoon salt
◄ ½ teaspoon dried oregano
◄ ½ teaspoon dried thyme
◄ ½ teaspoon garlic powder
◄ 4 cod fillets
◄ ½ white onion, thinly sliced
◄ 2 cups Swiss chard, washed, stemmed, and torn into pieces
◄ ¼ cup olive oil
◄ 1 lemon, quartered

1. Preheat the air fryer to 380°F(193°C). 2. In a small bowl, whisk together the salt, oregano, thyme, and garlic powder. 3. Tear off four pieces of aluminum foil, with each sheet being large enough to envelop one cod fillet and a quarter of the vegetables. 4. Place a cod fillet in the middle of each sheet of foil, then sprinkle on all sides with the spice mixture. 5. In each foil packet, place a quarter of the onion slices and ½ cup Swiss chard, then drizzle 1 tablespoon olive oil and squeeze ¼ lemon over the contents of each foil packet. 6. Fold and seal the sides of the foil packets and then place them into the air fryer basket. Steam for 12 minutes. 7. Remove from the basket, and carefully open each packet to avoid a steam burn.

Per Serving:

calories: 324 | fat: 15g | protein: 42g | carbs: 4g | fiber: 1g | sodium: 746mg

Seasoned Steamed Crab

Prep time: 10 minutes | Cook time: 3 minutes | Serves 2

◄ 1 tablespoon extra-virgin olive oil
◄ ½ teaspoon Old Bay seafood seasoning
◄ ½ teaspoon smoked paprika
◄ ¼ teaspoon cayenne pepper
◄ 2 cloves garlic, peeled and minced
◄ 2 (2-pound / 907-g) Dungeness crabs
◄ 1 cup water

1. In a medium bowl, combine oil, seafood seasoning, smoked paprika, cayenne pepper, and garlic. Mix well. Coat crabs in seasoning mixture and place in the steamer basket. 2. Add water to the Instant Pot® and place steamer basket inside. Close lid, set steam release to Sealing, press the Manual button, and set time to 3 minutes. 3. When the timer beeps, quick-release the pressure until the float valve drops. Press the Cancel button and open lid. Transfer crabs to a serving platter. Serve hot.

Per Serving:

calories: 185 | fat: 8g | protein: 25g | carbs: 1g | fiber: 0g | sodium: 434mg

Crispy Fish Sticks

Prep time: 15 minutes | Cook time: 10 minutes | Serves 4

◄ 1 ounce (28 g) pork rinds, finely ground
◄ ¼ cup blanched finely ground almond flour
◄ ½ teaspoon Old Bay
seasoning
◄ 1 tablespoon coconut oil
◄ 1 large egg
◄ 1 pound (454 g) cod fillet, cut into ¾-inch strips

1. Place ground pork rinds, almond flour, Old Bay seasoning, and coconut oil into a large bowl and mix together. In a medium bowl, whisk egg. 2. Dip each fish stick into the egg and then gently press into the flour mixture, coating as fully and evenly as possible. Place fish sticks into the air fryer basket. 3. Adjust the temperature to 400°F (204°C) and air fry for 10 minutes or until golden. 4. Serve immediately.

Per Serving:

calories: 223 | fat: 14g | protein: 21g | carbs: 2g | fiber: 1g | sodium: 390mg

Tuna Steak

Prep time: 10 minutes | Cook time: 12 minutes | Serves 4

◄ 1 pound (454 g) tuna steaks, boneless and cubed
◄ 1 tablespoon mustard
◄ 1 tablespoon avocado oil
◄ 1 tablespoon apple cider vinegar

1. Mix avocado oil with mustard and apple cider vinegar. 2. Then brush tuna steaks with mustard mixture and put in the air fryer basket. 3. Cook the fish at 360°F (182°C) for 6 minutes per side.

Per Serving:

calories: 197 | fat: 9g | protein: 27g | carbs: 0g | fiber: 0g | sodium: 87mg

Caramelized Fennel and Sardines with Penne

Prep time: 15 minutes | Cook time: 30 minutes | Serves 4

- 8 ounces (227 g) whole-wheat penne
- 2 tablespoons extra-virgin olive oil
- 1 bulb fennel, cored and thinly sliced, plus ¼ cup fronds
- 2 celery stalks, thinly sliced, plus ½ cup leaves
- 4 garlic cloves, sliced
- ¾ teaspoon kosher salt
- ¼ teaspoon freshly ground black pepper
- Zest of 1 lemon
- Juice of 1 lemon
- 2 (4.4-ounce / 125-g) cans boneless/skinless sardines packed in olive oil, undrained

1. Cook the penne according to the package directions. Drain, reserving 1 cup pasta water. 2. Heat the olive oil in a large skillet or sauté pan over medium heat. Add the fennel and celery and cook, stirring often, until tender and golden, about 10 to 12 minutes. Add the garlic and cook for 1 minute. 3. Add the penne, reserved pasta water, salt, and black pepper. Increase the heat to medium-high and cook for 1 to 2 minutes. 4. Remove the pan from the heat and stir in the lemon zest, lemon juice, fennel fronds, and celery leaves. Break the sardines into bite-size pieces and gently mix in, along with the oil they were packed in.

Per Serving:

calories: 400 | fat: 15g | protein: 22g | carbs: 46g | fiber: 6g | sodium: 530mg

Monkfish with Sautéed Leeks, Fennel, and Tomatoes

Prep time: 20 minutes | Cook time: 35 minutes | Serves 4

- 1 to 1½ pounds (454 to 680 g) monkfish
- 3 tablespoons lemon juice, divided
- 1 teaspoon kosher salt, divided
- ⅛ teaspoon freshly ground black pepper
- 2 tablespoons extra-virgin olive oil
- 1 leek, white and light green parts only, sliced in half lengthwise and thinly sliced
- ½ onion, julienned
- 3 garlic cloves, minced
- 2 bulbs fennel, cored and thinly sliced, plus ¼ cup fronds for garnish
- 1 (14½-ounce / 411-g) can no-salt-added diced tomatoes
- 2 tablespoons fresh parsley, chopped
- 2 tablespoons fresh oregano, chopped
- ¼ teaspoon red pepper flakes

1. Place the fish in a medium baking dish and add 2 tablespoons of the lemon juice, ¼ teaspoon of the salt, and the black pepper. Place in the refrigerator. 2. Heat the olive oil in a large skillet or sauté pan over medium heat. Add the leek and onion and sauté until translucent, about 3 minutes. Add the garlic and sauté for 30 seconds. Add the fennel and sauté 4 to 5 minutes. Add the tomatoes and simmer for 2 to 3 minutes. 3. Stir in the parsley, oregano, red pepper flakes, the remaining ¾ teaspoon salt, and the remaining 1 tablespoon lemon juice. Place the fish on top of the leek mixture,

cover, and simmer for 20 to 25 minutes, turning over halfway through, until the fish is opaque and pulls apart easily. Garnish with the fennel fronds.

Per Serving:

calories: 220 | fat: 9g | protein: 22g | carbs: 11g | fiber: 3g | sodium: 345mg

Red Snapper with Peppers and Potatoes

Prep time: 15 minutes | Cook time: 4 to 6 hours | Serves 4

- 1 pound (454 g) red potatoes, chopped
- 1 green bell pepper, seeded and sliced
- 1 red bell pepper, seeded and sliced
- ½ onion, sliced
- 1 (15-ounce / 425-g) can no-salt-added diced tomatoes
- ⅓ cup whole Kalamata olives, pitted
- 5 garlic cloves, minced
- 1 teaspoon dried thyme
- 1 teaspoon dried rosemary
- Juice of 1 lemon
- Sea salt
- Freshly ground black pepper
- 1½ to 2 pounds (680 to 907 g) fresh red snapper fillets
- 2 lemons, thinly sliced
- ¼ cup chopped fresh parsley

1. In a slow cooker, combine the potatoes, green and red bell peppers, onion, tomatoes, olives, garlic, thyme, rosemary, and lemon juice. Season with salt and black pepper. Stir to mix well. 2. Nestle the snapper into the vegetable mixture in a single layer, cutting it into pieces to fit if needed. Top it with lemon slices. 3. Cover the cooker and cook for 4 to 6 hours on Low heat, or until the potatoes are tender. 4. Garnish with fresh parsley for serving.

Per Serving:

calories: 350 | fat: 5g | protein: 45g | carbs: 41g | fiber: 8g | sodium: 241mg

White Wine–Sautéed Mussels

Prep time: 10 minutes | Cook time: 10 minutes | Serves 4

- 3 pounds (1.4 kg) live mussels, cleaned
- 4 tablespoons (½ stick) salted butter
- 2 shallots, finely chopped
- 2 tablespoons garlic, minced
- 2 cups dry white wine

1. Scrub the mussel shells to make sure they are clean; trim off any that have a beard (hanging string). Put the mussels in a large bowl of water, discarding any that are not tightly closed. 2. In a large pot over medium heat, cook the butter, shallots, and garlic for 2 minutes. 3. Add the wine to the pot, and cook for 1 minute. 4. Add the mussels to the pot, toss with the sauce, and cover with a lid. Let cook for 7 minutes. Discard any mussels that have not opened. 5. Serve in bowls with the wine broth.

Per Serving:

calories: 468 | fat: 15g | protein: 41g | carbs: 21g | fiber: 0g | sodium: 879mg

Seasoned Sole

Prep time: 5 minutes | Cook time: 2 to 4 hours | Serves 4

◄ Nonstick cooking spray
◄ 2 pounds (907 g) fresh sole fillets
◄ 3 tablespoons freshly squeezed lime juice
◄ 2 tablespoons extra-virgin
◄ olive oil
◄ 2 garlic cloves, minced
◄ 1 tablespoon ground cumin
◄ 1½ teaspoons paprika
◄ 1 teaspoon sea salt
◄ ¼ cup fresh cilantro

1. Coat a slow-cooker insert with cooking spray, or line the bottom and sides with parchment paper or aluminum foil. 2. Place the sole in the prepared slow cooker in a single layer, cutting it into pieces to fit if needed. 3. In a small bowl, whisk together the lime juice, olive oil, garlic, cumin, paprika, and salt until blended. Pour the sauce over the fish. 4. Cover the cooker and cook for 2 to 4 hours on Low heat. 5. Garnish with fresh cilantro for serving.

Per Serving:

calories: 234 | fat: 12g | protein: 29g | carbs: 2g | fiber: 1g | sodium: 713mg

Moroccan Crusted Sea Bass

Prep time: 15 minutes | Cook time: 40 minutes | Serves 4

◄ 1½ teaspoons ground turmeric, divided
◄ ¾ teaspoon saffron
◄ ½ teaspoon ground cumin
◄ ¼ teaspoon kosher salt
◄ ¼ teaspoon freshly ground black pepper
◄ 1½ pounds (680 g) sea bass fillets, about ½ inch thick
◄ 8 tablespoons extra-virgin olive oil, divided
◄ 8 garlic cloves, divided (4 minced cloves and 4 sliced)
◄ 6 medium baby portobello mushrooms, chopped
◄ 1 large carrot, sliced on an angle
◄ 2 sun-dried tomatoes, thinly sliced (optional)
◄ 2 tablespoons tomato paste
◄ 1 (15-ounce / 425-g) can chickpeas, drained and rinsed
◄ 1½ cups low-sodium vegetable broth
◄ ¼ cup white wine
◄ 1 tablespoon ground coriander (optional)
◄ 1 cup sliced artichoke hearts marinated in olive oil
◄ ½ cup pitted kalamata olives
◄ ½ lemon, juiced
◄ ½ lemon, cut into thin rounds
◄ 4 to 5 rosemary sprigs or 2 tablespoons dried rosemary
◄ Fresh cilantro, for garnish

1. In a small mixing bowl, combine 1 teaspoon turmeric and the saffron and cumin. Season with salt and pepper. Season both sides of the fish with the spice mixture. Add 3 tablespoons of olive oil and work the fish to make sure it's well coated with the spices and the olive oil. 2. In a large sauté pan or skillet, heat 2 tablespoons of olive oil over medium heat until shimmering but not smoking. Sear the top side of the sea bass for about 1 minute, or until golden. Remove and set aside. 3. In the same skillet, add the minced garlic and cook very briefly, tossing regularly, until fragrant. Add the mushrooms, carrot, sun-dried tomatoes (if using), and tomato paste. Cook for 3 to 4 minutes over medium heat, tossing frequently, until fragrant. Add the chickpeas, broth, wine, coriander (if using), and the sliced garlic. Stir in the remaining ½ teaspoon ground turmeric. Raise the heat, if needed, and bring to a boil, then lower

heat to simmer. Cover part of the way and let the sauce simmer for about 20 minutes, until thickened. 4. Carefully add the seared fish to the skillet. Ladle a bit of the sauce on top of the fish. Add the artichokes, olives, lemon juice and slices, and rosemary sprigs. Cook another 10 minutes or until the fish is fully cooked and flaky. Garnish with fresh cilantro.

Per Serving:

calories: 696 | fat: 41g | protein: 48g | carbs: 37g | fiber: 9g | sodium: 810mg

Lemon Salmon with Dill

Prep time: 10 minutes | Cook time: 3 minutes | Serves 4

◄ 1 cup water
◄ 4 (4-ounce / 113-g) skin-on salmon fillets
◄ ½ teaspoon salt
◄ ½ teaspoon ground black pepper
◄ ¼ cup chopped fresh dill
◄ 1 small lemon, thinly sliced
◄ 2 tablespoons extra-virgin olive oil
◄ 1 tablespoon chopped fresh parsley

1. Add water to the Instant Pot® and place rack inside. 2. Season fish fillets with salt and pepper. Place fillets on rack. Top each fillet with dill and two or three lemon slices. Close lid, set steam release to Sealing, press the Steam button, and set time to 3 minutes. 3. When the timer beeps, quick-release the pressure until the float valve drops. Press the Cancel button and open lid. Place fillets on a serving platter, drizzle with olive oil, and garnish with parsley. Serve immediately.

Per Serving:

calories: 160 | fat: 9g | protein: 19g | carbs: 0g | fiber: 0g | sodium: 545mg

Asian Swordfish

Prep time: 10 minutes | Cook time: 6 to 11 minutes | Serves 4

◄ 4 (4-ounce / 113-g) swordfish steaks
◄ ½ teaspoon toasted sesame oil
◄ 1 jalapeño pepper, finely minced
◄ 2 garlic cloves, grated
◄ 1 tablespoon grated fresh
◄ ginger
◄ ½ teaspoon Chinese five-spice powder
◄ ⅛ teaspoon freshly ground black pepper
◄ 2 tablespoons freshly squeezed lemon juice

1. Place the swordfish steaks on a work surface and drizzle with the sesame oil. 2. In a small bowl, mix the jalapeño, garlic, ginger, five-spice powder, pepper, and lemon juice. Rub this mixture into the fish and let it stand for 10 minutes. 3. Roast the swordfish in the air fryer at 380ºF (193ºC) for 6 to 11 minutes, or until the swordfish reaches an internal temperature of at least 140ºF (60ºC) on a meat thermometer. Serve immediately.

Per Serving:

calories: 175 | fat: 8g | protein: 22g | carbs: 2g | fiber: 0g | sodium: 93mg

Cod with Warm Tabbouleh Salad

Prep time: 10 minutes | Cook time: 6 minutes | Serves 4

- 1 cup medium-grind bulgur, rinsed
- 1 teaspoon table salt, divided
- 1 lemon, sliced ¼ inch thick, plus 2 tablespoons juice
- 4 (6-ounce / 170-g) skinless cod fillets, 1½ inches thick
- 3 tablespoons extra-virgin
- olive oil, divided, plus extra for drizzling
- ¼ teaspoon pepper
- 1 small shallot, minced
- 10 ounces (283 g) cherry tomatoes, halved
- 1 cup chopped fresh parsley
- ½ cup chopped fresh mint

1. Arrange trivet included with Instant Pot in base of insert and add ½ cup water. Fold sheet of aluminum foil into 16 by 6-inch sling, then rest 1½-quart round soufflé dish in center of sling. Combine 1 cup water, bulgur, and ½ teaspoon salt in dish. Using sling, lower soufflé dish into pot and onto trivet; allow narrow edges of sling to rest along sides of insert. 2. Lock lid in place and close pressure release valve. Select high pressure cook function and cook for 3 minutes. Turn off Instant Pot and quick-release pressure. Carefully remove lid, allowing steam to escape away from you. Using sling, transfer soufflé dish to wire rack; set aside to cool. Remove trivet; do not discard sling or water in pot. 3. Arrange lemon slices widthwise in 2 rows across center of sling. Brush cod with 1 tablespoon oil and sprinkle with remaining ½ teaspoon salt and pepper. Arrange cod skinned side down in even layer on top of lemon slices. Using sling, lower cod into Instant Pot; allow narrow edges of sling to rest along sides of insert. Lock lid in place and close pressure release valve. Select high pressure cook function and cook for 3 minutes. 4. Meanwhile, whisk remaining 2 tablespoons oil, lemon juice, and shallot together in large bowl. Add bulgur, tomatoes, parsley, and mint, and gently toss to combine. Season with salt and pepper to taste. 5. Turn off Instant Pot and quick-release pressure. Carefully remove lid, allowing steam to escape away from you. Using sling, transfer cod to large plate. Gently lift and tilt fillets with spatula to remove lemon slices. Serve cod with salad, drizzling individual portions with extra oil.

Per Serving:

calories: 380 | fat: 12g | protein: 36g | carbs: 32g | fiber: 6g | sodium: 690mg

Escabeche

Prep time: 10 minutes | Cook time: 20 minutes | Serves 4

- 1 pound (454 g) wild-caught Spanish mackerel fillets, cut into four pieces
- 1 teaspoon salt
- ½ teaspoon freshly ground black pepper
- 8 tablespoons extra-virgin olive oil, divided
- 1 bunch asparagus, trimmed
- and cut into 2-inch pieces
- 1 (13¾-ounce / 390-g) can artichoke hearts, drained and quartered
- 4 large garlic cloves, peeled and crushed
- 2 bay leaves
- ¼ cup red wine vinegar
- ½ teaspoon smoked paprika

1. Sprinkle the fillets with salt and pepper and let sit at room temperature for 5 minutes. 2. In a large skillet, heat 2 tablespoons olive oil over medium-high heat. Add the fish, skin-side up, and cook 5 minutes. Flip and cook 5 minutes on the other side, until browned and cooked through. Transfer to a serving dish, pour the cooking oil over the fish, and cover to keep warm. 3. Heat the remaining 6 tablespoons olive oil in the same skillet over medium heat. Add the asparagus, artichokes, garlic, and bay leaves and sauté until the vegetables are tender, 6 to 8 minutes. 4. Using a slotted spoon, top the fish with the cooked vegetables, reserving the oil in the skillet. Add the vinegar and paprika to the oil and whisk to combine well. Pour the vinaigrette over the fish and vegetables and let sit at room temperature for at least 15 minutes, or marinate in the refrigerator up to 24 hours for a deeper flavor. Remove the bay leaf before serving.

Per Serving:

calories: 459 | fat: 34g | protein: 26g | carbs: 13g | fiber: 6g | sodium: 597mg

Tuna and Fruit Kebabs

Prep time: 15 minutes | Cook time: 8 to 12 minutes | Serves 4

- 1 pound (454 g) tuna steaks, cut into 1-inch cubes
- ½ cup canned pineapple chunks, drained, juice reserved
- ½ cup large red grapes
- 1 tablespoon honey
- 2 teaspoons grated fresh ginger
- 1 teaspoon olive oil
- Pinch cayenne pepper

1. Thread the tuna, pineapple, and grapes on 8 bamboo or 4 metal skewers that fit in the air fryer. 2. In a small bowl, whisk the honey, 1 tablespoon of reserved pineapple juice, the ginger, olive oil, and cayenne. Brush this mixture over the kebabs. Let them stand for 10 minutes. 3. Air fry the kebabs at 370°F (188°C) for 8 to 12 minutes, or until the tuna reaches an internal temperature of at least 145°F (63°C) on a meat thermometer, and the fruit is tender and glazed, brushing once with the remaining sauce. Discard any remaining marinade. Serve immediately.

Per Serving:

calories: 213 | fat: 7g | protein: 27g | carbs: 11g | fiber: 1g | sodium: 45mg

Baked Salmon and Tomato Pockets

Prep time: 5 minutes | Cook time: 25 minutes | Serves 4

- 1 pint (2 cups) cherry tomatoes
- 3 tablespoons extra-virgin olive oil
- 3 tablespoons lemon juice
- 1 teaspoon oregano
- 3 tablespoons unsalted butter, melted
- ½ teaspoon salt
- 4 (5-ounce / 142-g) salmon fillets

1. Preheat the oven to 400°F (205°C). 2. Cut the tomatoes in half and put them in a bowl. 3. Add the olive oil, lemon juice, oregano, melted butter, and salt to the tomatoes and toss to combine. 4. Cut 4 pieces of foil, about 12-by-12 inches each. 5. Place the salmon in the middle of each piece of foil. 6. Divide the tomato mixture evenly over the 4 pieces of salmon. Bring the ends of the foil together and seal to form a closed pocket. 7. Place the 4 pockets on a baking sheet. Cook for 25 minutes. 8. To serve, place each pocket on a plate and let your guests open to reveal the baked salmon and tomatoes.

Per Serving:

calories: 410 | fat: 32g | protein: 30g | carbs: 4g | fiber: 1g | sodium: 370mg

Salmon with Lemon-Garlic Mashed Cauliflower

Prep time: 15 minutes | Cook time: 10 minutes | Serves 4

- 2 tablespoons extra-virgin olive oil
- 4 garlic cloves, peeled and smashed
- ½ cup chicken or vegetable broth
- ¾ teaspoon table salt, divided
- 1 large head cauliflower (3 pounds / 1.4 kg), cored and
- cut into 2-inch florets
- 4 (6-ounce / 170-g) skinless salmon fillets, 1½ inches thick
- ½ teaspoon ras el hanout
- ½ teaspoon grated lemon zest
- 3 scallions, sliced thin
- 1 tablespoon sesame seeds, toasted

1. Using highest sauté function, cook oil and garlic in Instant Pot until garlic is fragrant and light golden brown, about 3 minutes. Turn off Instant Pot, then stir in broth and ¼ teaspoon salt. Arrange cauliflower in pot in even layer. 2. Fold sheet of aluminum foil into 16 by 6-inch sling. Sprinkle flesh side of salmon with ras el hanout and remaining ½ teaspoon salt, then arrange skinned side down in center of sling. Using sling, lower salmon into Instant Pot on top of cauliflower; allow narrow edges of sling to rest along sides of insert. Lock lid in place and close pressure release valve. Select high pressure cook function and cook for 2 minutes. 3. Turn off Instant Pot and quick-release pressure. Carefully remove lid, allowing steam to escape away from you. Using sling, transfer salmon to large plate. Tent with foil and let rest while finishing cauliflower. 4. Using potato masher, mash cauliflower mixture until no large chunks remain. Using highest sauté function, cook cauliflower, stirring often, until slightly thickened, about 3 minutes. Stir in lemon zest and season with salt and pepper to taste. Serve salmon with cauliflower, sprinkling individual portions with scallions and sesame seeds.

Per Serving:

calories: 480 | fat: 31g | protein: 38g | carbs: 9g | fiber: 3g | sodium: 650mg

Tomato-Poached Fish

Prep time: 10 minutes | Cook time: 8 minutes | Serves 4

- 2 tablespoons olive oil
- 1 medium onion, peeled and chopped
- 2 cloves garlic, peeled and minced
- 1 tablespoon chopped fresh oregano
- 1 teaspoon fresh thyme leaves
- ½ teaspoon ground fennel
- ¼ teaspoon ground black
- pepper
- ¼ teaspoon crushed red pepper flakes
- 1 (14½-ounce / 411-g) can diced tomatoes
- 1 cup vegetable broth
- 1 pound (454 g) halibut fillets
- 2 tablespoons chopped fresh parsley

1. Press the Sauté button on the Instant Pot® and heat oil. Add onion and cook until soft, about 4 minutes. Add garlic, oregano, thyme, and fennel. Cook until fragrant, about 30 seconds, then add black pepper, red pepper flakes, tomatoes, and vegetable broth. Press the Cancel button. 2. Top vegetables with fish, close lid, set steam release to Sealing, press the Manual button, and set time to 3 minutes. 3. When the timer beeps, quick-release the pressure

until the float valve drops and open lid. Carefully transfer fillets to a serving platter and spoon sauce over fillets. Sprinkle with parsley and serve hot.

Per Serving:

calories: 212 | fat: 8g | protein: 24g | carbs: 10g | fiber: 2g | sodium: 449mg

Tuna Slow-Cooked in Olive Oil

Prep time: 5 minutes | Cook time: 45 minutes | Serves 4

- 1 cup extra-virgin olive oil, plus more if needed
- 4 (3- to 4-inch) sprigs fresh rosemary
- 8 (3- to 4-inch) sprigs fresh thyme
- 2 large garlic cloves, thinly
- sliced
- 2 (2-inch) strips lemon zest
- 1 teaspoon salt
- ½ teaspoon freshly ground black pepper
- 1 pound (454 g) fresh tuna steaks (about 1 inch thick)

1. Select a thick pot just large enough to fit the tuna in a single layer on the bottom. The larger the pot, the more olive oil you will need to use. Combine the olive oil, rosemary, thyme, garlic, lemon zest, salt, and pepper over medium-low heat and cook until warm and fragrant, 20 to 25 minutes, lowering the heat if it begins to smoke. 2. Remove from the heat and allow to cool for 25 to 30 minutes, until warm but not hot. 3. Add the tuna to the bottom of the pan, adding additional oil if needed so that tuna is fully submerged, and return to medium-low heat. Cook for 5 to 10 minutes, or until the oil heats back up and is warm and fragrant but not smoking. Lower the heat if it gets too hot. 4. Remove the pot from the heat and let the tuna cook in warm oil 4 to 5 minutes, to your desired level of doneness. For a tuna that is rare in the center, cook for 2 to 3 minutes. 5. Remove from the oil and serve warm, drizzling 2 to 3 tablespoons seasoned oil over the tuna. 6. To store for later use, remove the tuna from the oil and place in a container with a lid. Allow tuna and oil to cool separately. When both have cooled, remove the herb stems with a slotted spoon and pour the cooking oil over the tuna. Cover and store in the refrigerator for up to 1 week. Bring to room temperature to allow the oil to liquify before serving.

Per Serving:

calories: 606 | fat: 55g | protein: 28g | carbs: 1g | fiber: 0g | sodium: 631mg

Citrus–Marinated Scallops

Prep time: 10 minutes | Cook time: 10 minutes | Serves 4

- Juice and zest of 2 lemons
- ¼ cup extra-virgin olive oil
- Unrefined sea salt or salt, to taste
- Freshly ground black pepper,
- to taste
- 1 clove garlic, minced
- 1½ pounds (680 g) dry scallops, side muscle removed

1. In a large shallow bowl or baking dish, combine the lemon juice and zest, olive oil, salt, pepper, and garlic. Mix well to combine. Add the scallops to the marinade; cover and refrigerate 1 hour. 2. Heat a large skillet over medium-high heat. Drain the scallops and place them in skillet. Cook 4 to 5 minutes per side, until cooked through.

Per Serving:

calories: 243 | fat: 14g | protein: 21g | carbs: 7g | fiber: 0g | sodium: 567mg

Chapter 7 Snacks and Appetizers

Tirokafteri (Spicy Feta and Yogurt Dip)

Prep time: 10 minutes | Cook time: 0 minutes | Serves 8

- 1 teaspoon red wine vinegar
- 1 small green chili, seeded and sliced
- 2 teaspoons extra virgin
- olive oil
- 9 ounces (255 g) full-fat feta
- ¾ cup full-fat Greek yogurt

1. Combine the vinegar, chili, and olive oil in a food processor. Blend until smooth. 2. In a small bowl, combine the feta and Greek yogurt, and use a fork to mash the ingredients until a paste is formed. Add the pepper mixture and stir until blended. 3. Cover and transfer to the refrigerator to chill for at least 1 hour before serving. Store covered in the refrigerator for up to 3 days.

Per Serving:

calories: 109 | fat: 8g | protein: 6g | carbs: 4g | fiber: 0g | sodium: 311mg

Croatian Red Pepper Dip

Prep time: 10 minutes | Cook time: 30 minutes | Serves 4 to 6

- 4 or 5 medium red bell peppers
- 1 medium eggplant (about ¾ pound / 340 g)
- ¼ cup olive oil, divided
- 1 teaspoon salt, divided
- ½ teaspoon freshly ground black pepper, divided
- 4 cloves garlic, minced
- 1 tablespoon white vinegar

1. Preheat the broiler to high. 2. Line a large baking sheet with aluminum foil. 3. Brush the peppers and eggplant all over with 2 tablespoons of the olive oil and sprinkle with ½ teaspoon of the salt and ¼ teaspoon of the pepper. Place the peppers and the eggplant on the prepared baking sheet and broil, turning every few minutes, until the skins are charred on all sides. The peppers will take about 10 minutes and the eggplant will take about 20 minutes. 4. When the peppers are fully charred, remove them from the baking sheet, place them in a bowl, cover with plastic wrap, and let them steam while the eggplant continues to cook. When the eggplant is fully charred and soft in the center, remove it from the oven and set aside to cool. 5. When the peppers are cool enough to handle, slip the charred skins off. Discard the charred skins. Seed the peppers and place them in a food processor. 6. Add the garlic to the food processor and pulse until the vegetables are coarsely chopped. Add the rest of the olive oil, the vinegar, and remaining ½ teaspoon of salt and process to a smooth purée. 7. Transfer the vegetable mixture to a medium saucepan and bring to a simmer over medium-high heat. Lower the heat to medium-low and let simmer, stirring occasionally, for 30 minutes. Remove from the heat and cool to room temperature. Serve at room temperature.

Per Serving:

calories: 144 | fat: 11g | protein: 2g | carbs: 12g | fiber: 5g | sodium: 471mg

Sweet Potato Hummus

Prep time: 10 minutes | Cook time: 1 hour | Serves 8 to 10

- 1 pound (454 g) sweet potatoes (about 2)
- 1 (15-ounce / 425-g) can chickpeas, drained
- 4 garlic cloves, minced
- 2 tablespoons olive oil
- 2 tablespoons fresh lemon
- juice
- 2 teaspoons ground cumin
- 1 teaspoon Aleppo pepper or red pepper flakes
- Pita chips, pita bread, or fresh vegetables, for serving

1. Preheat the oven to 400ºF (205ºC). 2. Prick the sweet potatoes in a few places with a small, sharp knife and place them on a baking sheet. Roast until cooked through, about 1 hour, then set aside to cool. Peel the sweet potatoes and put the flesh in a blender or food processor. 3. Add the chickpeas, garlic, olive oil, lemon juice, cumin, and ⅓ cup water. Blend until smooth. Add the Aleppo pepper. 4. Serve with pita chips, pita bread, or as a dip for fresh vegetables.

Per Serving:

calories: 178 | fat: 5g | protein: 7g | carbs: 30g | fiber: 9g | sodium: 149mg

Savory Mediterranean Popcorn

Prep time: 5 minutes | Cook time: 2 minutes | Serves 4 to 6

- 3 tablespoons extra-virgin olive oil
- ¼ teaspoon garlic powder
- ¼ teaspoon freshly ground black pepper
- ¼ teaspoon sea salt
- ⅛ teaspoon dried thyme
- ⅛ teaspoon dried oregano
- 12 cups plain popped popcorn

1. In a large sauté pan or skillet, heat the oil over medium heat, until shimmering, and then add the garlic powder, pepper, salt, thyme, and oregano until fragrant. 2. In a large bowl, drizzle the oil over the popcorn, toss, and serve.

Per Serving:

calories: 183 | fat: 12g | protein: 3g | carbs: 19g | fiber: 4g | sodium: 146mg

Baked Eggplant Baba Ganoush

Prep time: 10 minutes | Cook time: 1 hour | Makes about 4 cups

- 2 pounds (907 g, about 2 medium to large) eggplant
- 3 tablespoons tahini
- Zest of 1 lemon
- 2 tablespoons lemon juice
- ¾ teaspoon kosher salt
- ½ teaspoon ground sumac, plus more for sprinkling (optional)
- ⅓ cup fresh parsley, chopped
- 1 tablespoon extra-virgin olive oil

1. Preheat the oven to 350°F (180°C). Place the eggplants directly on the rack and bake for 60 minutes, or until the skin is wrinkly. 2. In a food processor add the tahini, lemon zest, lemon juice, salt, and sumac. Carefully cut open the baked eggplant and scoop the flesh into the food processor. Process until the ingredients are well blended. 3. Place in a serving dish and mix in the parsley. Drizzle with the olive oil and sprinkle with sumac, if desired.

Per Serving:

calories: 50 | fat: 16g | protein: 4g | carbs: 2g | fiber: 1g | sodium: 110mg

Asiago Shishito Peppers

Prep time: 5 minutes | Cook time: 10 minutes | Serves 4

- Oil, for spraying
- 6 ounces (170 g) shishito peppers
- 1 tablespoon olive oil
- ½ teaspoon salt
- ½ teaspoon lemon pepper
- ⅓ cup grated Asiago cheese, divided

1. Line the air fryer basket with parchment and spray lightly with oil. 2. Rinse the shishitos and pat dry with paper towels. 3. In a large bowl, mix together the shishitos, olive oil, salt, and lemon pepper. Place the shishitos in the prepared basket. 4. Roast at 350°F (177°C) for 10 minutes, or until blistered but not burned. 5. Sprinkle with half of the cheese and cook for 1 more minute. 6. Transfer to a serving plate. Immediately sprinkle with the remaining cheese and serve.

Per Serving:

calories: 81 | fat: 6g | protein: 3g | carbs: 5g | fiber: 1g | sodium: 443mg

Smoky Baba Ghanoush

Prep time: 50 minutes | Cook time: 40 minutes | Serves 6

- 2 large eggplants, washed
- ¼ cup lemon juice
- 1 teaspoon garlic, minced
- 1 teaspoon salt
- ½ cup tahini paste
- 3 tablespoons extra-virgin olive oil

1. Grill the whole eggplants over a low flame using a gas stovetop or grill. Rotate the eggplant every 5 minutes to make sure that all sides are cooked evenly. Continue to do this for 40 minutes. 2. Remove the eggplants from the stove or grill and put them onto a plate or into a bowl; cover with plastic wrap. Let sit for 5 to 10 minutes. 3. Using your fingers, peel away and discard the charred skin of the eggplants. Cut off the stem. 4. Put the eggplants into a food processor fitted with a chopping blade. Add the lemon juice, garlic, salt, and tahini paste, and pulse the mixture 5 to 7 times. 5. Pour the eggplant mixture onto a serving plate. Drizzle with the olive oil. Serve chilled or at room temperature.

Per Serving:

calories: 230 | fat: 18g | protein: 5g | carbs: 16g | fiber: 7g | sodium: 416mg

Mini Lettuce Wraps

Prep time: 10 minutes | Cook time: 0 minutes | Makes about 1 dozen wraps

- 1 tomato, diced
- 1 cucumber, diced
- 1 red onion, sliced
- 1 ounce (28 g) low-fat feta cheese, crumbled
- Juice of 1 lemon
- 1 tablespoon olive oil
- Sea salt and freshly ground pepper, to taste
- 12 small, intact iceberg lettuce leaves

1. Combine the tomato, cucumber, onion, and feta in a bowl with the lemon juice and olive oil. 2. Season with sea salt and freshly ground pepper. 3. Without tearing the leaves, gently fill each leaf with a tablespoon of the veggie mixture. 4. Roll them as tightly as you can, and lay them seam-side-down on a serving platter.

Per Serving:

1 wrap: calories: 26 | fat: 2g | protein: 1g | carbs: 2g | fiber: 1g | sodium: 20mg

Flatbread with Ricotta and Orange-Raisin Relish

Prep time: 5 minutes | Cook time: 8 minutes | Serves 4 to 6

- ¾ cup golden raisins, roughly chopped
- 1 shallot, finely diced
- 1 tablespoon olive oil
- 1 tablespoon red wine vinegar
- 1 tablespoon honey
- 1 tablespoon chopped flat-leaf parsley
- 1 tablespoon fresh orange zest strips
- Pinch of salt
- 1 oval prebaked whole-wheat flatbread, such as naan or pocketless pita
- 8 ounces (227 g) whole-milk ricotta cheese
- ½ cup baby arugula

1. Preheat the oven to 450°F (235°C). 2. In a small bowl, stir together the raisins, shallot, olive oil, vinegar, honey, parsley, orange zest, and salt. 3. Place the flatbread on a large baking sheet and toast in the preheated oven until the edges are lightly browned, about 8 minutes. 4. Spoon the ricotta cheese onto the flatbread, spreading with the back of the spoon. Scatter the arugula over the cheese. Cut the flatbread into triangles and top each piece with a dollop of the relish. Serve immediately.

Per Serving:

calories: 195 | fat: 9g | protein: 6g | carbs: 25g | fiber: 1g | sodium: 135mg

Red Pepper Tapenade

Prep time: 5 minutes | Cook time: 5 minutes | Serves 4

- ◀ 1 large red bell pepper
- ◀ 2 tablespoons plus 1 teaspoon olive oil, divided
- ◀ ½ cup Kalamata olives,
- pitted and roughly chopped
- ◀ 1 garlic clove, minced
- ◀ ½ teaspoon dried oregano
- ◀ 1 tablespoon lemon juice

1. Preheat the air fryer to 380°F(193°C). 2. Brush the outside of a whole red pepper with 1 teaspoon olive oil and place it inside the air fryer basket. Roast for 5 minutes. 3. Meanwhile, in a medium bowl combine the remaining 2 tablespoons of olive oil with the olives, garlic, oregano, and lemon juice. 4. Remove the red pepper from the air fryer, then gently slice off the stem and remove the seeds. Roughly chop the roasted pepper into small pieces. 5. Add the red pepper to the olive mixture and stir all together until combined. 6. Serve with pita chips, crackers, or crusty bread.

Per Serving:

calories: 94 | fat: 9g | protein: 1g | carbs: 4g | fiber: 2g | sodium: 125mg

Five-Ingredient Falafel with Garlic-Yogurt Sauce

Prep time: 5 minutes | Cook time: 15 minutes | Serves 4

Falafel:
- ◀ 1 (15-ounce / 425-g) can chickpeas, drained and rinsed
- ◀ ½ cup fresh parsley
- ◀ 2 garlic cloves, minced

- ◀ ½ tablespoon ground cumin
- ◀ 1 tablespoon whole wheat flour
- ◀ Salt

Garlic-Yogurt Sauce:
- ◀ 1 cup nonfat plain Greek yogurt
- ◀ 1 garlic clove, minced

- ◀ 1 tablespoon chopped fresh dill
- ◀ 2 tablespoons lemon juice

Make the Falafel: 1. Preheat the air fryer to 360°F(182°C). 2. Put the chickpeas into a food processor. Pulse until mostly chopped, then add the parsley, garlic, and cumin and pulse for another 1 to 2 minutes, or until the ingredients are combined and turning into a dough. 3. Add the flour. Pulse a few more times until combined. The dough will have texture, but the chickpeas should be pulsed into small bits. 4. Using clean hands, roll the dough into 8 balls of equal size, then pat the balls down a bit so they are about ½-thick disks. 5. Spray the basket of the air fryer with olive oil cooking spray, then place the falafel patties in the basket in a single layer, making sure they don't touch each other. 6. Fry in the air fryer for 15 minutes. Make the garlic-yogurt sauce 7. In a small bowl, combine the yogurt, garlic, dill, and lemon juice. 8. Once the falafel are done cooking and nicely browned on all sides, remove them from the air fryer and season with salt. 9. Serve hot with a side of dipping sauce.

Per Serving:

calories: 150 | fat: 3g | protein: 10g | carbs: 23g | fiber: 6g | sodium: 194mg

Manchego Crackers

Prep time: 15 minutes | Cook time: 15 minutes | Makes 40 crackers

- ◀ 4 tablespoons butter, at room temperature
- ◀ 1 cup finely shredded Manchego cheese
- ◀ 1 cup almond flour
- ◀ 1 teaspoon salt, divided
- ◀ ¼ teaspoon freshly ground black pepper
- ◀ 1 large egg

1. Using an electric mixer, cream together the butter and shredded cheese until well combined and smooth. 2. In a small bowl, combine the almond flour with ½ teaspoon salt and pepper. Slowly add the almond flour mixture to the cheese, mixing constantly until the dough just comes together to form a ball. 3. Transfer to a piece of parchment or plastic wrap and roll into a cylinder log about 1½ inches thick. Wrap tightly and refrigerate for at least 1 hour. 4. Preheat the oven to 350°F(180°C). Line two baking sheets with parchment paper or silicone baking mats. 5. To make the egg wash, in a small bowl, whisk together the egg and remaining ½ teaspoon salt. 6. Slice the refrigerated dough into small rounds, about ¼ inch thick, and place on the lined baking sheets. 7. Brush the tops of the crackers with egg wash and bake until the crackers are golden and crispy, 12 to 15 minutes. Remove from the oven and allow to cool on a wire rack. 8. Serve warm or, once fully cooled, store in an airtight container in the refrigerator for up to 1 week.

Per Serving:

2 crackers: calories: 73 | fat: 7g | protein: 3g | carbs: 1g | fiber: 1g | sodium: 154mg

Romesco Dip

Prep time: 10 minutes |Cook time:minutes| Serves: 10

- ◀ 1 (12-ounce / 340-g) jar roasted red peppers, drained
- ◀ 1 (14½-ounce / 411-g) can diced tomatoes, undrained
- ◀ ½ cup dry-roasted almonds
- ◀ 2 garlic cloves
- ◀ 2 teaspoons red wine vinegar
- ◀ 1 teaspoon smoked paprika or ½ teaspoon cayenne pepper
- ◀ ¼ teaspoon kosher or sea
- salt
- ◀ ¼ teaspoon freshly ground black pepper
- ◀ ¼ cup extra-virgin olive oil
- ◀ ⅔ cup torn, day-old bread or toast (about 2 slices)
- ◀ Assortment of sliced raw vegetables such as carrots, celery, cucumber, green beans, and bell peppers, for serving

1. In a high-powered blender or food processor, combine the roasted peppers, tomatoes and their juices, almonds, garlic, vinegar, smoked paprika, salt, and pepper. 2. Begin puréeing the ingredients on medium speed, and slowly drizzle in the oil with the blender running. Continue to purée until the dip is thoroughly mixed. 3. Add the bread and purée. 4. Serve with raw vegetables for dipping, or store in a jar with a lid for up to one week in the refrigerator.

Per Serving:

calories: 133 | fat: 10g | protein: 3g | carbs: 10g | fiber: 2g | sodium: 515mg

Pea and Arugula Crostini with Pecorino Romano

Prep time: 10 minutes | Cook time: 15 minutes | Serves 6 to 8

- ◀ 1½ cups fresh or frozen peas
- ◀ 1 loaf crusty whole-wheat bread, cut into thin slices
- ◀ 3 tablespoons olive oil, divided
- ◀ 1 small garlic clove, finely mined or pressed
- ◀ Juice of ½ lemon
- ◀ ½ teaspoon salt
- ◀ ¼ teaspoon freshly ground black pepper
- ◀ 1 cup (packed) baby arugula
- ◀ ¼ cup thinly shaved Pecorino Romano

1. Preheat the oven to 350°F(180ºC). 2. Fill a small saucepan with about ½ inch of water. Bring to a boil over medium-high heat. Add the peas and cook for 3 to 5 minutes, until tender. Drain and rinse with cold water. 3. Arrange the bread slices on a large baking sheet and brush the tops with 2 tablespoons olive oil. Bake in the preheated oven for about 8 minutes, until golden brown. 4. Meanwhile, in a medium bowl, mash the peas gently with the back of a fork. They should be smashed but not mashed into a paste. Add the remaining 1 tablespoon olive oil, lemon juice, garlic, salt, and pepper and stir to mix. 5. Spoon the pea mixture onto the toasted bread slices and top with the arugula and cheese. Serve immediately.

Per Serving:

calories: 301 | fat: 13g | protein: 14g | carbs: 32g | fiber: 6g | sodium: 833mg

Lemon Shrimp with Garlic Olive Oil

Prep time: 5 minutes | Cook time: 6 minutes | Serves 4

- ◀ 1 pound (454 g) medium shrimp, cleaned and deveined
- ◀ ¼ cup plus 2 tablespoons olive oil, divided
- ◀ Juice of ½ lemon
- ◀ 3 garlic cloves, minced and
- divided
- ◀ ½ teaspoon salt
- ◀ ¼ teaspoon red pepper flakes
- ◀ Lemon wedges, for serving (optional)
- ◀ Marinara sauce, for dipping (optional)

1. Preheat the air fryer to 380°F(193ºC). 2. In a large bowl, combine the shrimp with 2 tablespoons of the olive oil, as well as the lemon juice, ⅓ of the minced garlic, salt, and red pepper flakes. Toss to coat the shrimp well. 3. In a small ramekin, combine the remaining ¼ cup of olive oil and the remaining minced garlic. 4. Tear off a 12-by-12-inch sheet of aluminum foil. Pour the shrimp into the center of the foil, then fold the sides up and crimp the edges so that it forms an aluminum foil bowl that is open on top. Place this packet into the air fryer basket. 5. Roast the shrimp for 4 minutes, then open the air fryer and place the ramekin with oil and garlic in the basket beside the shrimp packet. Cook for 2 more minutes. 6. Transfer the shrimp on a serving plate or platter with the ramekin of garlic olive oil on the side for dipping. You may also serve with lemon wedges and marinara sauce, if desired.

Per Serving:

calories: 283 | fat: 21g | protein: 23g | carbs: 1g | fiber: 0g | sodium: 427mg

Sfougato

Prep time: 10 minutes | Cook time: 8 minutes | Serves 4

- ◀ ½ cup crumbled feta cheese
- ◀ ¼ cup bread crumbs
- ◀ 1 medium onion, peeled and minced
- ◀ 4 tablespoons all-purpose flour
- ◀ 2 tablespoons minced fresh
- mint
- ◀ ½ teaspoon salt
- ◀ ½ teaspoon ground black pepper
- ◀ 1 tablespoon dried thyme
- ◀ 6 large eggs, beaten
- ◀ 1 cup water

1. In a medium bowl, mix cheese, bread crumbs, onion, flour, mint, salt, pepper, and thyme. Stir in eggs. 2. Spray an 8" round baking dish with nonstick cooking spray. Pour egg mixture into dish. 3. Place rack in the Instant Pot® and add water. Fold a long piece of foil in half lengthwise. Lay foil over rack to form a sling and top with dish. Cover loosely with foil. Close lid, set steam release to Sealing, press the Manual button, and set time to 8 minutes. 4. When the timer beeps, quick-release the pressure until the float valve drops. Open lid. Let stand 5 minutes, then remove dish from pot.

Per Serving:

calories: 226 | fat: 12g | protein: 14g | carbs: 15g | fiber: 1g | sodium: 621mg

Spicy Roasted Potatoes

Prep time: 20 minutes | Cook time: 25 minutes | Serves 5

- ◀ 1½ pounds (680 g) red potatoes or gold potatoes
- ◀ 3 tablespoons garlic, minced
- ◀ 1½ teaspoons salt
- ◀ ¼ cup extra-virgin olive oil
- ◀ ½ cup fresh cilantro,
- chopped
- ◀ ½ teaspoon freshly ground black pepper
- ◀ ¼ teaspoon cayenne pepper
- ◀ 3 tablespoons lemon juice

1. Preheat the oven to 450°F(235ºC). 2. Scrub the potatoes and pat dry. 3. Cut the potatoes into ½-inch pieces and put them into a bowl. 4. Add the garlic, salt, and olive oil and toss everything together to evenly coat. 5. Pour the potato mixture onto a baking sheet, spread the potatoes out evenly, and put them into the oven, roasting for 25 minutes. Halfway through roasting, turn the potatoes with a spatula; continue roasting for the remainder of time until the potato edges start to brown. 6. Remove the potatoes from the oven and let them cool on the baking sheet for 5 minutes. 7. Using a spatula, remove the potatoes from the pan and put them into a bowl. 8. Add the cilantro, black pepper, cayenne, and lemon juice to the potatoes and toss until well mixed. 9. Serve warm.

Per Serving:

calories: 203 | fat: 11g | protein: 3g | carbs: 24g | fiber: 3g | sodium: 728mg

Crunchy Basil White Beans

Prep time: 2 minutes | Cook time: 19 minutes | Serves 2

- 1 (15-ounce / 425-g) can cooked white beans
- 2 tablespoons olive oil
- 1 teaspoon fresh sage, chopped
- ¼ teaspoon garlic powder
- ¼ teaspoon salt, divided
- 1 teaspoon chopped fresh basil

1. Preheat the air fryer to 380°F(193°C). 2. In a medium bowl, mix together the beans, olive oil, sage, garlic, ⅛ teaspoon salt, and basil. 3. Pour the white beans into the air fryer and spread them out in a single layer. 4. Bake for 10 minutes. Stir and continue cooking for an additional 5 to 9 minutes, or until they reach your preferred level of crispiness. 5. Toss with the remaining ⅛ teaspoon salt before serving.

Per Serving:

calories: 418 | fat: 14g | protein: 21g | carbs: 54g | fiber: 14g | sodium: 304mg

Apple Chips with Chocolate Tahini

Prep time: 10 minutes | Cook time: 0 minutes | Serves 2

- 2 tablespoons tahini
- 1 tablespoon maple syrup
- 1 tablespoon unsweetened cocoa powder
- 1 to 2 tablespoons warm
- water (or more if needed)
- 2 medium apples
- 1 tablespoon roasted, salted sunflower seeds

1. In a small bowl, mix together the tahini, maple syrup, and cocoa powder. Add warm water, a little at a time, until thin enough to drizzle. Do not microwave it to thin it—it won't work. 2. Slice the apples crosswise into round slices, and then cut each piece in half to make a chip. 3. Lay the apple chips out on a plate and drizzle them with the chocolate tahini sauce. 4. Sprinkle sunflower seeds over the apple chips.

Per Serving:

calories: 261 | fat: 11g | protein: 5g | carbs: 43g | fiber: 8g | sodium: 21mg

Marinated Olives and Mushrooms

Prep time: 10 minutes | Cook time: 0 minutes | Serves 8

- 1 pound (454 g) white button mushrooms
- 1 pound (454 g) mixed, high-quality olives
- 2 tablespoons fresh thyme leaves
- 1 tablespoon white wine
- vinegar
- ½ tablespoon crushed fennel seeds
- Pinch chili flakes
- Olive oil, to cover
- Sea salt and freshly ground pepper, to taste

1. Clean and rinse mushrooms under cold water and pat dry. 2. Combine all ingredients in a glass jar or other airtight container. Cover with olive oil and season with sea salt and freshly ground

pepper. 3. Shake to distribute the ingredients. Allow to marinate for at least 1 hour. Serve at room temperature.

Per Serving:

calories: 61 | fat: 4g | protein: 2g | carbs: 5g | fiber: 2g | sodium: 420mg

Crispy Spiced Chickpeas

Prep time: 5 minutes | Cook time: 25 minutes | Serves 6

- 3 cans (15 ounces / 425 g each) chickpeas, drained and rinsed
- 1 cup olive oil
- 1 teaspoon paprika
- ½ teaspoon ground cumin
- ½ teaspoon kosher salt
- ¼ teaspoon ground cinnamon
- ¼ teaspoon ground black pepper

1. Spread the chickpeas on paper towels and pat dry. 2. In a large saucepan over medium-high heat, warm the oil until shimmering. Add 1 chickpea; if it sizzles right away, the oil is hot enough to proceed. 3. Add enough chickpeas to form a single layer in the saucepan. Cook, occasionally gently shaking the saucepan until golden brown, about 8 minutes. With a slotted spoon, transfer to a paper towel–lined plate to drain. Repeat with the remaining chickpeas until all the chickpeas are fried. Transfer to a large bowl. 4. In a small bowl, combine the paprika, cumin, salt, cinnamon, and pepper. Sprinkle all over the fried chickpeas and toss to coat. The chickpeas will crisp as they cool.

Per Serving:

calories: 175 | fat: 9g | protein: 6g | carbs: 20g | fiber: 5g | sodium: 509mg

Lemony Garlic Hummus

Prep time: 5 minutes |Cook time: 0 minutes| Serves: 6

- 1 (15-ounce / 425-g) can chickpeas, drained, liquid reserved
- 3 tablespoons freshly squeezed lemon juice (from about 1 large lemon)
- 2 tablespoons peanut butter
- 3 tablespoons extra-virgin
- olive oil, divided
- 2 garlic cloves
- ¼ teaspoon kosher or sea salt (optional)
- Raw veggies or whole-grain crackers, for serving (optional)

1. In the bowl of a food processor, combine the chickpeas and 2 tablespoons of the reserved chickpea liquid with the lemon juice, peanut butter, 2 tablespoons of oil, and the garlic. Process the mixture for 1 minute. Scrape down the sides of the bowl with a rubber spatula. Process for 1 more minute, or until smooth. 2. Put in a serving bowl, drizzle with the remaining 1 tablespoon of olive oil, sprinkle with the salt, if using, and serve with veggies or crackers, if desired.

Per Serving:

calories: 192 | fat: 11g | protein: 6g | carbs: 18g | fiber: 5g | sodium: 258mg

Crispy Chili Chickpeas

Prep time: 5 minutes | Cook time: 15 minutes | Serves 4

◄ 1 (15-ounce / 425-g) can cooked chickpeas, drained and rinsed
◄ 1 tablespoon olive oil
◄ ¼ teaspoon salt
◄ ⅛ teaspoon chili powder
◄ ⅛ teaspoon garlic powder
◄ ⅛ teaspoon paprika

1. Preheat the air fryer to 380°F(193°C). 2. In a medium bowl, toss all of the ingredients together until the chickpeas are well coated. 3. Pour the chickpeas into the air fryer and spread them out in a single layer. 4. Roast for 15 minutes, stirring once halfway through the cook time.

Per Serving:

calories: 177 | fat: 6g | protein: 8g | carbs: 24g | fiber: 7g | sodium: 374mg

Cinnamon-Apple Chips

Prep time: 10 minutes | Cook time: 32 minutes | Serves 4

◄ Oil, for spraying
◄ 2 Red Delicious or Honeycrisp apples
◄ ¼ teaspoon ground cinnamon, divided

1. Line the air fryer basket with parchment and spray lightly with oil. 2. Trim the uneven ends off the apples. Using a mandoline on the thinnest setting or a sharp knife, cut the apples into very thin slices. Discard the cores. 3. Place half of the apple slices in a single layer in the prepared basket and sprinkle with half of the cinnamon. 4. Place a metal air fryer trivet on top of the apples to keep them from flying around while they are cooking. 5. Air fry at 300°F (149°C) for 16 minutes, flipping every 5 minutes to ensure even cooking. Repeat with the remaining apple slices and cinnamon. 6. Let cool to room temperature before serving. The chips will firm up as they cool.

Per Serving:

calories: 63 | fat: 0g | protein: 0g | carbs: 15g | fiber: 3g | sodium: 1mg

Cream Cheese Wontons

Prep time: 15 minutes | Cook time: 6 minutes | Makes 20 wontons

◄ Oil, for spraying
◄ 20 wonton wrappers
◄ 4 ounces (113 g) cream cheese

1. Line the air fryer basket with parchment and spray lightly with oil. 2. Pour some water in a small bowl. 3. Lay out a wonton wrapper and place 1 teaspoon of cream cheese in the center. 4. Dip your finger in the water and moisten the edge of the wonton wrapper. Fold over the opposite corners to make a triangle and press the edges together. 5. Pinch the corners of the triangle together to form a classic wonton shape. Place the wonton in the prepared basket. Repeat with the remaining wrappers and cream cheese. You may need to work in batches, depending on the size of your air fryer. 6. Air fry at 400°F (204°C) for 6 minutes, or until golden brown around the edges.

Per Serving:

1 wonton: calories: 43 | fat: 2g | protein: 1g | carbs: 5g | fiber: 0g | sodium: 66mg

Garlic-Roasted Tomatoes and Olives

Prep time: 5 minutes | Cook time: 20 minutes | Serves 6

◄ 2 cups cherry tomatoes
◄ 4 garlic cloves, roughly chopped
◄ ½ red onion, roughly chopped
◄ 1 cup black olives
◄ 1 cup green olives
◄ 1 tablespoon fresh basil, minced
◄ 1 tablespoon fresh oregano, minced
◄ 2 tablespoons olive oil
◄ ¼ to ½ teaspoon salt

1. Preheat the air fryer to 380°F(193°C). 2. In a large bowl, combine all of the ingredients and toss together so that the tomatoes and olives are coated well with the olive oil and herbs. 3. Pour the mixture into the air fryer basket, and roast for 10 minutes. Stir the mixture well, then continue roasting for an additional 10 minutes. 4. Remove from the air fryer, transfer to a serving bowl, and enjoy.

Per Serving:

calories: 107 | fat: 9g | protein: 1g | carbs: 6g | fiber: 2g | sodium: 429mg

Black Olive and Lentil Pesto

Prep time: 10 minutes | Cook time: 20 minutes | Serves 10 to 12

◄ ¾ cup green lentils, rinsed
◄ ¼ teaspoon salt
◄ ½ cup pitted Kalamata olives
◄ 2 tablespoons fresh Greek oregano
◄ 2 garlic cloves, minced
◄ 2 tablespoons coarsely chopped fresh parsley
◄ 3 tablespoons fresh lemon juice
◄ 5 tablespoons olive oil

1. Place the lentils in a large saucepan and add cold water to cover by 1 inch. Bring the water to a boil; cover and simmer for 20 minutes, or until the lentils are soft but not disintegrating. Drain and let cool. 2. Shake the colander a few times to remove any excess water, then transfer the lentils to a blender or food processor. Add the salt, olives, oregano, garlic, and parsley. With the machine running, add the lemon juice, then the olive oil, and blend until smooth. 3. Serve with pita chips, pita bread, or as a dip for fresh vegetables.

Per Serving:

1 cup: calories: 70 | fat: 7g | protein: 1g | carbs: 2g | fiber: 1g | sodium: 99mg

Bite-Size Stuffed Peppers

Prep time: 15 minutes | Cook time: 10 minutes | Serves 8 to 10

◄ 20 to 25 mini sweet bell peppers, assortment of colors
◄ 1 tablespoon extra-virgin olive oil
◄ 4 ounces (113 g) goat cheese, at room temperature
◄ 4 ounces (113 g) mascarpone cheese, at room temperature
◄ 1 tablespoon fresh chives, chopped
◄ 1 tablespoon lemon zest

1. Preheat the oven to 400°F(205°C). 2. Remove the stem, cap, and any seeds from the peppers. Put them into a bowl and toss to coat with the olive oil. 3. Put the peppers onto a baking sheet; bake for 8 minutes. 4. Remove the peppers from the oven and let cool completely. 5. In a medium bowl, add the goat cheese, mascarpone cheese, chives, and lemon zest. Stir to combine, then spoon mixture into a piping bag. 6. Fill each pepper to the top with the cheese mixture, using the piping bag. 7. Chill the peppers in the fridge for at least 30 minutes before serving.

Per Serving:
calories: 141 | fat: 11g | protein: 4g | carbs: 6g | fiber: 2g | sodium: 73mg

Fried Baby Artichokes with Lemon-Garlic Aioli

Prep time: 5 minutes | Cook time: 50 minutes | Serves 10

Artichokes:
◄ 15 baby artichokes
◄ ½ lemon
Aioli:
◄ 1 egg
◄ 2 cloves garlic, chopped
◄ 1 tablespoon fresh lemon juice
◄ 3 cups olive oil
◄ Kosher salt, to taste

◄ ½ teaspoon Dijon mustard
◄ ½ cup olive oil
◄ Kosher salt and ground black pepper, to taste

Make the Artichokes: 1. Wash and drain the artichokes. With a paring knife, strip off the coarse outer leaves around the base and stalk, leaving the softer leaves on. Carefully peel the stalks and trim off all but 2' below the base. Slice off the top ½' of the artichokes. Cut each artichoke in half. Rub the cut surfaces with a lemon half to keep from browning. 2. In a medium saucepan fitted with a deep-fry thermometer over medium heat, warm the oil to about 280°F(138°C). Working in batches, cook the artichokes in the hot oil until tender, about 15 minutes. Using a slotted spoon, remove and drain on a paper towel–lined plate. Repeat with all the artichoke halves. 3. Increase the heat of the oil to 375°F(190°C). In batches, cook the precooked baby artichokes until browned at the edges and crisp, about 1 minute. Transfer to a paper towel–lined plate. Season with the salt to taste. Repeat with the remaining artichokes. Make the aioli: 4. In a blender, pulse together the egg, garlic, lemon juice, and mustard until combined. With the blender running, slowly drizzle in the oil a few drops at a time until the mixture thickens like mayonnaise, about 2 minutes. Transfer to a bowl and season to taste with the salt and pepper. 5. Serve the warm artichokes with the aioli on the side.

Per Serving:
calories: 236 | fat: 17g | protein: 6g | carbs: 21g | fiber: 10g | sodium: 283mg

Mixed-Vegetable Caponata

Prep time: 15 minutes | Cook time: 40 minutes | Serves 8

◄ 1 eggplant, chopped
◄ 1 zucchini, chopped
◄ 1 red bell pepper, seeded and chopped
◄ 1 small red onion, chopped
◄ 2 tablespoons extra-virgin olive oil, divided
◄ 1 cup canned tomato sauce
◄ 3 tablespoons red wine vinegar
◄ 1 tablespoon honey
◄ ¼ teaspoon red-pepper flakes
◄ ¼ teaspoon kosher salt
◄ ½ cup pitted, chopped green olives
◄ 2 tablespoons drained capers
◄ 2 tablespoons raisins
◄ 2 tablespoons chopped fresh flat-leaf parsley

1. Preheat the oven to 400°F(205°C). 2. On a large rimmed baking sheet, toss the eggplant, zucchini, bell pepper, and onion with 1 tablespoon of the oil. Roast until the vegetables are tender, about 30 minutes. 3. In a medium saucepan over medium heat, warm the remaining 1 tablespoon oil. Add the tomato sauce, vinegar, honey, pepper flakes, and salt and stir to combine. Add the roasted vegetables, olives, capers, raisins, and parsley and cook until bubbly and thickened, 10 minutes. 4. Remove from the heat and cool to room temperature. Serve immediately or store in an airtight container in the refrigerator for up to 1 week.

Per Serving:
calories: 100 | fat: 5g | protein: 2g | carbs: 13g | fiber: 4g | sodium: 464mg

Chapter 8 Vegetables and Sides

Coriander-Cumin Roasted Carrots

Prep time: 10 minutes | Cook time: 20 minutes | Serves 2

- ½ pound (227 g) rainbow carrots (about 4)
- 2 tablespoons fresh orange juice
- 1 tablespoon honey
- ½ teaspoon coriander
- Pinch salt

1. Preheat oven to 400°F(205°C) and set the oven rack to the middle position. 2. Peel the carrots and cut them lengthwise into slices of even thickness. Place them in a large bowl. 3. In a small bowl, mix together the orange juice, honey, coriander, and salt. 4. Pour the orange juice mixture over the carrots and toss well to coat. 5. Spread carrots onto a baking dish in a single layer. 6. Roast for 15 to 20 minutes, or until fork-tender.

Per Serving:

calories: 85 | fat: 0g | protein: 1g | carbs: 21g | fiber: 3g | sodium: 156mg

Roasted Broccoli with Tahini Yogurt Sauce

Prep time: 15 minutes | Cook time: 30 minutes | Serves 4

For the Broccoli:
- 1½ to 2 pounds (680 to 907 g) broccoli, stalk trimmed and cut into slices, head cut into florets
- 1 lemon, sliced into ¼-inch-thick rounds

For the Tahini Yogurt Sauce:
- ½ cup plain Greek yogurt
- 2 tablespoons tahini
- 1 tablespoon lemon juice
- 3 tablespoons extra-virgin olive oil
- ½ teaspoon kosher salt
- ¼ teaspoon freshly ground black pepper

- ¼ teaspoon kosher salt
- 1 teaspoon sesame seeds, for garnish (optional)

Make the Broccoli: 1. Preheat the oven to 425ºF (220ºC). Line a baking sheet with parchment paper or foil. 2. In a large bowl, gently toss the broccoli, lemon slices, olive oil, salt, and black pepper to combine. Arrange the broccoli in a single layer on the prepared baking sheet. Roast 15 minutes, stir, and roast another 15 minutes, until golden brown. Make the Tahini Yogurt Sauce: 3. In a medium bowl, combine the yogurt, tahini, lemon juice, and salt; mix well. 4. Spread the tahini yogurt sauce on a platter or large plate and top with the broccoli and lemon slices. Garnish with the sesame seeds (if desired).

Per Serving:

calories: 245 | fat: 16g | protein: 12g | carbs: 20g | fiber: 7g | sodium: 305mg

Potato Vegetable Hash

Prep time: 20 minutes | Cook time: 5 to 7 hours | Serves 4

- 1½ pounds (680 g) red potatoes, diced
- 8 ounces (227 g) green beans, trimmed and cut into ½-inch pieces
- 4 ounces (113 g) mushrooms, chopped
- 1 large tomato, chopped
- 1 large zucchini, diced
- 1 small onion, diced
- 1 red bell pepper, seeded and
- chopped
- ⅓ cup low-sodium vegetable broth
- 1 teaspoon sea salt
- ½ teaspoon garlic powder
- ½ teaspoon freshly ground black pepper
- ¼ teaspoon red pepper flakes
- ¼ cup shredded cheese of your choice (optional)

1. In a slow cooker, combine the potatoes, green beans, mushrooms, tomato, zucchini, onion, bell pepper, vegetable broth, salt, garlic powder, black pepper, and red pepper flakes. Stir to mix well. 2. Cover the cooker and cook for 5 to 7 hours on Low heat. 3. Garnish with cheese for serving (if using).

Per Serving:

calories: 183 | fat: 1g | protein: 7g | carbs: 41g | fiber: 8g | sodium: 642mg

Grits Casserole

Prep time: 5 minutes | Cook time: 28 to 30 minutes | Serves 4

- 10 fresh asparagus spears, cut into 1-inch pieces
- 2 cups cooked grits, cooled to room temperature
- 1 egg, beaten
- 2 teaspoons Worcestershire sauce
- ½ teaspoon garlic powder
- ¼ teaspoon salt
- 2 slices provolone cheese (about 1½ ounces / 43 g)
- Oil for misting or cooking spray

1. Mist asparagus spears with oil and air fry at 390ºF (199ºC) for 5 minutes, until crisp-tender. 2. In a medium bowl, mix together the grits, egg, Worcestershire, garlic powder, and salt. 3. Spoon half of grits mixture into a baking pan and top with asparagus. 4. Tear cheese slices into pieces and layer evenly on top of asparagus. 5. Top with remaining grits. 6. Bake at 360ºF (182ºC) for 23 to 25 minutes. The casserole will rise a little as it cooks. When done, the top will have browned lightly with just a hint of crispiness.

Per Serving:

calories: 161 | fat: 6g | protein: 8g | carbs: 20g | fiber: 2g | sodium: 704mg

Baked Tomatoes with Spiced Amaranth Stuffing

Prep time: 10 minutes | Cook time: 50 minutes | Serves 6

- 1 tablespoon olive oil
- 1 small onion, diced
- 1 clove garlic, minced
- 1 cup amaranth
- 1 cup vegetable broth or water
- 1 cup diced tomatoes, drained
- ¼ cup chopped fresh parsley
- ½ teaspoon ground cinnamon
- ½ cup golden raisins
- ½ cup toasted pine nuts
- ¾ teaspoon salt
- ½ teaspoon freshly ground black pepper
- 6 large ripe tomatoes

1. Preheat the oven to 375°F (190°C). 2. Heat the olive oil over medium heat in a medium saucepan. Add the onion and garlic and cook, stirring frequently, until the onion is softened, about 5 minutes. Stir in the amaranth and then the broth or water and bring to a boil over high heat. Lower the heat to low, cover, and cook, stirring occasionally, for about 20 minutes, until the amaranth is tender and the liquid has been absorbed. 3. Remove the pan from the heat and stir in the diced tomatoes, parsley, cinnamon, raisins, pine nuts, salt, and pepper. 4. Cut a slice off the bottom of each tomato to make a flat bottom for it to sit on. Scoop out the seeds and core of the tomato to make a shell for filling. Arrange the hollowed-out tomatoes in a baking dish. 5. Fill the tomatoes with the amaranth mixture and bake in the preheated oven for about 25 minutes, until the tomatoes have softened, but still hold their shape. Serve hot.

Per Serving:

calories: 306 | fat: 13g | protein: 10g | carbs: 43g | fiber: 7g | sodium: 439mg

Lightened-Up Eggplant Parmigiana

Prep time: 10 minutes | Cook time: 1 hour 20 minutes | Serves 3

- 2 medium globe eggplants, sliced into ¼-inch rounds
- 2 tablespoons extra virgin olive oil, divided
- 1 teaspoon fine sea salt, divided
- 1 medium onion (any variety), diced
- 1 garlic clove, finely chopped
- 20 ounces (567g) canned
- crushed tomatoes or tomato purée
- 3 tablespoons chopped fresh basil, divided
- ¼ teaspoon freshly ground black pepper
- 7 ounces (198 g) low-moisture mozzarella, thinly sliced or grated
- 2 ounces (57 g) grated Parmesan cheese

1. Line an oven rack with aluminum foil and preheat the oven to 350°F (180°C). 2. Place the eggplant slices in a large bowl and toss with 1 tablespoon of the olive oil and ½ teaspoon of the sea salt. Arrange the slices on the prepared oven rack. Place the oven rack in the middle position and roast the eggplant for 15–20 minutes or until soft. 3. While the eggplant slices are roasting, heat the remaining tablespoon of olive oil in a medium pan over medium heat. When the oil begins to shimmer, add the onions and sauté for 5 minutes, then add the garlic and sauté for 1 more minute. Add the crushed tomatoes, 1½ tablespoons of the basil, the remaining ½ teaspoon of sea salt, and black pepper. Reduce the heat to low and simmer for 15 minutes, then remove from the heat. 4. When the eggplant slices are done roasting, remove them from the oven. Begin assembling the dish by spreading ½ cup of the tomato sauce over the bottom of a 11 × 7-inch (30 × 20cm) casserole dish. Place a third of the eggplant rounds in a single layer in the dish, overlapping them slightly, if needed. Layer half of the mozzarella on top of the eggplant, then spread ¾ cup tomato sauce over the cheese slices and then sprinkle 2½ tablespoons of the grated Parmesan cheese over the top. Repeat the process with a second layer of eggplant, sauce, and cheese, then add the remaining eggplant in a single layer on top of the cheese. Top with the remaining sauce and then sprinkle the remaining 1½ tablespoons of basil over the top. 5. Bake for 40–45 minutes or until browned, then remove from oven and set aside to cool for 10 minutes before cutting into 6 equal-size pieces and serving. Store covered in the refrigerator for up to 3 days.

Per Serving:

calories: 453 | fat: 28g | protein: 28g | carbs: 26g | fiber: 4g | sodium: 842mg

Caponata (Sicilian Eggplant)

Prep time: 5 minutes | Cook time: 40 minutes | Serves 2

- 3 medium eggplant, cut into ½-inch cubes (about 1½ pounds / 680 g)
- ½ teaspoon fine sea salt
- ¼ cup extra virgin olive oil
- 1 medium onion (red or white), chopped
- 1 tablespoon dried oregano
- ½ cup green olives, pitted and halved
- 2 tablespoons capers, rinsed
- 3 medium tomatoes (about
- 15 ounces / 425 g), chopped
- 3 tablespoons red wine vinegar
- 2 tablespoons granulated sugar
- Salt to taste
- Freshly ground black pepper to taste
- 2 tablespoons chopped fresh basil
- 1 tablespoon toasted pine nuts (optional)

1. Place the eggplant in a large colander. Sprinkle ½ teaspoon sea salt over the top and set the eggplant aside to rest for about an hour. 2. Add the olive oil to a large pan over medium heat. When the oil starts to shimmer, add the eggplant and sauté until it starts to turn golden brown, about 5 minutes. Add the onions and continue sautéing until the onions become soft. 3. Add the oregano, olives, capers, and tomatoes (with juices) to the pan. Reduce the heat to medium-low and simmer for about 20–25 minutes. 4. While the onions and tomatoes are cooking, combine the vinegar and sugar in a small bowl. Stir until the sugar is completely dissolved, then add the mixture to the pan. Continue cooking for 2–3 more minutes or until you can no longer smell the vinegar and then remove the pan from the heat. 5. Season the mixture to taste with salt and black pepper. Just prior to serving, top each serving with a sprinkle of chopped basil and toasted pine nuts, if using. Store in the refrigerator for up to 3 days.

Per Serving:

calories: 473 | fat: 32g | protein: 6g | carbs: 47g | fiber: 15g | sodium: 702mg

Corn on the Cob

Prep time: 5 minutes | Cook time: 12 to 15 minutes | Serves 4

◀ 2 large ears fresh corn
◀ Olive oil for misting
◀ Salt, to taste (optional)

1. Shuck corn, remove silks, and wash. 2. Cut or break each ear in half crosswise. 3. Spray corn with olive oil. 4. Air fry at 390ºF (199ºC) for 12 to 15 minutes or until browned as much as you like. 5. Serve plain or with coarsely ground salt.

Per Serving:

calories: 67 | fat: 1g | protein: 2g | carbs: 14g | fiber: 2g | sodium: 156mg

Dill-and-Garlic Beets

Prep time: 10 minutes | Cook time: 30 minutes | Serves 4

◀ 4 beets, cleaned, peeled, and sliced
◀ 1 garlic clove, minced
◀ 2 tablespoons chopped fresh
   dill
◀ ¼ teaspoon salt
◀ ¼ teaspoon black pepper
◀ 3 tablespoons olive oil

1. Preheat the air fryer to 380°F(193°C). 2. In a large bowl, mix together all of the ingredients so the beets are well coated with the oil. 3. Pour the beet mixture into the air fryer basket, and roast for 15 minutes before stirring, then continue roasting for 15 minutes more.

Per Serving:

calories: 136 | fat: 2g | protein: 2g | carbs: 10g | fiber: 3g | sodium: 210mg

Garlicky Broccoli Rabe with Artichokes

Prep time: 5 minutes | Cook time: 10 minutes | Serves 4

◀ 2 pounds (907 g) fresh broccoli rabe
◀ ½ cup extra-virgin olive oil, divided
◀ 3 garlic cloves, finely minced
◀ 1 teaspoon salt
◀ 1 teaspoon red pepper flakes
◀ 1 (13¾-ounce / 390-g) can artichoke hearts, drained and quartered
◀ 1 tablespoon water
◀ 2 tablespoons red wine vinegar
◀ Freshly ground black pepper

1. Trim away any thick lower stems and yellow leaves from the broccoli rabe and discard. Cut into individual florets with a couple inches of thin stem attached. 2. In a large skillet, heat ¼ cup olive oil over medium-high heat. Add the trimmed broccoli, garlic, salt, and red pepper flakes and sauté for 5 minutes, until the broccoli begins to soften. Add the artichoke hearts and sauté for another 2 minutes. 3. Add the water and reduce the heat to low. Cover and simmer until the broccoli stems are tender, 3 to 5 minutes. 4. In a small bowl, whisk together remaining ¼ cup olive oil and the vinegar. Drizzle over the broccoli and artichokes. Season with

ground black pepper, if desired.

Per Serving:

calories: 341 | fat: 28g | protein: 11g | carbs: 18g | fiber: 12g | sodium: 750mg

Puréed Cauliflower Soup

Prep time: 15 minutes | Cook time: 11 minutes | Serves 6

◀ 2 tablespoons olive oil
◀ 1 medium onion, peeled and chopped
◀ 1 stalk celery, chopped
◀ 1 medium carrot, peeled and chopped
◀ 3 sprigs fresh thyme
◀ 4 cups cauliflower florets
◀ 2 cups vegetable stock
◀ ½ cup half-and-half
◀ ¼ cup low-fat plain Greek yogurt
◀ 2 tablespoons chopped fresh chives

1. Press the Sauté button on the Instant Pot® and heat oil. Add onion, celery, and carrot. Cook until just tender, about 6 minutes. Add thyme, cauliflower, and stock. Stir well, then press the Cancel button. 2. Close lid, set steam release to Sealing, press the Manual button, and set time to 5 minutes. When the timer beeps, let pressure release naturally, about 15 minutes. 3. Open lid, remove and discard thyme stems, and with an immersion blender, purée soup until smooth. Stir in half-and-half and yogurt. Garnish with chives and serve immediately.

Per Serving:

calories: 113 | fat: 7g | protein: 3g | carbs: 9g | fiber: 2g | sodium: 236mg

Brussels Sprouts with Pecans and Gorgonzola

Prep time: 10 minutes | Cook time: 25 minutes | Serves 4

◀ ½ cup pecans
◀ 1½ pounds (680 g) fresh Brussels sprouts, trimmed and quartered
◀ 2 tablespoons olive oil
◀ Salt and freshly ground black pepper, to taste
◀ ¼ cup crumbled Gorgonzola cheese

1. Spread the pecans in a single layer of the air fryer and set the heat to 350ºF (177ºC). Air fry for 3 to 5 minutes until the pecans are lightly browned and fragrant. Transfer the pecans to a plate and continue preheating the air fryer, increasing the heat to 400ºF (204ºC). 2. In a large bowl, toss the Brussels sprouts with the olive oil and season with salt and black pepper to taste. 3. Working in batches if necessary, arrange the Brussels sprouts in a single layer in the air fryer basket. Pausing halfway through the baking time to shake the basket, air fry for 20 to 25 minutes until the sprouts are tender and starting to brown on the edges. 4. Transfer the sprouts to a serving bowl and top with the toasted pecans and Gorgonzola. Serve warm or at room temperature.

Per Serving:

calories: 253 | fat: 18g | protein: 9g | carbs: 17g | fiber: 8g | sodium: 96mg

Greek Fasolakia (Green Beans)

Prep time: 10 minutes | Cook time: 6 to 8 hours | Serves 6

- 2 pounds (907 g) green beans, trimmed
- 1 (15-ounce / 425-g) can no-salt-added diced tomatoes, with juice
- 1 large onion, chopped
- 4 garlic cloves, chopped
- Juice of 1 lemon
- 1 teaspoon dried dill
- 1 teaspoon ground cumin
- 1 teaspoon dried oregano
- 1 teaspoon sea salt
- ½ teaspoon freshly ground black pepper
- ¼ cup feta cheese, crumbled

1. In a slow cooker, combine the green beans, tomatoes and their juice, onion, garlic, lemon juice, dill, cumin, oregano, salt, and pepper. Stir to mix well. 2. Cover the cooker and cook for 6 to 8 hours on Low heat. 3. Top with feta cheese for serving.

Per Serving:

calories: 94 | fat: 2g | protein: 5g | carbs: 18g | fiber: 7g | sodium: 497mg

Cauliflower with Lime Juice

Prep time: 10 minutes | Cook time: 7 minutes | Serves 4

- 2 cups chopped cauliflower florets
- 2 tablespoons coconut oil, melted
- 2 teaspoons chili powder
- ½ teaspoon garlic powder
- 1 medium lime
- 2 tablespoons chopped cilantro

1. In a large bowl, toss cauliflower with coconut oil. Sprinkle with chili powder and garlic powder. Place seasoned cauliflower into the air fryer basket. 2. Adjust the temperature to 350°F (177°C) and set the timer for 7 minutes. 3. Cauliflower will be tender and begin to turn golden at the edges. Place into a serving bowl. 4. Cut the lime into quarters and squeeze juice over cauliflower. Garnish with cilantro.

Per Serving:

calories: 80 | fat: 7g | protein: 1g | carbs: 5g | fiber: 2g | sodium: 55mg

Roasted Broccolini with Garlic and Romano

Prep time: 5 minutes | Cook time: 10 minutes | Serves 2

- 1 bunch broccolini (about 5 ounces / 142 g)
- 1 tablespoon olive oil
- ½ teaspoon garlic powder
- ¼ teaspoon salt
- 2 tablespoons grated Romano cheese

1. Preheat the oven to 400°F(205°C) and set the oven rack to the middle position. Line a sheet pan with parchment paper or foil. 2. Slice the tough ends off the broccolini and place in a medium bowl. Add the olive oil, garlic powder, and salt and toss to combine. Arrange broccolini on the lined sheet pan. 3. Roast for 7 minutes, flipping pieces over halfway through the roasting time. 4. Remove the pan from the oven and sprinkle the cheese over the broccolini. With a pair of tongs, carefully flip the pieces over to coat all sides. Return to the oven for another 2 to 3 minutes, or until the cheese melts and starts to turn golden.

Per Serving:

calories: 114 | fat: 9g | protein: 4g | carbs: 5g | fiber: 2g | sodium: 400mg

Spanish Green Beans

Prep time: 10 minutes | Cook time: 20 minutes | Serves 4

- ¼ cup extra-virgin olive oil
- 1 large onion, chopped
- 4 cloves garlic, finely chopped
- 1 pound (454 g) green beans, fresh or frozen, trimmed
- 1½ teaspoons salt, divided
- 1 (15-ounce / 425-g) can diced tomatoes
- ½ teaspoon freshly ground black pepper

1. In a large pot over medium heat, heat the olive oil, onion, and garlic; cook for 1 minute. 2. Cut the green beans into 2-inch pieces. 3. Add the green beans and 1 teaspoon of salt to the pot and toss everything together; cook for 3 minutes. 4. Add the diced tomatoes, remaining ½ teaspoon of salt, and black pepper to the pot; continue to cook for another 12 minutes, stirring occasionally. 5. Serve warm.

Per Serving:

calories: 200 | fat: 14g | protein: 4g | carbs: 18g | fiber: 6g | sodium: 844mg

Saffron Couscous with Almonds, Currants, and Scallions

Prep time: 5 minutes | Cook time: 35 minutes | Serves 8

- 2 cups whole wheat couscous
- 1 tablespoon olive oil
- 5 scallions, thinly sliced, whites and greens kept separate
- 1 large pinch saffron threads, crumbled
- 3 cups low-sodium chicken broth or vegetable broth
- ½ cup slivered almonds
- ¼ cup dried currants
- Kosher salt and ground black pepper, to taste

1. In a medium saucepan over medium heat, toast the couscous, stirring occasionally, until lightly browned, about 5 minutes. Transfer to a bowl. 2. In the same saucepan, add the oil and scallion whites. Cook, stirring, until lightly browned, about 5 minutes. Sprinkle in the saffron and stir to combine. Pour in the broth and bring to a boil. 3. Remove the saucepan from the heat, stir in the couscous, cover, and let sit until all the liquid is absorbed and the couscous is tender, about 15 minutes. 4. Fluff the couscous with a fork. Fluff in the scallion greens, almonds, and currants. Season to taste with the salt and pepper.

Per Serving:

calories: 212 | fat: 6g | protein: 8g | carbs: 34g | fiber: 4g | sodium: 148mg

Caesar Whole Cauliflower

Prep time: 20 minutes | Cook time: 30 minutes | Serves 2 to 4

- ◁ 3 tablespoons olive oil
- ◁ 2 tablespoons red wine vinegar
- ◁ 2 tablespoons Worcestershire sauce
- ◁ 2 tablespoons grated Parmesan cheese
- ◁ 1 tablespoon Dijon mustard
- ◁ 4 garlic cloves, minced
- ◁ 4 oil-packed anchovy fillets, drained and finely minced
- ◁ Kosher salt and freshly ground black pepper, to taste
- ◁ 1 small head cauliflower (about 1 pound / 454 g), green leaves trimmed and stem trimmed flush with the bottom of the head
- ◁ 1 tablespoon roughly chopped fresh flat-leaf parsley (optional)

1. In a liquid measuring cup, whisk together the olive oil, vinegar, Worcestershire, Parmesan, mustard, garlic, anchovies, and salt and pepper to taste. Place the cauliflower head upside down on a cutting board and use a paring knife to make an "x" through the full length of the core. Transfer the cauliflower head to a large bowl and pour half the dressing over it. Turn the cauliflower head to coat it in the dressing, then let it rest, stem-side up, in the dressing for at least 10 minutes and up to 30 minutes to allow the dressing to seep into all its nooks and crannies. 2. Transfer the cauliflower head, stem-side down, to the air fryer and air fry at 340°F (171°C) for 25 minutes. Drizzle the remaining dressing over the cauliflower and air fry at 400°F (204°C) until the top of the cauliflower is golden brown and the core is tender, about 5 minutes more. 3. Remove the basket from the air fryer and transfer the cauliflower to a large plate. Sprinkle with the parsley, if you like, and serve hot.

Per Serving:
calories: 187 | fat: 15g | protein: 5g | carbs: 9g | fiber: 2g | sodium: 453mg

Braised Cauliflower

Prep time: 10 minutes | Cook time: 35 minutes | Serves 3

- ◁ ½ cup extra virgin olive oil
- ◁ 1 medium head cauliflower (about 2 pounds / 907 g), washed and cut into medium-sized florets
- ◁ 1 medium russet or white potato, cut into 1-inch pieces
- ◁ ¼ teaspoon freshly ground black pepper
- ◁ 3 allspice berries
- ◁ 1 cinnamon stick
- ◁ 3 cloves
- ◁ 2 tablespoons tomato paste
- ◁ 1 teaspoon fine sea salt
- ◁ ¾ cup hot water

1. Add the olive oil to a large pot over medium heat. When the oil begins to shimmer, add the cauliflower, potatoes, black pepper, allspice berries, cinnamon stick, and cloves. Sauté for 4 minutes or until the cauliflower begins to brown. 2. Add the tomato paste and sea salt. Continue heating, using a wooden spoon to swirl the tomato paste around the pan until the color changes to a brick red. 3. Add the hot water and stir gently. Reduce the heat to low, cover, and simmer for about 30 minutes or until the cauliflower is tender and the sauce has thickened. (If the sauce is still watery, remove the lid and simmer until the sauce has thickened.) Remove the allspice berries, cinnamon stick, and cloves. 4. Remove the cauliflower from the heat and set it aside to cool for at least 10 minutes before serving. When ready to serve, transfer the cauliflower to a large serving bowl and spoon the sauce over the top. Store covered in the refrigerator for up to 3 days.

Per Serving:
calories: 406 | fat: 36g | protein: 4g | carbs: 19g | fiber: 3g | sodium: 813mg

Roasted Cauliflower with Lemon Tahini Sauce

Prep time: 10 minutes | Cook time: 20 minutes | Serves 2

- ◁ ½ large head cauliflower, stemmed and broken into florets (about 3 cups)
- ◁ 1 tablespoon olive oil
- ◁ 2 tablespoons tahini
- ◁ 2 tablespoons freshly squeezed lemon juice
- ◁ 1 teaspoon harissa paste
- ◁ Pinch salt

1. Preheat the oven to 400°F(205°C) and set the rack to the lowest position. Line a sheet pan with parchment paper or foil. 2. Toss the cauliflower florets with the olive oil in a large bowl and transfer to the sheet pan. Reserve the bowl to make the tahini sauce. 3. Roast the cauliflower for 15 minutes, turning it once or twice, until it starts to turn golden. 4. In the same bowl, combine the tahini, lemon juice, harissa, and salt. 5. When the cauliflower is tender, remove it from the oven and toss it with the tahini sauce. Return to the sheet pan and roast for 5 minutes more.

Per Serving:
calories: 205 | fat: 15g | protein: 7g | carbs: 15g | fiber: 7g | sodium: 161mg

Spicy Roasted Bok Choy

Prep time: 10 minutes | Cook time: 7 to 10 minutes | Serves 4

- ◁ 2 tablespoons olive oil
- ◁ 2 tablespoons reduced-sodium coconut aminos
- ◁ 2 teaspoons sesame oil
- ◁ 2 teaspoons chili-garlic sauce
- ◁ 2 cloves garlic, minced
- ◁ 1 head (about 1 pound / 454 g) bok choy, sliced lengthwise into quarters
- ◁ 2 teaspoons black sesame seeds

1. Preheat the air fryer to 400°F (204°C). 2. In a large bowl, combine the olive oil, coconut aminos, sesame oil, chili-garlic sauce, and garlic. Add the bok choy and toss, massaging the leaves with your hands if necessary, until thoroughly coated. 3. Arrange the bok choy in the basket of the air fryer. Pausing about halfway through the cooking time to shake the basket, air fry for 7 to 10 minutes until the bok choy is tender and the tips of the leaves begin to crisp. 4.Remove from the basket and let cool for a few minutes before coarsely chopping. Serve sprinkled with the sesame seeds.

Per Serving:
calories: 145 | fat: 13g | protein: 4g | carbs: 6g | fiber: 3g | sodium: 176mg

Vegetarian Skillet Lasagna

Prep time: 20 minutes | Cook time: 45 minutes | Serves 4

- 15 ounces (425 g) ricotta cheese
- ¼ cup chopped fresh Italian parsley
- ¼ teaspoon Italian seasoning
- 3 tablespoons olive oil
- 1 onion, coarsely chopped
- 3 garlic cloves, minced
- 2 yellow squash, quartered lengthwise and sliced into 1-inch pieces
- 8 ounces (227 g) cremini (baby bella) mushrooms, quartered
- 1 carrot, cut into long ribbons
- 6 ounces (170 g) baby spinach
- 1 (28-ounce / 794-g) can crushed tomatoes
- 1½ cups heavy (whipping) cream
- Sea salt
- Freshly ground black pepper
- 9 no-bake lasagna noodles, broken into 2-inch pieces
- 1 cup grated Parmesan cheese
- ½ cup shredded mozzarella cheese

1. Preheat the oven to 375°F (190°C). 2. In a medium bowl, stir together the ricotta, parsley, and Italian seasoning and set aside. 3. In a large oven-safe skillet, heat the olive oil over medium-high heat. Add the onion and garlic and sauté for 3 minutes. Add the squash and sauté for 2 minutes more. Add the mushrooms and sauté for 4 minutes. Add the carrot and spinach and sauté for 1 minute. 4. Add the crushed tomatoes and the cream and season with salt and pepper. Add the lasagna noodles and mix well, making sure all the noodles are entirely covered with the sauce. Dollop the ricotta mixture evenly over the tomato mixture, using the back of a spoon to gently spread it around. Evenly top with the Parmesan and mozzarella. Cover the skillet with a lid and transfer it to the oven. Bake for 20 minutes, then remove the lid and bake for 10 to 15 minutes more, until the cheese is golden brown. 5. Remove from the oven and serve.

Per Serving:

calories: 1026 | fat: 69g | protein: 37g | carbs: 71g | fiber: 9g | sodium: 933mg

Blackened Zucchini with Kimchi-Herb Sauce

Prep time: 10 minutes | Cook time: 15 minutes | Serves 2

- 2 medium zucchini, ends trimmed (about 6 ounces / 170 g each)
- 2 tablespoons olive oil
- ½ cup kimchi, finely chopped
- ¼ cup finely chopped fresh cilantro
- ¼ cup finely chopped fresh flat-leaf parsley, plus more for garnish
- 2 tablespoons rice vinegar
- 2 teaspoons Asian chili-garlic sauce
- 1 teaspoon grated fresh ginger
- Kosher salt and freshly ground black pepper, to taste

1. Brush the zucchini with half of the olive oil, place in the air fryer, and air fry at 400°F (204°C), turning halfway through, until lightly charred on the outside and tender, about 15 minutes. 2. Meanwhile, in a small bowl, combine the remaining 1 tablespoon olive oil, the kimchi, cilantro, parsley, vinegar, chili-garlic sauce, and ginger. 3. Once the zucchini is finished cooking, transfer it to a colander and let it cool for 5 minutes. Using your fingers, pinch and break the zucchini into bite-size pieces, letting them fall back into the colander. Season the zucchini with salt and pepper, toss to combine, then let sit a further 5 minutes to allow some of its liquid to drain. Pile the zucchini atop the kimchi sauce on a plate and sprinkle with more parsley to serve.

Per Serving:

calories: 172 | fat: 15g | protein: 4g | carbs: 8g | fiber: 3g | sodium: 102mg

Caramelized Eggplant with Harissa Yogurt

Prep time: 10 minutes | Cook time: 15 minutes | Serves 2

- 1 medium eggplant (about ¾ pound / 340 g), cut crosswise into ½-inch-thick slices and quartered
- 2 tablespoons vegetable oil
- Kosher salt and freshly ground black pepper, to
- taste
- ½ cup plain yogurt (not Greek)
- 2 tablespoons harissa paste
- 1 garlic clove, grated
- 2 teaspoons honey

1. In a bowl, toss together the eggplant and oil, season with salt and pepper, and toss to coat evenly. Transfer to the air fryer and air fry at 400°F (204°C), shaking the basket every 5 minutes, until the eggplant is caramelized and tender, about 15 minutes. 2. Meanwhile, in a small bowl, whisk together the yogurt, harissa, and garlic, then spread onto a serving plate. 3. Pile the warm eggplant over the yogurt and drizzle with the honey just before serving.

Per Serving:

calories: 247 | fat: 16g | protein: 5g | carbs: 25g | fiber: 8g | sodium: 34mg

Sautéed Mustard Greens and Red Peppers

Prep time: 10 minutes | Cook time: 5 minutes | Serves 4

- 1 tablespoon olive oil
- ½ red pepper, diced
- 2 cloves garlic, minced
- 1 bunch mustard greens
- Sea salt and freshly ground pepper, to taste
- 1 teaspoon white wine vinegar

1. Heat olive oil in a large saucepan over medium heat. Add bell pepper and garlic, and sauté for 1 minute, stirring often. 2. Add greens to pan and immediately cover to begin steaming. Set a timer for 2 minutes. 3. After 1 minute, lift lid and stir greens well, then immediately put lid back on for remaining minute. Remove the lid, season with sea salt and freshly ground pepper, sprinkle with vinegar, and serve.

Per Serving:

calories: 42 | fat: 4g | protein: 1g | carbs: 2g | fiber: 1g | sodium: 7mg

Garlic Zucchini and Red Peppers

Prep time: 5 minutes | Cook time: 15 minutes | Serves 6

◄ 2 medium zucchini, cubed
◄ 1 red bell pepper, diced
◄ 2 garlic cloves, sliced
◄ 2 tablespoons olive oil
◄ ½ teaspoon salt

1. Preheat the air fryer to 380°F(193°C). 2. In a large bowl, mix together the zucchini, bell pepper, and garlic with the olive oil and salt. 3. Pour the mixture into the air fryer basket, and roast for 7 minutes. Shake or stir, then roast for 7 to 8 minutes more.

Per Serving:

calories: 59 | fat: 5g | protein: 1g | carbs: 4g | fiber: 1g | sodium: 200mg

Garlic-Parmesan Crispy Baby Potatoes

Prep time: 10 minutes | Cook time: 15 minutes | Serves 4

◄ Oil, for spraying
◄ 1 pound (454 g) baby potatoes
◄ ½ cup grated Parmesan cheese, divided
◄ 3 tablespoons olive oil
◄ 2 teaspoons granulated garlic
◄ ½ teaspoon onion powder
◄ ½ teaspoon salt
◄ ¼ teaspoon freshly ground black pepper
◄ ¼ teaspoon paprika
◄ 2 tablespoons chopped fresh parsley, for garnish

1. Line the air fryer basket with parchment and spray lightly with oil. 2. Rinse the potatoes, pat dry with paper towels, and place in a large bowl. 3. In a small bowl, mix together ¼ cup of Parmesan cheese, the olive oil, garlic, onion powder, salt, black pepper, and paprika. Pour the mixture over the potatoes and toss to coat. 4. Transfer the potatoes to the prepared basket and spread them out in an even layer, taking care to keep them from touching. You may need to work in batches, depending on the size of your air fryer. 5. Air fry at 400°F (204°C) for 15 minutes, stirring after 7 to 8 minutes, or until easily pierced with a fork. Continue to cook for another 1 to 2 minutes, if needed. 6. Sprinkle with the parsley and the remaining Parmesan cheese and serve.

Per Serving:

calories: 234 | fat: 14g | protein: 6g | carbs: 22g | fiber: 3g | sodium: 525mg

Asparagus Fries

Prep time: 15 minutes | Cook time: 5 to 7 minutes per batch | Serves 4

◄ 12 ounces (340 g) fresh asparagus spears with tough ends trimmed off
◄ 2 egg whites
◄ ¼ cup water
◄ ¾ cup panko bread crumbs
◄ ¼ cup grated Parmesan cheese, plus 2 tablespoons
◄ ¼ teaspoon salt
◄ Oil for misting or cooking spray

1. Preheat the air fryer to 390°F (199°C). 2. In a shallow dish, beat egg whites and water until slightly foamy. 3. In another shallow dish, combine panko, Parmesan, and salt. 4. Dip asparagus spears in egg, then roll in crumbs. Spray with oil or cooking spray. 5. Place a layer of asparagus in air fryer basket, leaving just a little space in between each spear. Stack another layer on top, crosswise. Air fry at 390°F (199°C) for 5 to 7 minutes, until crispy and golden brown. 6. Repeat to cook remaining asparagus.

Per Serving:

calories: 132 | fat: 3g | protein: 8g | carbs: 19g | fiber: 3g | sodium: 436mg

Sweet-and-Sour Brussels Sprouts

Prep time: 10 minutes | Cook time: 20 minutes | Serves 2

◄ ¼ cup Thai sweet chili sauce
◄ 2 tablespoons black vinegar or balsamic vinegar
◄ ½ teaspoon hot sauce, such as Tabasco
◄ 8 ounces (227 g) Brussels sprouts, trimmed (large sprouts halved)
◄ 2 small shallots, cut into ¼-inch-thick slices
◄ Kosher salt and freshly ground black pepper, to taste
◄ 2 teaspoons lightly packed fresh cilantro leaves

1. In a large bowl, whisk together the chili sauce, vinegar, and hot sauce. Add the Brussels sprouts and shallots, season with salt and pepper, and toss to combine. Scrape the Brussels sprouts and sauce into a cake pan. 2. Place the pan in the air fryer and roast at 375°F (191°C), stirring every 5 minutes, until the Brussels sprouts are tender and the sauce is reduced to a sticky glaze, about 20 minutes. 3. Remove the pan from the air fryer and transfer the Brussels sprouts to plates. Sprinkle with the cilantro and serve warm.

Per Serving:

calories: 106 | fat: 0g | protein: 5g | carbs: 21g | fiber: 7g | sodium: 498mg

Maple-Roasted Tomatoes

Prep time: 15 minutes | Cook time: 20 minutes | Serves 2

◄ 10 ounces (283 g) cherry tomatoes, halved
◄ Kosher salt, to taste
◄ 2 tablespoons maple syrup
◄ 1 tablespoon vegetable oil
◄ 2 sprigs fresh thyme, stems removed
◄ 1 garlic clove, minced
◄ Freshly ground black pepper

1. Place the tomatoes in a colander and sprinkle liberally with salt. Let stand for 10 minutes to drain. 2. Transfer the tomatoes cut-side up to a cake pan, then drizzle with the maple syrup, followed by the oil. Sprinkle with the thyme leaves and garlic and season with pepper. Place the pan in the air fryer and roast at 325°F (163°C) until the tomatoes are soft, collapsed, and lightly caramelized on top, about 20 minutes. 3. Serve straight from the pan or transfer the tomatoes to a plate and drizzle with the juices from the pan to serve.

Per Serving:

calories: 139 | fat: 7g | protein: 1g | carbs: 20g | fiber: 2g | sodium: 10mg

Citrus Asparagus with Pistachios

Prep time: 10 minutes | Cook time: 15 minutes | Serves 4

- 5 tablespoons extra-virgin olive oil, divided
- Zest and juice of 2 clementines or 1 orange (about ¼ cup juice and 1 tablespoon zest)
- Zest and juice of 1 lemon
- 1 tablespoon red wine
- vinegar
- 1 teaspoon salt, divided
- ¼ teaspoon freshly ground black pepper
- ½ cup shelled pistachios
- 1 pound (454 g) fresh asparagus
- 1 tablespoon water

1. In a small bowl, whisk together 4 tablespoons olive oil, the clementine and lemon juices and zests, vinegar, ½ teaspoon salt, and pepper. Set aside. 2. In a medium dry skillet, toast the pistachios over medium-high heat until lightly browned, 2 to 3 minutes, being careful not to let them burn. Transfer to a cutting board and coarsely chop. Set aside. 3. Trim the rough ends off the asparagus, usually the last 1 to 2 inches of each spear. In a skillet, heat the remaining 1 tablespoon olive oil over medium-high heat. Add the asparagus and sauté for 2 to 3 minutes. Sprinkle with the remaining ½ teaspoon salt and add the water. Reduce the heat to medium-low, cover, and cook until tender, another 2 to 4 minutes, depending on the thickness of the spears. 4. Transfer the cooked asparagus to a serving dish. Add the pistachios to the dressing and whisk to combine. Pour the dressing over the warm asparagus and toss to coat.

Per Serving:

calories: 271 | fat: 24g | protein: 6g | carbs: 12g | fiber: 4g | sodium: 585mg

Artichokes Provençal

Prep time: 15 minutes | Cook time: 10 minutes | Serves 4

- 4 large artichokes
- 1 medium lemon, cut in half
- 2 tablespoons olive oil
- ½ medium white onion, peeled and sliced
- 4 cloves garlic, peeled and chopped
- 2 tablespoons chopped fresh oregano
- 2 tablespoons chopped fresh basil
- 2 sprigs fresh thyme
- 2 medium tomatoes, seeded and chopped
- ¼ cup chopped Kalamata olives
- ¼ cup red wine
- ¼ cup water
- ¼ teaspoon salt
- ¼ teaspoon ground black pepper

1. Run artichokes under running water, making sure water runs between leaves to flush out any debris. Slice off top ⅓ of artichoke, trim stem, and pull away any tough outer leaves. Rub all cut surfaces with lemon. 2. Press the Sauté button on the Instant Pot® and heat oil. Add onion and cook until just tender, about 2 minutes. Add garlic, oregano, basil, and thyme, and cook until fragrant, about 30 seconds. Add tomatoes and olives and gently mix, then add wine and water and cook for 30 seconds. Press the Cancel button, then add artichokes cut side down to the Instant Pot®. 3. Close lid, set steam release to Sealing, press the Manual button, and set time to 5 minutes. When the timer beeps, quick-release the

pressure until the float valve drops. Open lid and transfer artichokes to a serving platter. Pour sauce over top, then season with salt and pepper. Serve warm.

Per Serving:

calories: 449 | fat: 16g | protein: 20g | carbs: 40g | fiber: 12g | sodium: 762mg

Vibrant Green Beans

Prep time: 10 minutes | Cook time: 15 minutes | Serves 6

- 2 tablespoons olive oil
- 2 leeks, white parts only, sliced
- Sea salt and freshly ground pepper, to taste
- 1 pound (454 g) fresh green
- string beans, trimmed
- 1 tablespoon Italian seasoning
- 2 tablespoons white wine
- Zest of 1 lemon

1. Heat the olive oil over medium heat in a large skillet. 2. Add leeks and cook, stirring often, until they start to brown and become lightly caramelized. 3. Season with sea salt and freshly ground pepper. 4. Add green beans and Italian seasoning, cooking for a few minutes until beans are tender but still crisp to the bite. 5. Add the wine and continue cooking until beans are done to your liking and leeks are crispy and browned. 6. Sprinkle with lemon zest before serving.

Per Serving:

calories: 87 | fat: 5g | protein: 2g | carbs: 11g | fiber: 3g | sodium: 114mg

Walnut and Freekeh Pilaf

Prep time: 15 minutes | Cook time: 15 minutes | Serves 4

- 2½ cups freekeh
- 3 tablespoons extra-virgin olive oil, divided
- 2 medium onions, diced
- ¼ teaspoon ground cinnamon
- ¼ teaspoon ground allspice
- 5 cups chicken stock
- ½ cup chopped walnuts
- Salt
- Freshly ground black pepper
- ½ cup plain, unsweetened, full-fat Greek yogurt
- 1½ teaspoons freshly squeezed lemon juice
- ½ teaspoon garlic powder

1. In a small bowl, soak the freekeh covered in cold water for 5 minutes. Drain and rinse the freekeh, then rinse one more time. 2. In a large sauté pan or skillet, heat 2 tablespoons oil, then add the onions and cook until fragrant. Add the freekeh, cinnamon, and allspice. Stir periodically for 1 minute. 3. Add the stock and walnuts and season with salt and pepper. Bring to a simmer. 4. Cover and reduce the heat to low. Cook for 15 minutes. Once freekeh is tender, remove from the heat and allow to rest for 5 minutes. 5. In a small bowl, combine the yogurt, lemon juice, and garlic powder. You may need to add salt to bring out the flavors. Add the yogurt mixture to the freekeh and serve immediately.

Per Serving:

calories: 653 | fat: 25g | protein: 23g | carbs: 91g | fiber: 12g | sodium: 575mg

Parmesan Mushrooms

Prep time: 5 minutes | Cook time: 15 minutes | Serves 4

◄ Oil, for spraying
◄ 1 pound (454 g) cremini mushrooms, stems trimmed
◄ 2 tablespoons olive oil
◄ 2 teaspoons granulated garlic

◄ 1 teaspoon dried onion soup mix
◄ ½ teaspoon salt
◄ ¼ teaspoon freshly ground black pepper
◄ ⅓ cup grated Parmesan cheese, divided

1. Line the air fryer basket with parchment and spray lightly with oil. 2. In a large bowl, toss the mushrooms with the olive oil, garlic, onion soup mix, salt, and black pepper until evenly coated. 3. Place the mushrooms in the prepared basket. 4. Roast at 370ºF (188ºC) for 13 minutes. 5. Sprinkle half of the cheese over the mushrooms and cook for another 2 minutes. 6. Transfer the mushrooms to a serving bowl, add the remaining Parmesan cheese, and toss until evenly coated. Serve immediately.

Per Serving:

calories: 89 | fat: 9g | protein: 5g | carbs: 7g | fiber: 1g | sodium: 451mg

Cauliflower Steaks with Creamy Tahini Sauce

Prep time: 10 minutes | Cook time: 45 minutes | Serves 4

◄ ¼ cup olive oil
◄ 4 garlic cloves, minced
◄ 1 teaspoon sea salt
◄ 1 teaspoon freshly ground black pepper
◄ 2 large heads cauliflower, stem end trimmed (core left intact)

and cut from top to bottom into thick slabs
◄ ½ cup tahini
◄ Juice of 1 lemon
◄ ¼ cup chopped fresh Italian parsley

1. Preheat the oven to 400ºF (205ºC). Line a baking sheet with parchment paper. 2. In a small bowl, combine the olive oil, garlic, salt, and pepper. Brush this mixture on both sides of the cauliflower steaks and place them in a single layer on the baking sheet. Drizzle any remaining oil mixture over the cauliflower steaks. Bake for 45 minutes, or until the cauliflower is soft. 3. While the steaks are baking, in a small bowl, stir together the tahini and lemon juice. Season with salt and pepper. 4. Remove the cauliflower steaks from the oven and transfer them to four plates. Drizzle the lemon tahini sauce evenly over the cauliflower and garnish with the parsley. Serve.

Per Serving:

calories: 339 | fat: 30g | protein: 8g | carbs: 15g | fiber: 6g | sodium: 368mg

Chapter 9 Vegetarian Mains

Balsamic Marinated Tofu with Basil and Oregano

Prep time: 10 minutes | Cook time: 30 minutes | Serves 4

- ◄ ¼ cup extra-virgin olive oil
- ◄ ¼ cup balsamic vinegar
- ◄ 2 tablespoons low-sodium soy sauce or gluten-free tamari
- ◄ 3 garlic cloves, grated
- ◄ 2 teaspoons pure maple syrup
- ◄ Zest of 1 lemon
- ◄ 1 teaspoon dried basil
- ◄ 1 teaspoon dried oregano
- ◄ ½ teaspoon dried thyme
- ◄ ½ teaspoon dried sage
- ◄ ¼ teaspoon kosher salt
- ◄ ¼ teaspoon freshly ground black pepper
- ◄ ¼ teaspoon red pepper flakes (optional)
- ◄ 1 (16-ounce / 454-g) block extra firm tofu, drained and patted dry, cut into ½-inch or 1-inch cubes

1. In a bowl or gallon zip-top bag, mix together the olive oil, vinegar, soy sauce, garlic, maple syrup, lemon zest, basil, oregano, thyme, sage, salt, black pepper, and red pepper flakes, if desired. Add the tofu and mix gently. Put in the refrigerator and marinate for 30 minutes, or up to overnight if you desire. 2. Preheat the oven to 425°F (220°C). Line a baking sheet with parchment paper or foil. Arrange the marinated tofu in a single layer on the prepared baking sheet. Bake for 20 to 30 minutes, turning over halfway through, until slightly crispy on the outside and tender on the inside.

Per Serving:
calories: 225 | fat: 16g | protein: 13g | carbs: 9g | fiber: 2g | sodium: 265mg

Greek Frittata with Tomato-Olive Salad

Prep time: 10 minutes | Cook time: 25 minutes | Serves 4 to 6

Frittata:
- ◄ 2 tablespoons olive oil
- ◄ 6 scallions, thinly sliced
- ◄ 4 cups (about 5 ounces / 142 g) baby spinach leaves
- ◄ 8 eggs
- ◄ ¼ cup whole-wheat

Tomato-Olive Salad:
- ◄ 2 tablespoons olive oil
- ◄ 1 tablespoon lemon juice
- ◄ ¼ teaspoon dried oregano
- ◄ ½ teaspoon salt
- ◄ ¼ teaspoon freshly ground black pepper

- breadcrumbs, divided
- ◄ 1 cup (about 3 ounces / 85 g) crumbled feta cheese
- ◄ ¾ teaspoon salt
- ◄ ¼ teaspoon freshly ground black pepper

- ◄ 1 pint cherry, grape, or other small tomatoes, halved
- ◄ 3 pepperoncini, stemmed and chopped
- ◄ ½ cup coarsely chopped pitted Kalamata olives

1. Preheat the oven to 450°F(235°C). 2. Heat the olive oil in an oven-safe skillet set over medium-high heat. Add the scallions and spinach and cook, stirring frequently, for about 4 minutes, until the spinach wilts. 3. In a medium bowl, whisk together the eggs, 2 tablespoons breadcrumbs, cheese, ¾ cup water, salt, and pepper. Pour the egg mixture into the skillet with the spinach and onions and stir to mix. Sprinkle the remaining 2 tablespoons of breadcrumbs evenly over the top. Bake the frittata in the preheated oven for about 20 minutes, until the egg is set and the top is lightly browned. 4. While the frittata is cooking, make the salad. In a medium bowl, whisk together the olive oil, lemon juice, oregano, salt, and pepper. Add the tomatoes, pepperoncini, and olives and toss to mix well. 5. Invert the frittata onto a serving platter and slice it into wedges. Serve warm or at room temperature with the tomato-olive salad.

Per Serving:
calories: 246 | fat: 19g | protein: 11g | carbs: 8g | fiber: 1g | sodium: 832mg

Turkish Red Lentil and Bulgur Kofte

Prep time: 10 minutes | Cook time: 45 minutes | Serves 4

- ◄ ⅓ cup olive oil, plus 2 tablespoons, divided, plus more for brushing
- ◄ 1 cup red lentils
- ◄ ½ cup bulgur
- ◄ 1 teaspoon salt
- ◄ 1 medium onion, finely
- diced
- ◄ 2 tablespoons tomato paste
- ◄ 1 teaspoon ground cumin
- ◄ ¼ cup finely chopped flat-leaf parsley
- ◄ 3 scallions, thinly sliced
- ◄ Juice of ½ lemon

1. Preheat the oven to 400°F(205°C). 2. Brush a large, rimmed baking sheet with olive oil. 3. In a medium saucepan, combine the lentils with 2 cups water and bring to a boil. Reduce the heat to low and cook, stirring occasionally, for about 15 minutes, until the lentils are tender and have soaked up most of the liquid. Remove from the heat, stir in the bulgur and salt, cover, and let sit for 15 minutes or so, until the bulgur is tender. 4. Meanwhile, heat ⅓ cup olive oil in a medium skillet over medium-high heat. Add the onion and cook, stirring frequently, until softened, about 5 minutes. Stir in the tomato paste and cook for 2 minutes more. Remove from the heat and stir in the cumin. 5. Add the cooked onion mixture to the lentil-bulgur mixture and stir to combine. Add the parsley, scallions, and lemon juice and stir to mix well. 6. Shape the mixture into walnut-sized balls and place them on the prepared baking sheet. Brush the balls with the remaining 2 tablespoons of olive oil and bake for 15 to 20 minutes, until golden brown. Serve hot.

Per Serving:
calories: 460 | fat: 25g | protein: 16g | carbs: 48g | fiber: 19g | sodium: 604mg

Vegetable Burgers

Prep time: 10 minutes | Cook time: 12 minutes | Serves 4

- ◄ 8 ounces (227 g) cremini mushrooms
- ◄ 2 large egg yolks
- ◄ ½ medium zucchini, trimmed and chopped
- ◄ ¼ cup peeled and chopped
- ◄ yellow onion
- ◄ 1 clove garlic, peeled and finely minced
- ◄ ½ teaspoon salt
- ◄ ¼ teaspoon ground black pepper

1. Place all ingredients into a food processor and pulse twenty times until finely chopped and combined. 2. Separate mixture into four equal sections and press each into a burger shape. Place burgers into ungreased air fryer basket. Adjust the temperature to 375°F (191°C) and air fry for 12 minutes, turning burgers halfway through cooking. Burgers will be browned and firm when done. 3. Place burgers on a large plate and let cool 5 minutes before serving.

Per Serving:

calories: 50 | fat: 3g | protein: 3g | carbs: 4g | fiber: 1g | sodium: 299mg

Baked Tofu with Sun-Dried Tomatoes and Artichokes

Prep time: 15 minutes | Cook time: 30 minutes | Serves 4

- ◄ 1 (16-ounce / 454-g) package extra-firm tofu, drained and patted dry, cut into 1-inch cubes
- ◄ 2 tablespoons extra-virgin olive oil, divided
- ◄ 2 tablespoons lemon juice, divided
- ◄ 1 tablespoon low-sodium soy sauce or gluten-free tamari
- ◄ 1 onion, diced
- ◄ ½ teaspoon kosher salt
- ◄ 2 garlic cloves, minced
- ◄ 1 (14-ounce / 397-g) can artichoke hearts, drained
- ◄ 8 sun-dried tomato halves packed in oil, drained and chopped
- ◄ ¼ teaspoon freshly ground black pepper
- ◄ 1 tablespoon white wine vinegar
- ◄ Zest of 1 lemon
- ◄ ¼ cup fresh parsley, chopped

1. Preheat the oven to 400°F (205°C). Line a baking sheet with foil or parchment paper. 2. In a bowl, combine the tofu, 1 tablespoon of the olive oil, 1 tablespoon of the lemon juice, and the soy sauce. Allow to sit and marinate for 15 to 30 minutes. Arrange the tofu in a single layer on the prepared baking sheet and bake for 20 minutes, turning once, until light golden brown. 3. Heat the remaining 1 tablespoon olive oil in a large skillet or sauté pan over medium heat. Add the onion and salt; sauté until translucent, 5 to 6 minutes. Add the garlic and sauté for 30 seconds. Add the artichoke hearts, sun-dried tomatoes, and black pepper and sauté for 5 minutes. Add the white wine vinegar and the remaining 1 tablespoon lemon juice and deglaze the pan, scraping up any brown bits. Remove the pan from the heat and stir in the lemon zest and parsley. Gently mix in the baked tofu.

Per Serving:

calories: 230 | fat: 14g | protein: 14g | carbs: 13g | fiber: 5g | sodium: 500mg

Cauliflower Steak with Gremolata

Prep time: 15 minutes | Cook time: 25 minutes | Serves 4

- ◄ 2 tablespoons olive oil
- ◄ 1 tablespoon Italian seasoning
- ◄ 1 large head cauliflower, outer leaves removed and sliced lengthwise through the core into thick "steaks"
- ◄ Salt and freshly ground black pepper, to taste
- ◄ ¼ cup Parmesan cheese
- ◄ Gremolata:
- ◄ 1 bunch Italian parsley (about 1 cup packed)
- ◄ 2 cloves garlic
- ◄ Zest of 1 small lemon, plus 1 to 2 teaspoons lemon juice
- ◄ ½ cup olive oil
- ◄ Salt and pepper, to taste

1. Preheat the air fryer to 400°F (204°C). 2. In a small bowl, combine the olive oil and Italian seasoning. Brush both sides of each cauliflower "steak" generously with the oil. Season to taste with salt and black pepper. 3. Working in batches if necessary, arrange the cauliflower in a single layer in the air fryer basket. Pausing halfway through the cooking time to turn the "steaks," air fry for 15 to 20 minutes until the cauliflower is tender and the edges begin to brown. Sprinkle with the Parmesan and air fry for 5 minutes longer. 4. To make the gremolata: In a food processor fitted with a metal blade, combine the parsley, garlic, and lemon zest and juice. With the motor running, add the olive oil in a steady stream until the mixture forms a bright green sauce. Season to taste with salt and black pepper. Serve the cauliflower steaks with the gremolata spooned over the top.

Per Serving:

calories: 336 | fat: 30g | protein: 7g | carbs: 15g | fiber: 5g | sodium: 340mg

Moroccan Red Lentil and Pumpkin Stew

Prep time: 10 minutes | Cook time: 30 minutes | Serves 4

- ◄ 2 tablespoons olive oil
- ◄ 1 teaspoon ground cumin
- ◄ 1 teaspoon ground turmeric
- ◄ 1 tablespoon curry powder
- ◄ 1 large onion, diced
- ◄ 1 teaspoon salt
- ◄ 2 tablespoons minced fresh ginger
- ◄ 4 cloves garlic, minced
- ◄ 1 pound (454 g) pumpkin, peeled, seeded, and cut into 1-inch dice
- ◄ 1 red bell pepper, seeded and diced
- ◄ 1½ cups red lentils, rinsed
- ◄ 6 cups vegetable broth
- ◄ ¼ cup chopped cilantro, for garnish

1. Heat the olive oil in a stockpot over medium heat. Add the cumin, turmeric, and curry powder and cook, stirring, for 1 minute, until fragrant. Add the onion and salt and cook, stirring frequently, until softened, about 5 minutes. Add the ginger and garlic and cook, stirring frequently, for 2 more minutes. Stir in the pumpkin and bell pepper, and then the lentils and broth and bring to a boil. 2. Reduce the heat to low and simmer, uncovered, for about 20 minutes, until the lentils are very tender. Serve hot, garnished with cilantro.

Per Serving:

calories: 405 | fat: 9g | protein: 20g | carbs: 66g | fiber: 11g | sodium: 594mg

Stuffed Portobellos

Prep time: 10 minutes | Cook time: 8 minutes | Serves 4

◀ 3 ounces (85 g) cream cheese, softened
◀ ½ medium zucchini, trimmed and chopped
◀ ¼ cup seeded and chopped red bell pepper
◀ 1½ cups chopped fresh

◀ spinach leaves
◀ 4 large portobello mushrooms, stems removed
◀ 2 tablespoons coconut oil, melted
◀ ½ teaspoon salt

1. In a medium bowl, mix cream cheese, zucchini, pepper, and spinach. 2. Drizzle mushrooms with coconut oil and sprinkle with salt. Scoop ¼ zucchini mixture into each mushroom. 3. Place mushrooms into ungreased air fryer basket. Adjust the temperature to 400ºF (204ºC) and air fry for 8 minutes. Portobellos will be tender and tops will be browned when done. Serve warm.

Per Serving:

calories: 151 | fat: 13g | protein: 4g | carbs: 6g | fiber: 2g | sodium: 427mg

Parmesan Artichokes

Prep time: 10 minutes | Cook time: 10 minutes | Serves 4

◀ 2 medium artichokes, trimmed and quartered, center removed
◀ 2 tablespoons coconut oil
◀ 1 large egg, beaten
◀ ½ cup grated vegetarian

◀ Parmesan cheese
◀ ¼ cup blanched finely ground almond flour
◀ ½ teaspoon crushed red pepper flakes

1. In a large bowl, toss artichokes in coconut oil and then dip each piece into the egg. 2. Mix the Parmesan and almond flour in a large bowl. Add artichoke pieces and toss to cover as completely as possible, sprinkle with pepper flakes. Place into the air fryer basket. 3. Adjust the temperature to 400ºF (204ºC) and air fry for 10 minutes. 4. Toss the basket two times during cooking. Serve warm.

Per Serving:

calories: 207 | fat: 13g | protein: 10g | carbs: 15g | fiber: 5g | sodium: 211mg

Eggplant Parmesan

Prep time: 15 minutes | Cook time: 17 minutes | Serves 4

◀ 1 medium eggplant, ends trimmed, sliced into ½-inch rounds
◀ ¼ teaspoon salt
◀ 2 tablespoons coconut oil
◀ ½ cup grated Parmesan cheese

◀ 1 ounce (28 g) 100% cheese crisps, finely crushed
◀ ½ cup low-carb marinara sauce
◀ ½ cup shredded Mozzarella cheese

1. Sprinkle eggplant rounds with salt on both sides and wrap in a kitchen towel for 30 minutes. Press to remove excess water, then drizzle rounds with coconut oil on both sides. 2. In a medium bowl, mix Parmesan and cheese crisps. Press each eggplant slice into mixture to coat both sides. 3. Place rounds into ungreased air fryer basket. Adjust the temperature to 350ºF (177ºC) and air fry for 15 minutes, turning rounds halfway through cooking. They will be crispy around the edges when done. 4. Spoon marinara over rounds and sprinkle with Mozzarella. Continue cooking an additional 2 minutes at 350ºF (177ºC) until cheese is melted. Serve warm.

Per Serving:

calories: 208 | fat: 13g | protein: 12g | carbs: 13g | fiber: 5g | sodium: 531mg

Quinoa with Almonds and Cranberries

Prep time: 15 minutes | Cook time: 0 minutes | Serves 4

◀ 2 cups cooked quinoa
◀ ⅓ teaspoon cranberries or currants
◀ ¼ cup sliced almonds
◀ 2 garlic cloves, minced
◀ 1¼ teaspoons salt

◀ ½ teaspoon ground cumin
◀ ½ teaspoon turmeric
◀ ¼ teaspoon ground cinnamon
◀ ¼ teaspoon freshly ground black pepper

1. In a large bowl, toss the quinoa, cranberries, almonds, garlic, salt, cumin, turmeric, cinnamon, and pepper and stir to combine. Enjoy alone or with roasted cauliflower.

Per Serving:

calories: 194 | fat: 6g | protein: 7g | carbs: 31g | fiber: 4g | sodium: 727mg

One-Pan Mushroom Pasta with Mascarpone

Prep time: 10 minutes | Cook time: 20 minutes | Serves 2

◀ 2 tablespoons olive oil
◀ 1 large shallot, minced
◀ 8 ounces (227 g) baby bella (cremini) mushrooms, sliced
◀ ¼ cup dry sherry
◀ 1 teaspoon dried thyme
◀ 2 cups low-sodium vegetable

◀ stock
◀ 6 ounces (170 g) dry pappardelle pasta
◀ 2 tablespoons mascarpone cheese
◀ Salt
◀ Freshly ground black pepper

1. Heat olive oil in a large sauté pan over medium-high heat. Add the shallot and mushrooms and sauté for 10 minutes, or until the mushrooms have given up much of their liquid. 2. Add the sherry, thyme, and vegetable stock. Bring the mixture to a boil. 3. Add the pasta, breaking it up as needed so it fits into the pan and is covered by the liquid. Return the mixture to a boil. Cover, and reduce the heat to medium-low. Let the pasta cook for 10 minutes, or until al dente. Stir it occasionally so it doesn't stick. If the sauce gets too dry, add some water or additional chicken stock. 4. When the pasta is tender, stir in the mascarpone cheese and season with salt and pepper. 5. The sauce will thicken up a bit when it's off the heat.

Per Serving:

calories: 517 | fat: 18g | protein: 16g | carbs: 69g | fiber: 3g | sodium: 141mg

Cauliflower Steaks with Olive Citrus Sauce

Prep time: 15 minutes | Cook time: 30 minutes | Serves 4

- 1 or 2 large heads cauliflower (at least 2 pounds / 907 g, enough for 4 portions)
- ⅓ cup extra-virgin olive oil
- ¼ teaspoon kosher salt
- ⅛ teaspoon ground black pepper
- Juice of 1 orange
- Zest of 1 orange
- ¼ cup black olives, pitted and chopped
- 1 tablespoon Dijon or grainy mustard
- 1 tablespoon red wine vinegar
- ½ teaspoon ground coriander

1. Preheat the oven to 400ºF (205ºC). Line a baking sheet with parchment paper or foil. 2. Cut off the stem of the cauliflower so it will sit upright. Slice it vertically into four thick slabs. Place the cauliflower on the prepared baking sheet. Drizzle with the olive oil, salt, and black pepper. Bake for about 30 minutes, turning over once, until tender and golden brown. 3. In a medium bowl, combine the orange juice, orange zest, olives, mustard, vinegar, and coriander; mix well. 4. Serve the cauliflower warm or at room temperature with the sauce.

Per Serving:

calories: 265 | fat: 21g | protein: 5g | carbs: 19g | fiber: 4g | sodium: 310mg

Beet and Carrot Fritters with Yogurt Sauce

Prep time: 15 minutes | Cook time: 15 minutes | Serves 2

For the Yogurt Sauce:
- ⅓ cup plain Greek yogurt
- 1 tablespoon freshly squeezed lemon juice
- Zest of ½ lemon
- ¼ teaspoon garlic powder
- ¼ teaspoon salt

For the Fritters:
- 1 large carrot, peeled
- 1 small potato, peeled
- 1 medium golden or red beet, peeled
- 1 scallion, minced
- 2 tablespoons fresh minced parsley
- ¼ cup brown rice flour or
- unseasoned bread crumbs
- ¼ teaspoon garlic powder
- ¼ teaspoon salt
- 1 large egg, beaten
- ¼ cup feta cheese, crumbled
- 2 tablespoons olive oil (more if needed)

Make the Yogurt Sauce: In a small bowl, mix together the yogurt, lemon juice and zest, garlic powder, and salt. Set aside. Make the Fritters: 1. Shred the carrot, potato, and beet in a food processor with the shredding blade. You can also use a mandoline with a julienne shredding blade or a vegetable peeler. Squeeze out any moisture from the vegetables and place them in a large bowl. 2. Add the scallion, parsley, rice flour, garlic powder, salt, and egg. Stir the mixture well to combine. Add the feta cheese and stir briefly, leaving chunks of feta cheese throughout. 3. Heat a large nonstick sauté pan over medium-high heat and add 1 tablespoon of the olive oil. 4. Make the fritters by scooping about 3 tablespoons of the vegetable mixture into your hands and flattening it into a firm disc about 3 inches in diameter. 5. Place 2 fritters at a time in the pan and let them cook for about two minutes. Check to see if the underside is golden, and then flip and repeat on the other side. Remove from the heat, add the rest of the olive oil to the pan, and repeat with the remaining vegetable mixture. 6. To serve, spoon about 1 tablespoon of the yogurt sauce on top of each fritter.

Per Serving:

calories: 295 | fat: 14g | protein: 6g | carbs: 44g | fiber: 5g | sodium: 482mg

Mediterranean Baked Chickpeas

Prep time: 15 minutes | Cook time: 15 minutes | Serves 4

- 1 tablespoon extra-virgin olive oil
- ½ medium onion, chopped
- 3 garlic cloves, chopped
- 2 teaspoons smoked paprika
- ¼ teaspoon ground cumin
- 4 cups halved cherry tomatoes
- 2 (15-ounce / 425-g) cans chickpeas, drained and rinsed
- ½ cup plain, unsweetened, full-fat Greek yogurt, for serving
- 1 cup crumbled feta, for serving

1. Preheat the oven to 425ºF (220ºC). 2. In an oven-safe sauté pan or skillet, heat the oil over medium heat and sauté the onion and garlic. Cook for about 5 minutes, until softened and fragrant. Stir in the paprika and cumin and cook for 2 minutes. Stir in the tomatoes and chickpeas. 3. Bring to a simmer for 5 to 10 minutes before placing in the oven. 4. Roast in oven for 25 to 30 minutes, until bubbling and thickened. To serve, top with Greek yogurt and feta.

Per Serving:

calories: 412 | fat: 15g | protein: 20g | carbs: 51g | fiber: 13g | sodium: 444mg

Freekeh, Chickpea, and Herb Salad

Prep time: 15 minutes | Cook time: 10 minutes | Serves 4 to 6

- 1 (15-ounce / 425-g) can chickpeas, rinsed and drained
- 1 cup cooked freekeh
- 1 cup thinly sliced celery
- 1 bunch scallions, both white and green parts, finely chopped
- ½ cup chopped fresh flat-leaf parsley
- ¼ cup chopped fresh mint
- 3 tablespoons chopped celery leaves
- ½ teaspoon kosher salt
- ⅓ cup extra-virgin olive oil
- ¼ cup freshly squeezed lemon juice
- ¼ teaspoon cumin seeds
- 1 teaspoon garlic powder

1. In a large bowl, combine the chickpeas, freekeh, celery, scallions, parsley, mint, celery leaves, and salt and toss lightly. 2. In a small bowl, whisk together the olive oil, lemon juice, cumin seeds, and garlic powder. Once combined, add to freekeh salad.

Per Serving:

calories: 350 | fat: 19g | protein: 9g | carbs: 38g | fiber: 9g | sodium: 329mg

Roasted Portobello Mushrooms with Kale and Red Onion

Prep time: 15 minutes | Cook time: 30 minutes | Serves 4

- ¼ cup white wine vinegar
- 3 tablespoons extra-virgin olive oil, divided
- ½ teaspoon honey
- ¾ teaspoon kosher salt, divided
- ¼ teaspoon freshly ground black pepper
- 4 large (4 to 5 ounces / 113 to 142 g each) portobello
- mushrooms, stems removed
- 1 red onion, julienned
- 2 garlic cloves, minced
- 1 (8-ounce / 227-g) bunch kale, stemmed and chopped small
- ¼ teaspoon red pepper flakes
- ¼ cup grated Parmesan or Romano cheese

1. Line a baking sheet with parchment paper or foil. In a medium bowl, whisk together the vinegar, 1½ tablespoons of the olive oil, honey, ¼ teaspoon of the salt, and the black pepper. Arrange the mushrooms on the baking sheet and pour the marinade over them. Marinate for 15 to 30 minutes. 2. Meanwhile, preheat the oven to 400°F (205°C). 3. Bake the mushrooms for 20 minutes, turning over halfway through. 4. Heat the remaining 1½ tablespoons olive oil in a large skillet or ovenproof sauté pan over medium-high heat. Add the onion and the remaining ½ teaspoon salt and sauté until golden brown, 5 to 6 minutes. Add the garlic and sauté for 30 seconds. Add the kale and red pepper flakes and sauté until the kale cooks down, about 5 minutes. 5. Remove the mushrooms from the oven and increase the temperature to broil. 6. Carefully pour the liquid from the baking sheet into the pan with the kale mixture; mix well. 7. Turn the mushrooms over so that the stem side is facing up. Spoon some of the kale mixture on top of each mushroom. Sprinkle 1 tablespoon Parmesan cheese on top of each. 8. Broil until golden brown, 3 to 4 minutes.

Per Serving:

calories: 200 | fat: 13g | protein: 8g | carbs: 16g | fiber: 4g | sodium: 365mg

Pistachio Mint Pesto Pasta

Prep time: 10 minutes | Cook time: 10 minutes | Serves 4

- 8 ounces (227 g) whole-wheat pasta
- 1 cup fresh mint
- ½ cup fresh basil
- ⅓ cup unsalted pistachios,
- shelled
- 1 garlic clove, peeled
- ½ teaspoon kosher salt
- Juice of ½ lime
- ⅓ cup extra-virgin olive oil

1. Cook the pasta according to the package directions. Drain, reserving ½ cup of the pasta water, and set aside. 2. In a food processor, add the mint, basil, pistachios, garlic, salt, and lime juice. Process until the pistachios are coarsely ground. Add the olive oil in a slow, steady stream and process until incorporated. 3. In a large bowl, mix the pasta with the pistachio pesto; toss well to incorporate. If a thinner, more saucy consistency is desired, add some of the reserved pasta water and toss well.

Per Serving:

calories: 420 | fat: 3g | protein: 11g | carbs: 48g | fiber: 2g | sodium: 150mg

Cauliflower Rice-Stuffed Peppers

Prep time: 10 minutes | Cook time: 15 minutes | Serves 4

- 2 cups uncooked cauliflower rice
- ¾ cup drained canned petite diced tomatoes
- 2 tablespoons olive oil
- 1 cup shredded Mozzarella cheese
- ¼ teaspoon salt
- ¼ teaspoon ground black pepper
- 4 medium green bell peppers, tops removed, seeded

1. In a large bowl, mix all ingredients except bell peppers. Scoop mixture evenly into peppers. 2. Place peppers into ungreased air fryer basket. Adjust the temperature to 350°F (177°C) and air fry for 15 minutes. Peppers will be tender and cheese will be melted when done. Serve warm.

Per Serving:

calories: 144 | fat: 7g | protein: 11g | carbs: 11g | fiber: 5g | sodium: 380mg

Provençal Ratatouille with Herbed Breadcrumbs and Goat Cheese

Prep time: 10 minutes | Cook time: 1 hour 5 minutes | Serves 4

- 6 tablespoons olive oil, divided
- 2 medium onions, diced
- 2 cloves garlic, minced
- 2 medium eggplants, halved lengthwise and cut into ¾-inch thick half rounds
- 3 medium zucchini, halved lengthwise and cut into ¾-inch thick half rounds
- 2 red bell peppers, seeded and cut into 1½-inch pieces
- 1 green bell pepper, seeded and cut into 1½-inch pieces
- 1 (14-ounce / 397-g) can
- diced tomatoes, drained
- 1 teaspoon salt
- ½ teaspoon freshly ground black pepper
- 8 ounces (227 g) fresh breadcrumbs
- 1 tablespoon chopped fresh parsley
- 1 tablespoon chopped fresh basil
- 1 tablespoon chopped fresh chives
- 6 ounces (170 g) soft, fresh goat cheese

1. Preheat the oven to 375°F(190°C). 2. Heat 5 tablespoons of the olive oil in a large skillet over medium heat. Add the onions and garlic and cook, stirring frequently, until the onions are soft and beginning to turn golden, about 8 minutes. Add the eggplant, zucchini, and bell peppers and cook, turning the vegetables occasionally, for another 10 minutes. Stir in the tomatoes, salt, and pepper and let simmer for 15 minutes. 3. While the vegetables are simmering, stir together the breadcrumbs, the remaining tablespoon of olive oil, the parsley, basil, and chives. 4. Transfer the vegetable mixture to a large baking dish, spreading it out into an even layer. Crumble the goat cheese over the top, then sprinkle the breadcrumb mixture evenly over the top. Bake in the preheated oven for about 30 minutes, until the topping is golden brown and crisp. Serve hot.

Per Serving:

calories: 644 | fat: 37g | protein: 21g | carbs: 63g | fiber: 16g | sodium: 861mg

Pesto Spinach Flatbread

Prep time: 10 minutes | Cook time: 8 minutes | Serves 4

- 1 cup blanched finely ground almond flour
- 2 ounces (57 g) cream cheese
- 2 cups shredded Mozzarella
- cheese
- 1 cup chopped fresh spinach leaves
- 2 tablespoons basil pesto

1. Place flour, cream cheese, and Mozzarella in a large microwave-safe bowl and microwave on high 45 seconds, then stir. 2. Fold in spinach and microwave an additional 15 seconds. Stir until a soft dough ball forms. 3. Cut two pieces of parchment paper to fit air fryer basket. Separate dough into two sections and press each out on ungreased parchment to create 6-inch rounds. 4. Spread 1 tablespoon pesto over each flatbread and place rounds on parchment into ungreased air fryer basket. Adjust the temperature to 350ºF (177ºC) and air fry for 8 minutes, turning crusts halfway through cooking. Flatbread will be golden when done. 5. Let cool 5 minutes before slicing and serving.

Per Serving:

calories: 387 | fat: 28g | protein: 28g | carbs: 10g | fiber: 5g | sodium: 556mg

Zucchini Lasagna

Prep time: 15 minutes | Cook time: 1 hour | Serves 8

- ½ cup extra-virgin olive oil, divided
- 4 to 5 medium zucchini squash
- 1 teaspoon salt
- 8 ounces (227 g) frozen spinach, thawed and well drained (about 1 cup)
- 2 cups whole-milk ricotta cheese
- ¼ cup chopped fresh basil or
- 2 teaspoons dried basil
- 1 teaspoon garlic powder
- ½ teaspoon freshly ground black pepper
- 2 cups shredded fresh whole-milk mozzarella cheese
- 1¾ cups shredded Parmesan cheese
- ½ (24-ounce / 680-g) jar low-sugar marinara sauce (less than 5 grams sugar)

1. Preheat the oven to 425ºF (220ºC). 2. Line two baking sheets with parchment paper or aluminum foil and drizzle each with 2 tablespoons olive oil, spreading evenly. 3. Slice the zucchini lengthwise into ¼-inch-thick long slices and place on the prepared baking sheet in a single layer. Sprinkle with ½ teaspoon salt per sheet. Bake until softened, but not mushy, 15 to 18 minutes. Remove from the oven and allow to cool slightly before assembling the lasagna. 4. Reduce the oven temperature to 375ºF (190ºC). 5. While the zucchini cooks, prep the filling. In a large bowl, combine the spinach, ricotta, basil, garlic powder, and pepper. In a small bowl, mix together the mozzarella and Parmesan cheeses. In a medium bowl, combine the marinara sauce and remaining ¼ cup olive oil and stir to fully incorporate the oil into sauce. 6. To assemble the lasagna, spoon a third of the marinara sauce mixture into the bottom of a 9-by-13-inch glass baking dish and spread evenly. Place 1 layer of softened zucchini slices to fully cover the sauce, then add a third of the ricotta-spinach mixture and spread evenly on top of the zucchini. Sprinkle a third of the mozzarella-Parmesan mixture on top of the ricotta. Repeat with 2 more cycles of these layers: marinara, zucchini, ricotta-spinach, then cheese blend. 7. Bake until the cheese is bubbly and melted, 30 to 35 minutes. Turn the broiler to low and broil until the top is golden brown, about 5 minutes. Remove from the oven and allow to cool slightly before slicing.

Per Serving:

calories: 473 | fat: 36g | protein: 23g | carbs: 17g | fiber: 3g | sodium: 868mg

Eggplants Stuffed with Walnuts and Feta

Prep time: 10 minutes | Cook time: 55 minutes | Serves 6

- 3 medium eggplants, halved lengthwise
- 2 teaspoons salt, divided
- ¼ cup olive oil, plus 2 tablespoons, divided
- 2 medium onions, diced
- 1½ pints cherry or grape tomatoes, halved
- ¾ cup roughly chopped walnut pieces
- 2¼ teaspoons ground cinnamon
- 1½ teaspoons dried oregano
- ½ teaspoon freshly ground black pepper
- ¼ cup whole-wheat breadcrumbs
- ⅔ cup (about 3 ounces / 85 g) crumbled feta cheese

1. Scoop out the flesh of the eggplants, leaving a ½-inch thick border of flesh in the skins. Dice the flesh that you removed and place it in a colander set over the sink. Sprinkle 1½ teaspoons of salt over the diced eggplant and inside the eggplant shells and let stand for 30 minutes. Rinse the shells and the pieces and pat dry with paper towels. 2. Heat ¼ cup of olive oil in a large skillet over medium heat. Add the eggplant shells, skin-side down, and cook for about 4 minutes, until browned and softened. Turn over and cook on the cut side until golden brown and soft, about 4 minutes more. Transfer to a plate lined with paper towel to drain. 3. Drain off all but about 1 to 2 tablespoons of the oil in the skillet and heat over medium-high heat. Add the onions and cook, stirring, until beginning to soften, about 3 minutes. Add the diced eggplant, tomatoes, walnuts, cinnamon, oregano, ¼ cup water, the remaining ½ teaspoon of salt, and the pepper. Cook, stirring occasionally, until the vegetables are golden brown and softened, about 8 minutes. 4. Preheat the broiler to high. 5. In a small bowl, toss together the breadcrumbs and 1 tablespoon olive oil. 6. Arrange the eggplant shells cut-side up on a large, rimmed baking sheet. Brush each shell with about ½ teaspoon of olive oil. Cook under the broiler until tender and just starting to turn golden brown, about 5 minutes. Remove the eggplants from the broiler and reduce the heat of the oven to 375ºF (190ºC). 7. Spoon the sautéed vegetable mixture into the eggplant shells, dividing equally. Sprinkle the breadcrumbs over the tops of the filled eggplants, dividing equally. Sprinkle the cheese on top, again dividing equally. Bake in the oven until the filling and shells are heated through and the topping is nicely browned and crisp, about 35 minutes.

Per Serving:

calories: 274 | fat: 15g | protein: 7g | carbs: 34g | fiber: 13g | sodium: 973mg

Crispy Eggplant Rounds

Prep time: 15 minutes | Cook time: 10 minutes | Serves 4

- ◄ 1 large eggplant, ends trimmed, cut into ½-inch slices
- ◄ ½ teaspoon salt
- ◄ 2 ounces (57 g) Parmesan

100% cheese crisps, finely ground
- ◄ ½ teaspoon paprika
- ◄ ¼ teaspoon garlic powder
- ◄ 1 large egg

1. Sprinkle eggplant rounds with salt. Place rounds on a kitchen towel for 30 minutes to draw out excess water. Pat rounds dry. 2. In a medium bowl, mix cheese crisps, paprika, and garlic powder. In a separate medium bowl, whisk egg. Dip each eggplant round in egg, then gently press into cheese crisps to coat both sides. 3. Place eggplant rounds into ungreased air fryer basket. Adjust the temperature to 400°F (204°C) and air fry for 10 minutes, turning rounds halfway through cooking. Eggplant will be golden and crispy when done. Serve warm.

Per Serving:

calories: 113 | fat: 5g | protein: 7g | carbs: 10g | fiber: 4g | sodium: 567mg

Quinoa Lentil "Meatballs" with Quick Tomato Sauce

Prep time: 25 minutes | Cook time: 45 minutes | Serves 4

For the Meatballs:
- ◄ Olive oil cooking spray
- ◄ 2 large eggs, beaten
- ◄ 1 tablespoon no-salt-added tomato paste
- ◄ ½ teaspoon kosher salt
- ◄ ½ cup grated Parmesan

For the Tomato Sauce:
- ◄ 1 tablespoon extra-virgin olive oil
- ◄ 1 onion, minced
- ◄ ½ teaspoon dried oregano
- ◄ ½ teaspoon kosher salt

cheese
- ◄ ½ onion, roughly chopped
- ◄ ¼ cup fresh parsley
- ◄ 1 garlic clove, peeled
- ◄ 1½ cups cooked lentils
- ◄ 1 cup cooked quinoa

- ◄ 2 garlic cloves, minced
- ◄ 1 (28-ounce / 794-g) can no-salt-added crushed tomatoes
- ◄ ½ teaspoon honey
- ◄ ¼ cup fresh basil, chopped

Make the Meatballs: 1. Preheat the oven to 400°F (205°C). Lightly grease a 12-cup muffin pan with olive oil cooking spray. 2. In a large bowl, whisk together the eggs, tomato paste, and salt until fully combined. Mix in the Parmesan cheese. 3. In a food processor, add the onion, parsley, and garlic. Process until minced. Add to the egg mixture and stir together. Add the lentils to the food processor and process until puréed into a thick paste. Add to the large bowl and mix together. Add the quinoa and mix well. 4. Form balls, slightly larger than a golf ball, with ¼ cup of the quinoa mixture. Place each ball in a muffin pan cup. Note: The mixture will be somewhat soft but should hold together. 5. Bake 25 to 30 minutes, until golden brown. Make the Tomato Sauce: 6. Heat the olive oil in a large saucepan over medium heat. Add the onion, oregano, and salt and sauté until light golden brown, about 5 minutes. Add the garlic and cook for 30 seconds. 7. Stir in the tomatoes and honey. Increase the heat to high and cook, stirring often, until simmering, then decrease the heat to medium-low and cook for 10 minutes. Remove from the heat and stir in the basil. Serve with the meatballs.

Per Serving:

3 meatballs: calories: 360 | fat: 10g | protein: 20g | carbs: 48g | fiber: 14g | sodium: 520mg

Herbed Ricotta–Stuffed Mushrooms

Prep time: 10 minutes | Cook time: 30 minutes | Serves 4

- ◄ 6 tablespoons extra-virgin olive oil, divided
- ◄ 4 portobello mushroom caps, cleaned and gills removed
- ◄ 1 cup whole-milk ricotta cheese
- ◄ ⅓ cup chopped fresh herbs (such as basil, parsley,

rosemary, oregano, or thyme)
- ◄ 2 garlic cloves, finely minced
- ◄ ½ teaspoon salt
- ◄ ¼ teaspoon freshly ground black pepper

1. Preheat the oven to 400°F (205°C). 2. Line a baking sheet with parchment or foil and drizzle with 2 tablespoons olive oil, spreading evenly. Place the mushroom caps on the baking sheet, gill-side up. 3. In a medium bowl, mix together the ricotta, herbs, 2 tablespoons olive oil, garlic, salt, and pepper. Stuff each mushroom cap with one-quarter of the cheese mixture, pressing down if needed. Drizzle with remaining 2 tablespoons olive oil and bake until golden brown and the mushrooms are soft, 30 to 35 minutes, depending on the size of the mushrooms.

Per Serving:

calories: 308 | fat: 29g | protein: 9g | carbs: 6g | fiber: 1g | sodium: 351mg

Spinach-Artichoke Stuffed Mushrooms

Prep time: 10 minutes | Cook time: 10 to 14 minutes | Serves 4

- ◄ 2 tablespoons olive oil
- ◄ 4 large portobello mushrooms, stems removed and gills scraped out
- ◄ ½ teaspoon salt
- ◄ ¼ teaspoon freshly ground pepper
- ◄ 4 ounces (113 g) goat cheese, crumbled

- ◄ ½ cup chopped marinated artichoke hearts
- ◄ 1 cup frozen spinach, thawed and squeezed dry
- ◄ ½ cup grated Parmesan cheese
- ◄ 2 tablespoons chopped fresh parsley

1. Preheat the air fryer to 400°F (204°C). 2. Rub the olive oil over the portobello mushrooms until thoroughly coated. Sprinkle both sides with the salt and black pepper. Place top-side down on a clean work surface. 3. In a small bowl, combine the goat cheese, artichoke hearts, and spinach. Mash with the back of a fork until thoroughly combined. Divide the cheese mixture among the mushrooms and sprinkle with the Parmesan cheese. 4. Air fry for 10 to 14 minutes until the mushrooms are tender and the cheese has begun to brown. Top with the fresh parsley just before serving.

Per Serving:

calories: 284 | fat: 21g | protein: 16g | carbs: 10g | fiber: 4g | sodium: 686mg

Moroccan Vegetable Tagine

Prep time: 20 minutes | Cook time: 1 hour | Serves 6

◄ ½ cup extra-virgin olive oil
◄ 2 medium yellow onions, sliced
◄ 6 celery stalks, sliced into ¼-inch crescents
◄ 6 garlic cloves, minced
◄ 1 teaspoon ground cumin
◄ 1 teaspoon ginger powder
◄ 1 teaspoon salt
◄ ½ teaspoon paprika
◄ ½ teaspoon ground cinnamon
◄ ¼ teaspoon freshly ground black pepper

◄ 2 cups vegetable stock
◄ 1 medium eggplant, cut into 1-inch cubes
◄ 2 medium zucchini, cut into ½-inch-thick semicircles
◄ 2 cups cauliflower florets
◄ 1 (13¾-ounce / 390-g) can artichoke hearts, drained and quartered
◄ 1 cup halved and pitted green olives
◄ ½ cup chopped fresh flat-leaf parsley, for garnish
◄ ½ cup chopped fresh cilantro leaves, for garnish
◄ Greek yogurt, for garnish (optional)

1. In a large, thick soup pot or Dutch oven, heat the olive oil over medium-high heat. Add the onion and celery and sauté until softened, 6 to 8 minutes. Add the garlic, cumin, ginger, salt, paprika, cinnamon, and pepper and sauté for another 2 minutes. 2. Add the stock and bring to a boil. Reduce the heat to low and add the eggplant, zucchini, and cauliflower. Simmer on low heat, covered, until the vegetables are tender, 30 to 35 minutes. Add the artichoke hearts and olives, cover, and simmer for another 15 minutes. 3. Serve garnished with parsley, cilantro, and Greek yogurt (if using).

Per Serving:
calories: 265 | fat: 21g | protein: 5g | carbs: 19g | fiber: 9g | sodium: 858mg

Orzo-Stuffed Tomatoes

Prep time: 15 minutes | Cook time: 30 minutes | Serves 2

◄ 1 tablespoon olive oil
◄ 1 small zucchini, minced
◄ ½ medium onion, minced
◄ 1 garlic clove, minced
◄ ⅔ cup cooked orzo (from ¼ cup dry orzo, cooked according to

package instructions, or precooked)
◄ ½ teaspoon salt
◄ 2 teaspoons dried oregano
◄ 6 medium round tomatoes (not Roma)

1. Preheat the oven to 350ºF (180ºC). 2. Heat the olive oil in a large sauté pan over medium-high heat. Add the zucchini, onion, and garlic and sauté for 15 minutes, or until the vegetables turn golden. 3. Add the orzo, salt, and oregano and stir to heat through. Remove the pan from the heat and set aside. 4. Cut about ½ inch from the top of each tomato. With a paring knife, cut around the inner core of the tomato to remove about half of the flesh. Reserve for another recipe or a salad. 5. Stuff each tomato with the orzo mixture. 6. If serving hot, put the tomatoes in a baking dish, or, if they'll fit, a muffin tin. Roast the tomatoes for about 15 minutes, or until they're soft. Don't overcook them or they won't hold together. If desired, this can also be served without roasting the tomatoes.

Per Serving:
calories: 241 | fat: 8g | protein: 7g | carbs: 38g | fiber: 6g | sodium: 301mg

Cheese Stuffed Zucchini

Prep time: 20 minutes | Cook time: 8 minutes | Serves 4

◄ 1 large zucchini, cut into four pieces
◄ 2 tablespoons olive oil
◄ 1 cup Ricotta cheese, room temperature
◄ 2 tablespoons scallions, chopped
◄ 1 heaping tablespoon fresh parsley, roughly chopped

◄ 1 heaping tablespoon coriander, minced
◄ 2 ounces (57 g) Cheddar cheese, preferably freshly grated
◄ 1 teaspoon celery seeds
◄ ½ teaspoon salt
◄ ½ teaspoon garlic pepper

1. Cook your zucchini in the air fryer basket for approximately 10 minutes at 350ºF (177ºC). Check for doneness and cook for 2-3 minutes longer if needed. 2. Meanwhile, make the stuffing by mixing the other items. 3. When your zucchini is thoroughly cooked, open them up. Divide the stuffing among all zucchini pieces and bake an additional 5 minutes.

Per Serving:
calories: 242 | fat: 20g | protein: 12g | carbs: 5g | fiber: 1g | sodium: 443mg

Chapter 10 Desserts

Creamy Spiced Almond Milk

Prep time: 5 minutes | Cook time: 1 minute | Serves 6

- 1 cup raw almonds
- 5 cups filtered water, divided
- 1 teaspoon vanilla bean
- paste
- ½ teaspoon pumpkin pie spice

1. Add almonds and 1 cup water to the Instant Pot®. Close lid, set steam release to Sealing, press the Manual button, and set time to 1 minute. 2. When the timer beeps, quick-release the pressure until the float valve drops. Press the Cancel button and open lid. Strain almonds and rinse under cool water. Transfer to a high-powered blender with remaining 3.cups water. Purée for 2 minutes on high speed. 4. Pour mixture into a nut milk bag set over a large bowl. Squeeze bag to extract all liquid. Stir in vanilla and pumpkin pie spice. Transfer to a Mason jar or sealed jug and refrigerate for 8 hours. Stir or shake gently before serving.

Per Serving:

calories: 86 | fat: 8g | protein: 3g | carbs: 3g | fiber: 2g | sodium: 0mg

Date and Nut Balls

Prep time: 10 minutes | Cook time: 10 minutes | Serves 6 to 8

- 1 cup walnuts or pistachios
- 1 cup unsweetened shredded coconut
- 14 medjool dates, pits
- removed
- 8 tablespoons (1 stick) butter, melted

1. Preheat the oven to 350°F. 2. Put the nuts on a baking sheet. Toast the nuts for 5 minutes. 3. Put the shredded coconut on a clean baking sheet; toast just until it turns golden brown, about 3 to 5 minutes (coconut burns fast so keep an eye on it). Once done, remove it from the oven and put it in a shallow bowl. 4. In a food processor fitted with a chopping blade, process the nuts until they have a medium chop. Put the chopped nuts into a medium bowl. 5. Add the dates and melted butter to the food processor and blend until the dates become a thick paste. Pour the chopped nuts into the food processor with the dates and pulse just until the mixture is combined, about 5 to 7 pulses. 6. Remove the mixture from the food processor and scrape it into a large bowl. 7. To make the balls, spoon 1 to 2 tablespoons of the date mixture into the palm of your hand and roll around between your hands until you form a ball. Put the ball on a clean, lined baking sheet. Repeat until all the mixture is formed into balls. 8. Roll each ball in the toasted coconut until the outside of the ball is coated, put the ball back on the baking sheet, and repeat. 9. Put all the balls into the fridge for 20 minutes

before serving so that they firm up. You can also store any leftovers in the fridge in an airtight container.

Per Serving:

calories: 489 | fat: 35g | protein: 5g | carbs: 48g | fiber: 7g | sodium: 114mg

Crunchy Sesame Cookies

Prep time: 10 minutes | Cook time: 15 minutes | Yield 14 to 16

- 1 cup sesame seeds, hulled
- 1 cup sugar
- 8 tablespoons (1 stick) salted
- butter, softened
- 2 large eggs
- 1¼ cups flour

1. Preheat the oven to 350°F(180°C). Toast the sesame seeds on a baking sheet for 3 minutes. Set aside and let cool. 2. Using a mixer, cream together the sugar and butter. 3. Add the eggs one at a time until well-blended. 4. Add the flour and toasted sesame seeds and mix until well-blended. 5. Drop spoonfuls of cookie dough onto a baking sheet and form them into round balls, about 1-inch in diameter, similar to a walnut. 6. Put in the oven and bake for 5 to 7 minutes or until golden brown. 7. Let the cookies cool and enjoy.

Per Serving:

calories: 218 | fat: 12g | protein: 4g | carbs: 25g | fiber: 2g | sodium: 58mg

Dark Chocolate Lava Cake

Prep time: 5 minutes | Cook time: 10 minutes | Serves 4

- Olive oil cooking spray
- ¼ cup whole wheat flour
- 1 tablespoon unsweetened dark chocolate cocoa powder
- ⅛ teaspoon salt
- ½ teaspoon baking powder
- ¼ cup raw honey
- 1 egg
- 2 tablespoons olive oil

1. Preheat the air fryer to 380°F(193°C). Lightly coat the insides of four ramekins with olive oil cooking spray. 2. In a medium bowl, combine the flour, cocoa powder, salt, baking powder, honey, egg, and olive oil. 3. Divide the batter evenly among the ramekins. 4. Place the filled ramekins inside the air fryer and bake for 10 minutes. 5. Remove the lava cakes from the air fryer and slide a knife around the outside edge of each cake. Turn each ramekin upside down on a saucer and serve.

Per Serving:

calories: 179 | fat: 8g | protein: 3g | carbs: 26g | fiber: 1g | sodium: 95mg

Pomegranate-Quinoa Dark Chocolate Bark

Prep time: 10 minutes |Cook time: 10 minutes|
Serves: 6

- Nonstick cooking spray
- ½ cup uncooked tricolor or regular quinoa
- ½ teaspoon kosher or sea salt
- 8 ounces (227 g) dark chocolate or 1 cup dark chocolate chips
- ½ cup fresh pomegranate seeds

1. In a medium saucepan coated with nonstick cooking spray over medium heat, toast the uncooked quinoa for 2 to 3 minutes, stirring frequently. Do not let the quinoa burn. Remove the pan from the stove, and mix in the salt. Set aside 2 tablespoons of the toasted quinoa to use for the topping. 2. Break the chocolate into large pieces, and put it in a gallon-size zip-top plastic bag. Using a metal ladle or a meat pounder, pound the chocolate until broken into smaller pieces. (If using chocolate chips, you can skip this step.) Dump the chocolate out of the bag into a medium, microwave-safe bowl and heat for 1 minute on high in the microwave. Stir until the chocolate is completely melted. Mix the toasted quinoa (except the topping you set aside) into the melted chocolate. 3. Line a large, rimmed baking sheet with parchment paper. Pour the chocolate mixture onto the sheet and spread it evenly until the entire pan is covered. Sprinkle the remaining 2 tablespoons of quinoa and the pomegranate seeds on top. Using a spatula or the back of a spoon, press the quinoa and the pomegranate seeds into the chocolate. 4. Freeze the mixture for 10 to 15 minutes, or until set. Remove the bark from the freezer, and break it into about 2-inch jagged pieces. Store in a sealed container or zip-top plastic bag in the refrigerator until ready to serve.

Per Serving:

calories: 290 | fat: 17g | protein: 5g | carbs: 29g | fiber: 6g | sodium: 202mg

Tortilla Fried Pies

Prep time: 10 minutes | Cook time: 5 minutes per batch |
Makes 12 pies

- 12 small flour tortillas (4-inch diameter)
- ½ cup fig preserves
- ¼ cup sliced almonds
- 2 tablespoons shredded, unsweetened coconut
- Oil for misting or cooking spray

1. Wrap refrigerated tortillas in damp paper towels and heat in microwave 30 seconds to warm. 2. Working with one tortilla at a time, place 2 teaspoons fig preserves, 1 teaspoon sliced almonds, and ½ teaspoon coconut in the center of each. 3. Moisten outer edges of tortilla all around. 4. Fold one side of tortilla over filling to make a half-moon shape and press down lightly on center. Using the tines of a fork, press down firmly on edges of tortilla to seal in filling. 5. Mist both sides with oil or cooking spray. 6. Place hand pies in air fryer basket close but not overlapping. It's fine to lean some against the sides and corners of the basket. You may need to cook in 2 batches. 7. Air fry at 390ºF (199ºC) for 5 minutes or until lightly browned. Serve hot. 8. Refrigerate any leftover pies

in a closed container. To serve later, toss them back in the air fryer basket and cook for 2 or 3 minutes to reheat.

Per Serving:

1 pie: calories: 137 | fat: 4g | protein: 4g | carbs: 22g | fiber: 2g | sodium: 279mg

Honey-Vanilla Apple Pie with Olive Oil Crust

Prep time: 10 minutes | Cook time: 45 minutes | Serves 8

For the crust:
- ¼ cup olive oil
- 1½ cups whole-wheat flour
- ½ teaspoon sea salt
- 2 tablespoons ice water

For the filling:
- 4 large apples of your choice, peeled, cored, and sliced
- Juice of 1 lemon
- 1 tablespoon pure vanilla
- extract
- 1 tablespoon honey
- ½ teaspoon sea salt
- Olive oil

Make the crust: 1. Put the olive oil, flour, and sea salt in a food processor and process until dough forms. 2. Slowly add the water and pulse until you have a stiff dough. 3. Form the dough into 2 equal-sized balls, wrap in plastic wrap, and put in the refrigerator while you make the filling. Make the filling: 1. Combine the apples, lemon juice, vanilla, honey, and sea salt in a large bowl. 2. Stir and allow to sit for at least 10 minutes. Preheat oven to 400ºF (205ºC). 3. Roll 1 crust out on a lightly floured surface. Transfer to a 9-inch pie plate and top with filling. 4. Roll the other ball of dough out and put on top of the pie. Cut a few slices in the top to vent the pie, and lightly brush the top of the pie with olive oil. 5. Bake for 45 minutes, or until top is browned and apples are bubbly. 6. Allow to cool completely before slicing and serving with your favorite frozen yogurt.

Per Serving:

calories: 208 | fat: 8g | protein: 3g | carbs: 34g | fiber: 5g | sodium: 293mg

Vanilla-Poached Apricots

Prep time: 10 minutes | Cook time: 1 minute | Serves 6

- 1¼ cups water
- ¼ cup marsala wine
- ¼ cup sugar
- 1 teaspoon vanilla bean
- paste
- 8 medium apricots, sliced in half and pitted

1. Place all ingredients in the Instant Pot®. Stir to combine. Close lid, set steam release to Sealing, press the Manual button, and set time to 1 minute. 2. When the timer beeps, quick-release the pressure until the float valve drops. Press the Cancel button and open lid. Let stand for 10 minutes. Carefully remove apricots from poaching liquid with a slotted spoon. Serve warm or at room temperature.

Per Serving:

calories: 62 | fat: 0g | protein: 2g | carbs: 14g | fiber: 1g | sodium: 10mg

Ricotta-Lemon Cheesecake

Prep time: 5 minutes | Cook time: 1 hour | Serves 8 to 10

- 2 (8-ounce / 227-g) packages full-fat cream cheese
- 1 (16-ounce / 454-g) container full-fat ricotta cheese
- 1½ cups granulated sugar
- 1 tablespoon lemon zest
- 5 large eggs
- Nonstick cooking spray

1. Preheat the oven to 350°F (180°C) . 2. Using a mixer, blend together the cream cheese and ricotta cheese. 3. Blend in the sugar and lemon zest. 4. Blend in the eggs; drop in 1 egg at a time, blend for 10 seconds, and repeat. 5. Line a 9-inch springform pan with parchment paper and nonstick spray. Wrap the bottom of the pan with foil. Pour the cheesecake batter into the pan. 6. To make a water bath, get a baking or roasting pan larger than the cheesecake pan. Fill the roasting pan about ⅓ of the way up with warm water. Put the cheesecake pan into the water bath. Put the whole thing in the oven and let the cheesecake bake for 1 hour. 7. After baking is complete, remove the cheesecake pan from the water bath and remove the foil. Let the cheesecake cool for 1 hour on the countertop. Then put it in the fridge to cool for at least 3 hours before serving.

Per Serving:

calories: 489 | fat: 31g | protein: 15g | carbs: 42g | fiber: 0g | sodium: 264mg

Lemon Coconut Cake

Prep time: 5 minutes | Cook time: 40 minutes | Serves 9

Base:
- 6 large eggs, separated
- ⅓ cup melted ghee or virgin coconut oil
- 1 tablespoon fresh lemon juice
- Zest of 2 lemons
- 2 cups almond flour
- ½ cup coconut flour

Topping:
- ½ cup unsweetened large coconut flakes
- 1 cup heavy whipping cream or coconut cream
- ¼ cup mascarpone, more

- ¼ cup collagen powder
- 1 teaspoon baking soda
- 1 teaspoon vanilla powder or 1 tablespoon unsweetened vanilla extract
- Optional: low-carb sweetener, to taste

heavy whipping cream, or coconut cream
- ½ teaspoon vanilla powder or 1½ teaspoons unsweetened vanilla extract

1. Preheat the oven to 285°F (140°C) fan assisted or 320°F (160°C) conventional. Line a baking tray with parchment paper (or use a silicone tray). A square 8 × 8–inch (20 × 20 cm) or a rectangular tray of similar size will work best. 2. Make the base: Whisk the egg whites in a bowl until stiff peaks form. In a separate bowl, whisk the egg yolks, melted ghee, lemon juice, and lemon zest. In a third bowl, mix the almond flour, coconut flour, collagen, baking soda, vanilla and optional sweetener. 3. Add the whisked egg yolk–ghee mixture into the dry mixture and combine well. Gently fold in the egg whites, trying not to deflate them. 4. Pour into the baking tray. Bake for 35 to 40 minutes, until lightly golden on top and set inside. Remove from the oven and let cool completely before adding the topping. 5. Make the topping: Preheat the oven to 350°F (175°C) fan assisted or 380°F (195°C) conventional. Place the coconut flakes on a baking tray and bake for 2 to 3 minutes. Remove from the oven and set aside to cool. 6. Once the cake is cool, place the cream, mascarpone, and vanilla in a bowl. Whip until soft peaks form. Spread on top of the cooled cake and top with the toasted coconut flakes. 7. To store, refrigerate for up to 5 days or freeze for up to 3 months. Coconut flakes will soften in the fridge. If you want to keep them crunchy, sprinkle on top of each slice before serving.

Per Serving:

calories: 342 | fat: 31g | protein: 9g | carbs: 10g | fiber: 4g | sodium: 208mg

Honeyed Roasted Apples with Walnuts

Prep time: 5 minutes | Cook time: 12 to 15 minutes | Serves 4

- 2 Granny Smith apples
- ¼ cup certified gluten-free rolled oats
- 2 tablespoons honey
- ½ teaspoon ground
- cinnamon
- 2 tablespoons chopped walnuts
- Pinch salt
- 1 tablespoon olive oil

1. Preheat the air fryer to 380°F(193°C). 2. Core the apples and slice them in half. 3. In a medium bowl, mix together the oats, honey, cinnamon, walnuts, salt, and olive oil. 4. Scoop a quarter of the oat mixture onto the top of each half apple. 5. Place the apples in the air fryer basket, and roast for 12 to 15 minutes, or until the apples are fork-tender.

Per Serving:

calories: 144 | fat: 6g | protein: 1g | carbs: 22g | fiber: 3g | sodium: 2mg

Fruit Compote

Prep time: 15 minutes | Cook time: 11 minutes | Serves 6

- 1 cup apple juice
- 1 cup dry white wine
- 2 tablespoons honey
- 1 cinnamon stick
- ¼ teaspoon ground nutmeg
- 1 tablespoon grated lemon zest
- 1½ tablespoons grated orange zest
- 3 large apples, peeled, cored, and chopped
- 3 large pears, peeled, cored, and chopped
- ½ cup dried cherries

1. Place all ingredients in the Instant Pot® and stir well. Close lid, set steam release to Sealing, press the Manual button, and set time to 1 minute. When the timer beeps, quick-release the pressure until the float valve drops. Press the Cancel button and open lid. 2. Use a slotted spoon to transfer fruit to a serving bowl. Remove and discard cinnamon stick. Press the Sauté button and bring juice in the pot to a boil. Cook, stirring constantly, until reduced to a syrup that will coat the back of a spoon, about 10 minutes. 3. Stir syrup into fruit mixture. Allow to cool slightly, then cover with plastic wrap and refrigerate overnight.

Per Serving:

calories: 211 | fat: 1g | protein: 2g | carbs: 44g | fiber: 5g | sodium: 7mg

Crispy Apple Phyllo Tart

Prep time: 15 minutes | Cook time: 30 minutes | Serves 4

- 5 teaspoons extra virgin olive oil
- 2 teaspoons fresh lemon juice
- ¼ teaspoon ground cinnamon
- 1½ teaspoons granulated
- sugar, divided
- 1 large apple (any variety), peeled and cut into ⅛-inch thick slices
- 5 phyllo sheets, defrosted
- 1 teaspoon all-purpose flour
- 1½ teaspoons apricot jam

1. Preheat the oven to 350°F (180°C). Line a baking sheet with parchment paper, and pour the olive oil into a small dish. Set aside. 2. In a separate small bowl, combine the lemon juice, cinnamon, 1 teaspoon of the sugar, and the apple slices. Mix well to ensure the apple slices are coated in the seasonings. Set aside. 3. On a clean working surface, stack the phyllo sheets one on top of the other. Place a large bowl with an approximate diameter of 15 inches on top of the sheets, then draw a sharp knife around the edge of the bowl to cut out a circle through all 5 sheets. Discard the remaining phyllo. 4. Working quickly, place the first sheet on the lined baking sheet and then brush with the olive oil. Repeat the process by placing a second sheet on top of the first sheet, then brushing the second sheet with olive oil. Repeat until all the phyllo sheets are in a single stack. 5. Sprinkle the flour and remaining sugar over the top of the sheets. Arrange the apples in overlapping circles 4 inches from the edge of the phyllo. 6. Fold the edges of the phyllo in and then twist them all around the apple filling to form a crust edge. Brush the edge with the remaining olive oil. Bake for 30 minutes or until the crust is golden and the apples are browned on the edges. 7. While the tart is baking, heat the apricot jam in a small sauce pan over low heat until it's melted. 8. When the tart is done baking, brush the apples with the jam sauce. Slice the tart into 4 equal servings and serve warm. Store at room temperature, covered in plastic wrap, for up to 2 days.

Per Serving:

calories: 165 | fat: 7g | protein: 2g | carbs: 24g | fiber: 2g | sodium: 116mg

Baklava and Honey

Prep time: 40 minutes | Cook time: 1 hour | Serves 6 to 8

- 2 cups very finely chopped walnuts or pecans
- 1 teaspoon cinnamon
- 1 cup (2 sticks) of unsalted butter, melted
- 1 (16-ounce / 454-g) package phyllo dough, thawed
- 1 (12-ounce / 340-g) jar honey

1. Preheat the oven to 350°F(180°C). 2. In a bowl, combine the chopped nuts and cinnamon. 3. Using a brush, butter the sides and bottom of a 9-by-13-inch inch baking dish. 4. Remove the phyllo dough from the package and cut it to the size of the baking dish using a sharp knife. 5. Place one sheet of phyllo dough on the bottom of the dish, brush with butter, and repeat until you have 8 layers. 6. Sprinkle ⅓ cup of the nut mixture over the phyllo layers. Top with a sheet of phyllo dough, butter that sheet, and repeat until you have 4 sheets of buttered phyllo dough. 7. Sprinkle ⅓ cup of

the nut mixture for another layer of nuts. Repeat the layering of nuts and 4 sheets of buttered phyllo until all the nut mixture is gone. The last layer should be 8 buttered sheets of phyllo. 8. Before you bake, cut the baklava into desired shapes; traditionally this is diamonds, triangles, or squares. 9. Bake the baklava for 1 hour or until the top layer is golden brown. 10. While the baklava is baking, heat the honey in a pan just until it is warm and easy to pour. 11. Once the baklava is done baking, immediately pour the honey evenly over the baklava and let it absorb it, about 20 minutes. Serve warm or at room temperature.

Per Serving:

calories: 1235 | fat: 89g | protein: 18g | carbs: 109g | fiber: 7g | sodium: 588mg

Honey Ricotta with Espresso and Chocolate Chips

Prep time: 5 minutes | Cook time: 0 minutes | Serves 2

- 8 ounces (227 g) ricotta cheese
- 2 tablespoons honey
- 2 tablespoons espresso,
- chilled or room temperature
- 1 teaspoon dark chocolate chips or chocolate shavings

1. In a medium bowl, whip together the ricotta cheese and honey until light and smooth, 4 to 5 minutes. 2. Spoon the ricotta cheese-honey mixture evenly into 2 dessert bowls. Drizzle 1 tablespoon espresso into each dish and sprinkle with chocolate chips or shavings.

Per Serving:

calories: 235 | fat: 10g | protein: 13g | carbs: 25g | fiber: 0g | sodium: 115mg

Tahini Baklava Cups

Prep time: 10 minutes | Cook time: 25 minutes | Serves 8

- 1 box (about 16) mini phyllo dough cups, thawed
- ⅓ cup tahini
- ¼ cup shelled pistachios or walnuts, chopped, plus more for garnish
- 4 tablespoons honey, divided
- 1 teaspoon ground cinnamon
- Pinch of kosher salt
- ½ teaspoon rosewater (optional)

1. Preheat the oven to 350°F(180°C). Remove the phyllo cups from the packaging and place on a large rimmed baking sheet. 2. In a small bowl, stir together the tahini, nuts, 1 tablespoon of the honey, the cinnamon, and salt. Divide this mixture among the phyllo cups and top each with a few more nuts. Bake until golden and warmed through, 10 minutes. Remove from the oven and cool for 5 minutes. 3. Meanwhile, in a small saucepan or in a microwaveable bowl, stir together the remaining 3 tablespoons honey and the rosewater, if using, and heat until warmed, about 5 minutes over medium heat .

Per Serving:

calories: 227 | fat: 9g | protein: 5g | carbs: 32g | fiber: 2g | sodium: 195mg

Dark Chocolate Bark with Fruit and Nuts

Prep time: 15 minutes | Cook time: 0 minutes | Serves 2

- 2 tablespoons chopped nuts (almonds, pecans, walnuts, hazelnuts, pistachios, or any combination of those)
- 3 ounces (85 g) good-quality dark chocolate chips (about
- ⅔ cup)
- ¼ cup chopped dried fruit (apricots, blueberries, figs, prunes, or any combination of those)

1. Line a sheet pan with parchment paper. 2. Place the nuts in a skillet over medium-high heat and toast them for 60 seconds, or just until they're fragrant. 3. Place the chocolate in a microwave-safe glass bowl or measuring cup and microwave on high for 1 minute. Stir the chocolate and allow any unmelted chips to warm and melt. If necessary, heat for another 20 to 30 seconds, but keep a close eye on it to make sure it doesn't burn. 4. Pour the chocolate onto the sheet pan. Sprinkle the dried fruit and nuts over the chocolate evenly and gently pat in so they stick. 5. Transfer the sheet pan to the refrigerator for at least 1 hour to let the chocolate harden. 6. When solid, break into pieces. Store any leftover chocolate in the refrigerator or freezer.

Per Serving:

calories: 284 | fat: 16g | protein: 4g | carbs: 39g | fiber: 2g | sodium: 2mg

Lightened-Up Baklava Rolls

Prep time: 2 minutes | Cook time: 1 hour 15 minutes | Serves 12

- 4 ounces (113 g) shelled walnuts
- 1¼ teaspoons ground cinnamon
- 1½ teaspoons granulated sugar
- 5 teaspoons unseasoned breadcrumbs
- 1 teaspoon extra virgin olive
- oil plus 2 tablespoons for brushing
- 6 phyllo sheets, defrosted
- Syrup:
- ¼ cup water
- ½ cup granulated sugar
- 1½ tablespoons fresh lemon juice

1. Preheat the oven to 350°F (180°C). 2. Make the syrup by combining the water and sugar in a small pan placed over medium heat. Bring to a boil, cook for 2 minutes, then remove the pan from the heat. Add the lemon juice, and stir. Set aside to cool. 3. In a food processor, combine the walnuts, cinnamon, sugar, breadcrumbs, and 1 teaspoon of the olive oil. Pulse until combined and grainy, but not chunky. 4. Place 1 phyllo sheet on a clean working surface and brush with the olive oil. Place a second sheet on top of the first sheet, brush with olive oil, and repeat the process with a third sheet. Cut the sheets in half crosswise, and then cut each half into 3 pieces crosswise. 5. Scatter 1 tablespoon of the walnut mixture over the phyllo sheet. Start rolling the phyllo and filling into a log shape while simultaneously folding the sides in (like a burrito) until the filling is encased in each piece of dough. The rolls should be about 3½ inches long. Place the rolls one next to the other in a large baking pan, then repeat the process with the remaining 3 phyllo sheets. You should have a total of 12 rolls. 6. Lightly brush the rolls with the remaining olive oil. Place in the oven to bake for 30 minutes or until the rolls turn golden brown, then remove from the oven and promptly drizzle the cold syrup over the top. 7. Let the rolls sit for 20 minutes, then flip them over and let them sit for an additional 20 minutes. Turn them over once more and sprinkle any remining walnut mixture over the rolls before serving. Store uncovered at room temperature for 2 days (to retain crispiness) and then cover with plastic wrap and store at room temperature for up to 10 days.

Per Serving:

calories: 148 | fat: 9g | protein: 2g | carbs: 16g | fiber: 1g | sodium: 53mg

Chocolate Turtle Hummus

Prep time: 15 minutes | Cook time: 0 minutes | Serves 2

For the Caramel:
- 2 tablespoons coconut oil
- 1 tablespoon maple syrup

For the Hummus:
- ½ cup chickpeas, drained and rinsed
- 2 tablespoons unsweetened cocoa powder
- 1 tablespoon maple syrup,

- 1 tablespoon almond butter
- Pinch salt

  plus more to taste
- 2 tablespoons almond milk, or more as needed, to thin
- Pinch salt
- 2 tablespoons pecans

Make the caramel 1. put the coconut oil in a small microwave-safe bowl. If it's solid, microwave it for about 15 seconds to melt it. 2. Stir in the maple syrup, almond butter, and salt. 3. Place the caramel in the refrigerator for 5 to 10 minutes to thicken. Make the hummus 1. In a food processor, combine the chickpeas, cocoa powder, maple syrup, almond milk, and pinch of salt, and process until smooth. Scrape down the sides to make sure everything is incorporated. 2. If the hummus seems too thick, add another tablespoon of almond milk. 3. Add the pecans and pulse 6 times to roughly chop them. 4. Transfer the hummus to a serving bowl and when the caramel is thickened, swirl it into the hummus. Gently fold it in, but don't mix it in completely. 5. Serve with fresh fruit or pretzels.

Per Serving:

calories: 321 | fat: 22g | protein: 7g | carbs: 30g | fiber: 6g | sodium: 100mg

Fresh Figs with Chocolate Sauce

Prep time: 5 minutes | Cook time: 0 minutes | Serves 4

- ¼ cup honey
- 2 tablespoons cocoa powder
- 8 fresh figs

1. Combine the honey and cocoa powder in a small bowl, and mix well to form a syrup. 2. Cut the figs in half and place cut side up. Drizzle with the syrup and serve.

Per Serving:

calories: 112 | fat: 1g | protein: 1g | carbs: 30g | fiber: 3g | sodium: 3mg

Brown Betty Apple Dessert

Prep time: 15 minutes | Cook time: 10 minutes | Serves 8

- ◄ 2 cups dried bread crumbs
- ◄ ½ cup sugar
- ◄ 1 teaspoon ground cinnamon
- ◄ 3 tablespoons lemon juice
- ◄ 1 tablespoon grated lemon
- zest
- ◄ 1 cup olive oil, divided
- ◄ 8 medium apples, peeled, cored, and diced
- ◄ 2 cups water

1. Combine crumbs, sugar, cinnamon, lemon juice, lemon zest, and ½ cup oil in a medium mixing bowl. Set aside. 2. In a greased oven-safe dish that will fit in your cooker loosely, add a thin layer of crumbs, then one diced apple. Continue filling the container with alternating layers of crumbs and apples until all ingredients are finished. Pour remaining ½ cup oil on top. 3. Add water to the Instant Pot® and place rack inside. Make a foil sling by folding a long piece of foil in half lengthwise and lower the uncovered container into the pot using the sling. 4. Close lid, set steam release to Sealing, press the Manual button, and set time to 10 minutes. When the timer beeps, let pressure release naturally, about 20 minutes. Press the Cancel button and open lid. 5. Using the sling, remove the baking dish from the pot and let stand for 5 minutes before serving.

Per Serving:

calories: 422 | fat: 27g | protein: 0g | carbs: 40g | fiber: 4g | sodium: 474mg

Flourless Chocolate Brownies with Raspberry Balsamic Sauce

Prep time: 10 minutes | Cook time: 20 minutes | Serves 2

For the raspberry sauce
- ◄ ¼ cup good-quality balsamic vinegar
- ◄ 1 cup frozen raspberries

For the brownie
- ◄ ½ cup black beans with no added salt, rinsed
- ◄ 1 large egg
- ◄ 1 tablespoon olive oil
- ◄ ½ teaspoon vanilla extract
- ◄ 4 tablespoons unsweetened
- cocoa powder
- ◄ ¼ cup sugar
- ◄ ¼ teaspoon baking powder
- ◄ Pinch salt
- ◄ ¼ cup dark chocolate chips

Make the raspberry sauce: Combine the balsamic vinegar and raspberries in a saucepan and bring the mixture to a boil. Reduce the heat to medium and let the sauce simmer for 15 minutes, or until reduced to ½ cup. If desired, strain the seeds and set the sauce aside until the brownie is ready. Make the brownie: 1. Preheat the oven to 350°F (180°C) and set the rack to the middle position. Grease two 8-ounce ramekins and place them on a baking sheet. 2. In a food processor, combine the black beans, egg, olive oil, and vanilla. Purée the mixture for 1 to 2 minutes, or until it's smooth and the beans are completely broken down. Scrape down the sides of the bowl a few times to make sure everything is well-incorporated. 3. Add the cocoa powder, sugar, baking powder, and salt and purée again to combine the dry ingredients, scraping down

the sides of the bowl as needed. 4. Stir the chocolate chips into the batter by hand. Reserve a few if you like, to sprinkle over the top of the brownies when they come out of the oven. 5. Pour the brownies into the prepared ramekins and bake for 15 minutes, or until firm. The center will look slightly undercooked. If you prefer a firmer brownie, leave it in the oven for another 5 minutes, or until a toothpick inserted in the middle comes out clean. 6. Remove the brownies from the oven. If desired, sprinkle any remaining chocolate chips over the top and let them melt into the warm brownies. 7. Let the brownies cool for a few minutes and top with warm raspberry sauce to serve.

Per Serving:

calories: 510 | fat: 16g | protein: 10g | carbs: 88g | fiber: 14g | sodium: 124mg

Whipped Greek Yogurt with Chocolate

Prep time: 10 minutes | Cook time: 0 minutes | Serves 4

- ◄ 4 cups plain full-fat Greek yogurt
- ◄ ½ cup heavy (whipping) cream
- ◄ 2 ounces (57 g) dark chocolate (at least 70% cacao), grated, for topping

1. In the bowl of a stand mixer fitted with the whisk attachment or in a large bowl using a handheld mixer, whip the yogurt and cream for about 5 minutes, or until peaks form. 2. Evenly divide the whipped yogurt mixture among bowls and top with the grated chocolate. Serve.

Per Serving:

calories: 337 | fat: 25g | protein: 10g | carbs: 19g | fiber: 2g | sodium: 127mg

Date and Honey Almond Milk Ice Cream

Prep time: 10 minutes | Cook time: 5 minutes | Serves 4

- ◄ ¾ cup (about 4 ounces/ 113 g) pitted dates
- ◄ ¼ cup honey
- ◄ ½ cup water
- ◄ 2 cups cold unsweetened almond milk
- ◄ 2 teaspoons vanilla extract

1. Combine the dates and water in a small saucepan and bring to a boil over high heat. Remove the pan from the heat, cover, and let stand for 15 minutes. 2. In a blender, combine the almond milk, dates, the date soaking water, honey, and the vanilla and process until very smooth. 3. Cover the blender jar and refrigerate the mixture until cold, at least 1 hour. 4. Transfer the mixture to an electric ice cream maker and freeze according to the manufacturer's instructions. 5. Serve immediately or transfer to a freezer-safe storage container and freeze for 4 hours (or longer). Serve frozen.

Per Serving:

calories: 106 | fat: 2g | protein: 1g | carbs: 23g | fiber: 3g | sodium: 92mg

Blueberry Compote

Prep time: 10 minutes | Cook time: 5 minutes | Serves 8

◄ 1 (16-ounce/ 454-g) bag frozen blueberries, thawed
◄ ¼ cup sugar
◄ 1 tablespoon lemon juice
◄ 2 tablespoons cornstarch
◄ 2 tablespoons water
◄ ¼ teaspoon vanilla extract
◄ ¼ teaspoon grated lemon zest

1. Add blueberries, sugar, and lemon juice to the Instant Pot®. Close lid, set steam release to Sealing, press the Manual button, and set time to 1 minute. 2. When the timer beeps, quick-release the pressure until the float valve drops. Press the Cancel button and open lid. 3. Press the Sauté button. In a small bowl, combine cornstarch and water. Stir into blueberry mixture and cook until mixture comes to a boil and thickens, about 3–4 minutes. Press the Cancel button and stir in vanilla and lemon zest. Serve immediately or refrigerate until ready to serve.

Per Serving:
calories: 57 | fat: 0g | protein: 0g | carbs: 14g | fiber: 2g | sodium: 0mg

Strawberry-Pomegranate Molasses Sauce

Prep time: 10 minutes | Cook time: 5 minutes | Serves 6

◄ 3 tablespoons olive oil
◄ ¼ cup honey
◄ 2 pints strawberries, hulled and halved
◄ 1 to 2 tablespoons
pomegranate molasses
◄ 2 tablespoons chopped fresh mint
◄ Greek yogurt, for serving

1. In a medium saucepan, heat the olive oil over medium heat. Add the strawberries; cook until their juices are released. Stir in the honey and cook for 1 to 2 minutes. Stir in the molasses and mint. Serve warm over Greek yogurt.

Per Serving:
calories: 189 | fat: 7g | protein: 4g | carbs: 24g | fiber: 3g | sodium: 12mg

Light and Lemony Olive Oil Cupcakes

Prep time: 10 minutes | Cook time: 24 minutes | Serves 18

◄ 2 cups all-purpose flour
◄ 4 teaspoons baking powder
◄ 1 cup granulated sugar
◄ 1 cup extra virgin olive oil
◄ 2 eggs
◄ 7 ounces (198 g) 2% Greek yogurt
◄ 1 teaspoon pure vanilla
extract
◄ 4 tablespoons fresh lemon juice
◄ Zest of 2 lemons
◄ Glaze:
◄ 1 tablespoon lemon juice
◄ 5 tablespoons powdered sugar

1. Preheat the oven to 350°F (180°C). Line a 12-cup muffin pan with cupcake liners and then line a second pan with 6 liners. Set aside. 2. In a medium bowl, combine the flour and baking powder. Whisk and set aside. 3. In a large bowl, combine the sugar and olive oil, and mix until smooth. Add the eggs, one at a time, and mix well. Add the Greek yogurt, vanilla extract, lemon juice, and lemon zest. Mix until well combined. 4. Add the flour mixture to the batter, ½ cup at a time, while continuously mixing. 5. Spoon the batter into the liners, filling each liner two-thirds full. Bake for 22–25 minutes or until a toothpick inserted into the center of a cupcake comes out clean. 6. While the cupcakes are baking, make the glaze by combining the lemon juice and powdered sugar in a small bowl. Stir until smooth, then set aside. 7. Set the cupcakes aside to cool in the pans for about 5 minutes, then remove the cupcakes from the pans and transfer to a wire rack to cool completely. 8. Drizzle the glaze over the cooled cupcakes. Store in the refrigerator for up to 4 days.

Per Serving:
calories: 225 | fat: 13g | protein: 3g | carbs: 25g | fiber: 1g | sodium: 13mg

Mascarpone and Fig Crostini

Prep time: 10 minutes | Cook time: 10 minutes | Serves 6 to 8

◄ 1 long French baguette
◄ 4 tablespoons (½ stick) salted butter, melted
◄ 1 (8-ounce / 227-g) tub
mascarpone cheese
◄ 1 (12-ounce / 340-g) jar fig jam

1. Preheat the oven to 350°F(180°C). 2. Slice the bread into ¼-inch-thick slices. 3. Arrange the sliced bread on a baking sheet and brush each slice with the melted butter. 4. Put the baking sheet in the oven and toast the bread for 5 to 7 minutes, just until golden brown. 5. Let the bread cool slightly. Spread about a teaspoon or so of the mascarpone cheese on each piece of bread. 6. Top with a teaspoon or so of the jam. Serve immediately.

Per Serving:
calories: 445 | fat: 24g | protein: 3g | carbs: 48g | fiber: 5g | sodium: 314mg

Figs with Mascarpone and Honey

Prep time: 5 minutes | Cook time: 5 minutes | Serves 4

◄ ⅓ cup walnuts, chopped
◄ 8 fresh figs, halved
◄ ¼ cup mascarpone cheese
◄ 1 tablespoon honey
◄ ¼ teaspoon flaked sea salt

1. In a skillet over medium heat, toast the walnuts, stirring often, 3 to 5 minutes. 2. Arrange the figs cut-side up on a plate or platter. Using your finger, make a small depression in the cut side of each fig and fill with mascarpone cheese. Sprinkle with a bit of the walnuts, drizzle with the honey, and add a tiny pinch of sea salt.

Per Serving:
calories: 200 | fat: 13g | protein: 3g | carbs: 24g | fiber: 3g | sodium: 105mg

Spanish Cream

Prep time: 5 minutes | Cook time: 0 minutes | Serves 6

- 3 large eggs
- 1¼ cups unsweetened almond milk, divided
- 1 tablespoon gelatin powder
- 1¼ cups goat's cream, heavy whipping cream, or coconut cream
- 1 teaspoon vanilla powder or 1 tablespoon unsweetened vanilla

- extract
- 1 teaspoon cinnamon, plus more for dusting
- ½ ounce (14 g) grated 100% chocolate, for topping
- Optional: low-carb sweetener, to taste

1. Separate the egg whites from the egg yolks. Place ½ cup (120 ml) of the almond milk in a small bowl, then add the gelatin and let it bloom. 2. Place the yolks, cream, and the remaining ¾ cup (180 ml) almond milk in a heatproof bowl placed over a small saucepan filled with 1 cup (240 ml) of water, placed over medium heat, ensuring that the bottom of the bowl doesn't touch the water. Whisk while heating until the mixture is smooth and thickened. 3. Stir in the vanilla, cinnamon, sweetener (if using), and the bloomed gelatin. Cover with plastic wrap pressed to the surface, and chill for 30 minutes. At this point the mixture will look runny. Don't panic! This is absolutely normal. It will firm up. 4. In a bowl with a hand mixer, or in a stand mixer, whisk the egg whites until stiff, then fold them through the cooled custard. Divide among six serving glasses and chill until fully set, 3 to 4 hours. Sprinkle with the grated chocolate and, optionally, add the sweetener and a dusting of cinnamon. Store covered in the refrigerator for up to 5 days.

Per Serving:

calories: 172 | fat: 13g | protein: 5g | carbs: 7g | fiber: 1g | sodium: 83mg

Chapter 11 Salads

Tabbouleh

Prep time: 15 minutes | Cook time: 12 minutes | Serves 4 to 6

- 1 cup water
- ½ cup dried bulgur
- ½ English cucumber, quartered lengthwise and sliced
- 2 tomatoes on the vine, diced
- 2 scallions, chopped
- Juice of 1 lemon
- 2 cups coarsely chopped fresh Italian parsley
- ⅓ cup coarsely chopped fresh mint leaves
- 1 garlic clove
- ¼ cup extra-virgin olive oil
- Sea salt
- Freshly ground black pepper

1. In a medium saucepan, combine the water and bulgur and bring to a boil over medium heat. Reduce the heat to low, cover, and cook until the bulgur is tender, about 12 minutes. Drain off any excess liquid, fluff the bulgur with a fork, and set aside to cool. 2. In a large bowl, toss together the bulgur, cucumber, tomatoes, scallions, and lemon juice. 3. In a food processor, combine the parsley, mint, and garlic and process until finely chopped. 4. Add the chopped herb mixture to the bulgur mixture and stir to combine. Add the olive oil and stir to incorporate. 5. Season with salt and pepper and serve.

Per Serving:

calories: 215 | fat: 14g | protein: 4g | carbs: 21g | fiber: 5g | sodium: 66mg

Citrus Fennel Salad

Prep time: 15 minutes | Cook time: 0 minutes | Serves 2

For the Dressing:
- 2 tablespoons fresh orange juice
- 3 tablespoons olive oil
- 1 tablespoon blood orange vinegar, other orange
For the Salad:
- 2 cups packed baby kale
- 1 medium navel or blood orange, segmented
- ½ small fennel bulb, stems and leaves removed, sliced

- vinegar, or cider vinegar
- 1 tablespoon honey
- Salt
- Freshly ground black pepper

- into matchsticks
- 3 tablespoons toasted pecans, chopped
- 2 ounces (57 g) goat cheese, crumbled

Make the Dressing: Combine the orange juice, olive oil, vinegar, and honey in a small bowl and whisk to combine. Season with salt and pepper. Set the dressing aside. Make the Salad: 1. Divide the baby kale, orange segments, fennel, pecans, and goat cheese evenly between two plates. 2. Drizzle half of the dressing over each salad.

Per Serving:

calories: 502 | fat: 39g | protein: 13g | carbs: 31g | fiber: 6g | sodium: 158mg

Spinach-Arugula Salad with Nectarines and Lemon Dressing

Prep time: 15 minutes | Cook time: 0 minutes | Serves 6

- 1 (7-ounce / 198-g) package baby spinach and arugula blend
- 3 tablespoons fresh lemon juice
- 5 tablespoons olive oil
- ⅛ teaspoon salt
- Pinch (teaspoon) sugar
- Freshly ground black pepper, to taste
- ½ red onion, thinly sliced
- 3 ripe nectarines, pitted and sliced into wedges
- 1 cucumber, peeled, seeded, and sliced
- ½ cup crumbled feta cheese

1. Place the spinach-arugula blend in a large bowl. 2. In a small bowl, whisk together the lemon juice, olive oil, salt, and sugar and season with pepper. Taste and adjust the seasonings. 3. Add the dressing to the greens and toss. Top with the onion, nectarines, cucumber, and feta. 4. Serve immediately.

Per Serving:

1 cup: calories: 178 | fat: 14g | protein: 4g | carbs: 11g | fiber: 2g | sodium: 193mg

Tomato and Pepper Salad

Prep time: 10 minutes | Cook time: 0 minutes | Serves 6

- 3 large yellow peppers
- ¼ cup olive oil
- 1 small bunch fresh basil leaves
- 2 cloves garlic, minced
- 4 large tomatoes, seeded and diced
- Sea salt and freshly ground pepper, to taste

1. Preheat broiler to high heat and broil the peppers until blackened on all sides. 2. Remove from heat and place in a paper bag. Seal and allow peppers to cool. 3. Once cooled, peel the skins off the peppers, then seed and chop them. 4. Add half of the peppers to a food processor along with the olive oil, basil, and garlic, and pulse several times to make the dressing. 5. Combine the rest of the peppers with the tomatoes and toss with the dressing. 6. Season the salad with sea salt and freshly ground pepper. Allow salad to come to room temperature before serving.

Per Serving:

calories: 129 | fat: 9g | protein: 2g | carbs: 11g | fiber: 2g | sodium: 8mg

Pipirrana (Spanish Summer Salad)

Prep time: 15 minutes | Cook time: 0 minutes | Serves 2

- 1 medium red onion, diced
- 2 large tomatoes, cut into small cubes
- 1 large Persian or mini cucumber, cut into small cubes
- 1 large green bell pepper, seeded and diced
- 2 garlic cloves, minced
- Pinch of ground cumin
- ½ teaspoon salt plus a pinch for the garlic paste
- 3 tablespoons extra virgin olive oil plus a few drops for the garlic paste
- 2 tablespoons red wine vinegar

1. Place the onions in a small bowl filled with water. Set aside to soak. 2. Place the tomatoes, cucumber, and bell pepper in a medium bowl. Drain the onions and then combine them with the rest of the vegetables. Mix well. 3. In a mortar or small bowl, combine the garlic, cumin, a pinch of salt, and a few drops of olive oil, then roll or mash the ingredients until a paste is formed. 4. In another small bowl, combine 3 tablespoons of the olive oil, vinegar, and ½ teaspoon of the salt. Add the garlic paste and mix well. 5. Add the dressing to the salad and mix well. 6. Cover and refrigerate for 30 minutes before serving. Store in the refrigerator for up to 2 days.

Per Serving:

calories: 274 | fat: 21g | protein: 4g | carbs: 20g | fiber: 6g | sodium: 600mg

Roasted Golden Beet, Avocado, and Watercress Salad

Prep time: 15 minutes | Cook time: 1 hour | Serves 4

- 1 bunch (about 1½ pounds / 680 g) golden beets
- 1 tablespoon extra-virgin olive oil
- 1 tablespoon white wine vinegar
- ½ teaspoon kosher salt
- ¼ teaspoon freshly ground black pepper
- 1 bunch (about 4 ounces / 113 g) watercress
- 1 avocado, peeled, pitted, and diced
- ¼ cup crumbled feta cheese
- ¼ cup walnuts, toasted
- 1 tablespoon fresh chives, chopped

1. Preheat the oven to 425ºF (220ºC). Wash and trim the beets (cut an inch above the beet root, leaving the long tail if desired), then wrap each beet individually in foil. Place the beets on a baking sheet and roast until fully cooked, 45 to 60 minutes depending on the size of each beet. Start checking at 45 minutes; if easily pierced with a fork, the beets are cooked. 2. Remove the beets from the oven and allow them to cool. Under cold running water, slough off the skin. Cut the beets into bite-size cubes or wedges. 3. In a large bowl, whisk together the olive oil, vinegar, salt, and black pepper. Add the watercress and beets and toss well. Add the avocado, feta, walnuts, and chives and mix gently.

Per Serving:

calories: 235 | fat: 16g | protein: 6g | carbs: 21g | fiber: 8g | sodium: 365mg

Roasted Cauliflower "Steak" Salad

Prep time: 10 minutes | Cook time: 50 minutes | Serves 4

- 2 tablespoons olive oil, divided
- 2 large heads cauliflower (about 3 pounds / 1.4 kg each), trimmed of outer leaves
- 2 teaspoons za'atar
- 1½ teaspoons kosher salt, divided
- 1¼ teaspoons ground black pepper, divided
- 1 teaspoon ground cumin
- 2 large carrots
- 8 ounces (227 g) dandelion greens, tough stems removed
- ½ cup low-fat plain Greek yogurt
- 2 tablespoons tahini
- 2 tablespoons fresh lemon juice
- 1 tablespoon water
- 1 clove garlic, minced

1. Preheat the oven to 450°F(235ºC). Brush a large baking sheet with some of the oil. 2. Place the cauliflower on a cutting board, stem side down. Cut down the middle, through the core and stem, and then cut two 1'-thick "steaks" from the middle. Repeat with the other cauliflower head. Set aside the remaining cauliflower for another use. Brush both sides of the steaks with the remaining oil and set on the baking sheet. 3. Combine the za'atar, 1 teaspoon of the salt, 1 teaspoon of the pepper, and the cumin. Sprinkle on the cauliflower steaks. Bake until the bottom is deeply golden, about 30 minutes. Flip and bake until tender, 10 to 15 minutes. 4. Meanwhile, set the carrots on a cutting board and use a vegetable peeler to peel them into ribbons. Add to a large bowl with the dandelion greens. 5. In a small bowl, combine the yogurt, tahini, lemon juice, water, garlic, the remaining ½ teaspoon salt, and the remaining ¼ teaspoon pepper. 6. Dab 3 tablespoons of the dressing onto the carrot-dandelion mix. With a spoon or your hands, massage the dressing into the mix for 5 minutes. 7. Remove the steaks from the oven and transfer to individual plates. Drizzle each with 2 tablespoons of the dressing and top with 1 cup of the salad.

Per Serving:

calories: 214 | fat: 12g | protein: 9g | carbs: 21g | fiber: 7g | sodium: 849mg

Four-Bean Salad

Prep time: 20 minutes | Cook time: 0 minutes | Serves 4

- ½ cup white beans, cooked
- ½ cup black-eyed peas, cooked
- ½ cup fava beans, cooked
- ½ cup lima beans, cooked
- 1 red bell pepper, diced
- 1 small bunch flat-leaf
- parsley, chopped
- 2 tablespoons olive oil
- 1 teaspoon ground cumin
- Juice of 1 lemon
- Sea salt and freshly ground pepper, to taste

1. You can cook the beans a day or two in advance to speed up the preparation of this dish. 2. Combine all ingredients in a large bowl and mix well. Season to taste. 3. Allow to sit for 30 minutes, so the flavors can come together before serving.

Per Serving:

calories: 189 | fat: 7g | protein: 8g | carbs: 24g | fiber: 7g | sodium: 14mg

Beets with Goat Cheese and Chermoula

Prep time: 10 minutes | Cook time: 40 minutes | Serves 4

- 6 beets, trimmed
- Chermoula:
- 1 cup fresh cilantro leaves
- 1 cup fresh flat-leaf parsley leaves
- ¼ cup fresh lemon juice
- 3 cloves garlic, minced
- 2 teaspoons ground cumin
- 1 teaspoon smoked paprika
- ½ teaspoon kosher salt
- ¼ teaspoon chili powder (optional)
- ¼ cup extra-virgin olive oil
- 2 ounces (57 g) goat cheese, crumbled

1. Preheat the oven to 400°F(205°C). 2. Wrap the beets in a piece of foil and place on a baking sheet. Roast until the beets are tender enough to be pierced with a fork, 30 to 40 minutes. When cool enough to handle, remove the skins and slice the beets into ¼' rounds. Arrange the beet slices on a large serving platter. 3. Make the chermoula: In a food processor, pulse the cilantro, parsley, lemon juice, garlic, cumin, paprika, salt, and chili powder (if using) until the herbs are just coarsely chopped and the ingredients are combined. Stir in the oil. 4. To serve, dollop the chermoula over the beets and scatter the cheese on top.

Per Serving:

calories: 249 | fat: 19g | protein: 6g | carbs: 15g | fiber: 5g | sodium: 472mg

Pistachio Quinoa Salad with Pomegranate Citrus Vinaigrette

Prep time: 15 minutes | Cook time: 15 minutes | Serves 6

For the Quinoa:
- 1½ cups water
- 1 cup quinoa
- ¼ teaspoon kosher salt
- For the Dressing:
- 1 cup extra-virgin olive oil
- ½ cup pomegranate juice
- ½ cup freshly squeezed orange juice

For the Salad:
- 3 cups baby spinach
- ½ cup fresh parsley, coarsely chopped
- ½ cup fresh mint, coarsely chopped
- Approximately ¾ cup

- 1 small shallot, minced
- 1 teaspoon pure maple syrup
- 1 teaspoon za'atar
- ½ teaspoon ground sumac
- ½ teaspoon kosher salt
- ¼ teaspoon freshly ground black pepper

- pomegranate seeds, or 2 pomegranates
- ¼ cup pistachios, shelled and toasted
- ¼ cup crumbled blue cheese

Make the Quinoa: Bring the water, quinoa, and salt to a boil in a small saucepan. Reduce the heat and cover; simmer for 10 to 12 minutes. Fluff with a fork. Make the Dressing: 1. In a medium bowl, whisk together the olive oil, pomegranate juice, orange juice, shallot, maple syrup, za'atar, sumac, salt, and black pepper. 2. In a large bowl, add about ½ cup of dressing. 3. Store the remaining dressing in a glass jar or airtight container and refrigerate. The dressing can be kept up to 2 weeks. Let the chilled dressing reach room temperature before using. Make the Salad: 4. Combine the spinach, parsley, and mint in the bowl with the dressing and toss gently together. 5. Add the quinoa. Toss gently. 6. Add the pomegranate seeds. 7. Or, if using whole pomegranates: Cut the pomegranates in half. Fill a large bowl with water and hold the pomegranate half, cut side-down. Using a wooden spoon, hit the back of the pomegranate so the seeds fall into the water. Immerse the pomegranate in the water and gently pull out any remaining seeds. Repeat with the remaining pomegranate. Skim the white pith off the top of the water. Drain the seeds and add them to the greens. 8. Add the pistachios and cheese and toss gently.

Per Serving:

calories: 300 | fat: 19g | protein: 8g | carbs: 28g | fiber: 5g | sodium: 225mg

Classic Tabouli

Prep time: 30 minutes | Cook time: 0 minutes | Serves 8 to 10

- 1 cup bulgur wheat, grind
- 4 cups Italian parsley, finely chopped
- 2 cups ripe tomato, finely diced
- 1 cup green onion, finely

- chopped
- ½ cup lemon juice
- ½ cup extra-virgin olive oil
- 1½ teaspoons salt
- 1 teaspoon dried mint

1. Before you chop the vegetables, put the bulgur in a small bowl. Rinse with water, drain, and let stand in the bowl while you prepare the other ingredients. 2. Put the parsley, tomatoes, green onion, and bulgur into a large bowl. 3. In a small bowl, whisk together the lemon juice, olive oil, salt, and mint. 4. Pour the dressing over the tomato, onion, and bulgur mixture, tossing everything together. Add additional salt to taste. Serve immediately or store in the fridge for up to 2 days.

Per Serving:

calories: 207 | fat: 14g | protein: 4g | carbs: 20g | fiber: 5g | sodium: 462mg

Warm Fennel, Cherry Tomato, and Spinach Salad

Prep time: 15 minutes | Cook time: 0 minutes | Serves 2

- 4 tablespoons chicken broth
- 4 cups baby spinach leaves
- 10 cherry tomatoes, halved
- Sea salt and freshly ground

- pepper, to taste
- 1 fennel bulb, sliced
- ¼ cup olive oil
- Juice of 2 lemons

1. In a large sauté pan, heat the chicken broth over medium heat. Add the spinach and tomatoes and cook until spinach is wilted. Season with sea salt and freshly ground pepper to taste. 2. Remove from heat and toss fennel slices in with the spinach and tomatoes. Let the fennel warm in the pan, then transfer to a large bowl. 3. Drizzle with the olive oil and lemon juice, and serve immediately.

Per Serving:

calories: 319 | fat: 28g | protein: 5g | carbs: 18g | fiber: 6g | sodium: 123mg

Greek Potato Salad

Prep time: 15 minutes | Cook time: 15 to 18 minutes | Serves 6

- ◀ 1½ pounds (680 g) small red or new potatoes
- ◀ ½ cup olive oil
- ◀ ⅓ cup red wine vinegar
- ◀ 1 teaspoon fresh Greek oregano
- ◀ 4 ounces (113 g) feta cheese, crumbled, if desired, or 4 ounces (113 g) grated Swiss
- cheese (for a less salty option)
- ◀ 1 green bell pepper, seeded and chopped (1¼ cups)
- ◀ 1 small red onion, halved and thinly sliced (generous 1 cup)
- ◀ ½ cup Kalamata olives, pitted and halved

1. Put the potatoes in a large saucepan and add water to cover. Bring the water to a boil and cook until tender, 15 to 18 minutes. Drain and set aside until cool enough to handle. 2. Meanwhile, in a large bowl, whisk together the olive oil, vinegar, and oregano. 3. When the potatoes are just cool enough to handle, cut them into 1-inch pieces and add them to the bowl with the dressing. Toss to combine. Add the cheese, bell pepper, onion, and olives and toss gently. Let stand for 30 minutes before serving.

Per Serving:

calories: 315 | fat: 23g | protein: 5g | carbs: 21g | fiber: 3g | sodium: 360mg

Israeli Salad with Nuts and Seeds

Prep time: 15 minutes | Cook time: 0 minutes | Serves 4

- ◀ ¼ cup pine nuts
- ◀ ¼ cup shelled pistachios
- ◀ ¼ cup coarsely chopped walnuts
- ◀ ¼ cup shelled pumpkin seeds
- ◀ ¼ cup shelled sunflower seeds
- ◀ 2 large English cucumbers, unpeeled and finely chopped
- ◀ 1 pint cherry tomatoes, finely chopped
- ◀ ½ small red onion, finely chopped
- ◀ ½ cup finely chopped fresh flat-leaf Italian parsley
- ◀ ¼ cup extra-virgin olive oil
- ◀ 2 to 3 tablespoons freshly squeezed lemon juice (from 1 lemon)
- ◀ 1 teaspoon salt
- ◀ ¼ teaspoon freshly ground black pepper
- ◀ 4 cups baby arugula

1. In a large dry skillet, toast the pine nuts, pistachios, walnuts, pumpkin seeds, and sunflower seeds over medium-low heat until golden and fragrant, 5 to 6 minutes, being careful not to burn them. Remove from the heat and set aside. 2. In a large bowl, combine the cucumber, tomatoes, red onion, and parsley. 3. In a small bowl, whisk together olive oil, lemon juice, salt, and pepper. Pour over the chopped vegetables and toss to coat. 4. Add the toasted nuts and seeds and arugula and toss with the salad to blend well. Serve at room temperature or chilled.

Per Serving:

calories: 404 | fat: 36g | protein: 10g | carbs: 16g | fiber: 5g | sodium: 601mg

No-Mayo Florence Tuna Salad

Prep time: 10 minutes | Cook time: 0 minutes | Serves 4

- ◀ 4 cups spring mix greens
- ◀ 1 (15-ounce / 425-g) can cannellini beans, drained
- ◀ 2 (5-ounce / 142-g) cans water-packed, white albacore tuna, drained (I prefer Wild Planet brand)
- ◀ ⅔ cup crumbled feta cheese
- ◀ ½ cup thinly sliced sun-dried tomatoes
- ◀ ¼ cup sliced pitted kalamata
- olives
- ◀ ¼ cup thinly sliced scallions, both green and white parts
- ◀ 3 tablespoons extra-virgin olive oil
- ◀ ½ teaspoon dried cilantro
- ◀ 2 or 3 leaves thinly chopped fresh sweet basil
- ◀ 1 lime, zested and juiced
- ◀ Kosher salt
- ◀ Freshly ground black pepper

1. In a large bowl, combine greens, beans, tuna, feta, tomatoes, olives, scallions, olive oil, cilantro, basil, and lime juice and zest. Season with salt and pepper, mix, and enjoy!

Per Serving:

1 cup: calories: 355 | fat: 19g | protein: 22g | carbs: 25g | fiber: 8g | sodium: 744mg

Quinoa with Zucchini, Mint, and Pistachios

Prep time: 20 to 30 minutes | Cook time: 20 minutes | Serves 4

For the Quinoa:
- ◀ 1½ cups water
- ◀ 1 cup quinoa

For the Salad:
- ◀ 2 tablespoons extra-virgin olive oil
- ◀ 1 zucchini, thinly sliced into rounds
- ◀ 6 small radishes, sliced
- ◀ 1 shallot, julienned
- ◀ ¾ teaspoon kosher salt
- ◀ ¼ teaspoon freshly ground
- ◀ ¼ teaspoon kosher salt

- black pepper
- ◀ 2 garlic cloves, sliced
- ◀ Zest of 1 lemon
- ◀ 2 tablespoons lemon juice
- ◀ ¼ cup fresh mint, chopped
- ◀ ¼ cup fresh basil, chopped
- ◀ ¼ cup pistachios, shelled and toasted

Make the Quinoa: Bring the water, quinoa, and salt to a boil in a medium saucepan. Reduce to a simmer, cover, and cook for 10 to 12 minutes. Fluff with a fork. Make the Salad: 1. Heat the olive oil in a large skillet or sauté pan over medium-high heat. Add the zucchini, radishes, shallot, salt, and black pepper, and sauté for 7 to 8 minutes. Add the garlic and cook 30 seconds to 1 minute more. 2. In a large bowl, combine the lemon zest and lemon juice. Add the quinoa and mix well. Add the cooked zucchini mixture and mix well. Add the mint, basil, and pistachios and gently mix.

Per Serving:

calories: 220 | fat: 12g | protein: 6g | carbs: 25g | fiber: 5g | sodium: 295mg

Endive with Shrimp

Prep time: 15 minutes | Cook time: 2 minutes | Serves 4

- ¼ cup olive oil
- 1 small shallot, minced
- 1 tablespoon Dijon mustard
- Juice and zest of 1 lemon
- Sea salt and freshly ground pepper, to taste
- 2 cups salted water
- 14 shrimp, peeled and deveined
- 1 head endive
- ½ cup tart green apple, diced
- 2 tablespoons toasted walnuts

1. For the vinaigrette, whisk together the first five ingredients in a small bowl until creamy and emulsified. 2. Refrigerate for at least 2 hours for best flavor. 3. In a small pan, boil salted water. Add the shrimp and cook 1–2 minutes, or until the shrimp turns pink. Drain and cool under cold water. 4. To assemble the salad, wash and break the endive. Place on serving plates and top with the shrimp, green apple, and toasted walnuts. 5. Drizzle with the vinaigrette before serving.

Per Serving:

calories: 194 | fat: 16g | protein: 6g | carbs: 8g | fiber: 5g | sodium: 191mg

Arugula and Artichokes

Prep time: 20 minutes | Cook time: 0 minutes | Serves 6

- 4 tablespoons olive oil
- 2 tablespoons balsamic vinegar
- 1 teaspoon Dijon mustard
- 1 clove garlic, minced
- 6 cups baby arugula leaves
- 6 oil-packed artichoke
- hearts, sliced
- 6 low-salt olives, pitted and chopped
- 1 cup cherry tomatoes, sliced in half
- 4 fresh basil leaves, thinly sliced

1. Make the dressing by whisking together the olive oil, vinegar, Dijon, and garlic until you have a smooth emulsion. Set aside. 2. Toss the arugula, artichokes, olives, and tomatoes together. 3. Drizzle the salad with the dressing, garnish with the fresh basil, and serve.

Per Serving:

calories: 133 | fat: 12g | protein: 2g | carbs: 6g | fiber: 3g | sodium: 75mg

Orange-Tarragon Chicken Salad Wrap

Prep time: 15 minutes | Cook time: 0 minutes | Serves 4

- ½ cup plain whole-milk Greek yogurt
- 2 tablespoons Dijon mustard
- 2 tablespoons extra-virgin olive oil
- 2 tablespoons chopped fresh tarragon or 1 teaspoon dried tarragon
- ½ teaspoon salt
- ¼ teaspoon freshly ground
- black pepper
- 2 cups cooked shredded chicken
- ½ cup slivered almonds
- 4 to 8 large Bibb lettuce leaves, tough stem removed
- 2 small ripe avocados, peeled and thinly sliced
- Zest of 1 clementine, or ½ small orange (about 1

tablespoon)

1. In a medium bowl, combine the yogurt, mustard, olive oil, tarragon, orange zest, salt, and pepper and whisk until creamy. 2. Add the shredded chicken and almonds and stir to coat. 3. To assemble the wraps, place about ½ cup chicken salad mixture in the center of each lettuce leaf and top with sliced avocados.

Per Serving:

calories: 491 | fat: 38g | protein: 28g | carbs: 14g | fiber: 9g | sodium: 454mg

Arugula and Fennel Salad with Fresh Basil

Prep time: 5 minutes | Cook time: 0 minutes | Serves 4

- 3 tablespoons olive oil
- 3 tablespoons lemon juice
- 1 teaspoon honey
- ½ teaspoon salt
- 1 medium bulb fennel, very thinly sliced
- 1 small cucumber, very
- thinly sliced
- 2 cups arugula
- ¼ cup toasted pine nuts
- ½ cup crumbled feta cheese
- ¼ cup julienned fresh basil leaves

1. In a medium bowl, whisk together the olive oil, lemon juice, honey, and salt. Add the fennel and cucumber and toss to coat and let sit for 10 minutes or so. 2. Put the arugula in a large salad bowl. Add the marinated cucumber and fennel, along with the dressing, to the bowl and toss well. Serve immediately, sprinkled with pine nuts, feta cheese, and basil.

Per Serving:

calories: 237 | fat: 21g | protein: 6g | carbs: 11g | fiber: 3g | sodium: 537mg

Marinated Greek Salad with Oregano and Goat Cheese

Prep time: 10 minutes | Cook time: 0 minutes | Serves 4

- ½ cup white wine vinegar
- 1 small garlic clove, minced
- 1 teaspoon crumbled dried Greek oregano
- ½ teaspoon salt
- ¼ teaspoon freshly ground black pepper
- 2 Persian cucumbers, sliced thinly
- 4 to 6 long, skinny red or yellow banana peppers or other mild peppers
- 1 medium red onion, cut into rings
- 1 pint mixed small heirloom tomatoes, halved
- 2 ounces (57 g) crumbled goat cheese or feta

1. In a large, nonreactive (glass, ceramic, or plastic) bowl, whisk together the vinegar, garlic, oregano, salt, and pepper. Add the cucumbers, peppers, and onion and toss to mix. Cover and refrigerate for at least 1 hour. 2. Add the tomatoes to the bowl and toss to coat. Serve topped with the cheese.

Per Serving:

calories: 98 | fat: 4g | protein: 4g | carbs: 13g | fiber: 3g | sodium: 460mg

Tuna Niçoise

Prep time: 15 minutes | Cook time: 20 minutes | Serves 4

- 1 pound (454 g) small red or fingerling potatoes, halved
- 1 pound (454 g) green beans or haricots verts, trimmed
- 1 head romaine lettuce, chopped or torn into bite-size pieces
- ½ pint cherry tomatoes, halved
- 8 radishes, thinly sliced
- ½ cup olives, pitted (any kind you like)
- 2 (5-ounce / 142-g) cans no-salt-added tuna packed in olive oil, drained
- 8 anchovies (optional)

1. Fill a large pot fitted with a steamer basket with 2 to 3 inches of water. Put the potatoes in the steamer basket and lay the green beans on top of the potatoes. Bring the water to a boil over high heat, lower the heat to low and simmer, cover, and cook for 7 minutes, or until the green beans are tender but crisp. Remove the green beans and continue to steam the potatoes for an additional 10 minutes. 2. Place the romaine lettuce on a serving platter. Group the potatoes, green beans, tomatoes, radishes, olives, and tuna in different areas of the platter. If using the anchovies, place them around the platter.

Per Serving:

calories: 315 | fat: 9g | protein: 28g | carbs: 33g | fiber: 9g | sodium: 420mg

Flank Steak Spinach Salad

Prep time: 15 minutes | Cook time: 10 minutes | Serves 4

- 1 pound (454 g) flank steak
- 1 teaspoon extra-virgin olive oil
- 1 tablespoon garlic powder
- ½ teaspoon salt
- ½ teaspoon freshly ground black pepper
- 4 cups baby spinach leaves
- 10 cherry tomatoes, halved
- 10 cremini or white mushrooms, sliced
- 1 small red onion, thinly sliced
- ½ red bell pepper, thinly sliced

1. Preheat the broiler. Line a baking sheet with aluminum foil. 2. Rub the top of the flank steak with the olive oil, garlic powder, salt, and pepper and let sit for 10 minutes before placing under the broiler. Broil for 5 minutes on each side for medium rare. Allow the meat to rest on a cutting board for 10 minutes. 3. Meanwhile, in a large bowl, combine the spinach, tomatoes, mushrooms, onion, and bell pepper and toss well. 4. To serve, divide the salad among 4 dinner plates. Slice the steak on the diagonal and place 4 to 5 slices on top of each salad. Serve with your favorite vinaigrette.

Per Serving:

calories: 211 | fat: 7g | protein: 28g | carbs: 9g | fiber: 2g | sodium: 382mg

Mediterranean Potato Salad

Prep time: 10 minutes |Cook time: 20 minutes| Serves: 6

- 2 pounds (907 g) Yukon Gold baby potatoes, cut into 1-inch cubes
- 3 tablespoons freshly squeezed lemon juice (from about 1 medium lemon)
- 3 tablespoons extra-virgin olive oil
- 1 tablespoon olive brine
- ¼ teaspoon kosher or sea salt
- 1 (2¼-ounce / 35-g) can sliced olives (about ½ cup)
- 1 cup sliced celery (about 2 stalks) or fennel
- 2 tablespoons chopped fresh oregano
- 2 tablespoons torn fresh mint

1. In a medium saucepan, cover the potatoes with cold water until the waterline is one inch above the potatoes. Set over high heat, bring the potatoes to a boil, then turn down the heat to medium-low. Simmer for 12 to 15 minutes, until the potatoes are just fork tender. 2. While the potatoes are cooking, in a small bowl, whisk together the lemon juice, oil, olive brine, and salt. 3. Drain the potatoes in a colander and transfer to a serving bowl. Immediately pour about 3 tablespoons of the dressing over the potatoes. Gently mix in the olives and celery. 4. Before serving, gently mix in the oregano, mint, and the remaining dressing.

Per Serving:

calories: 192 | fat: 8g | protein: 3g | carbs: 28g | fiber: 4g | sodium: 195mg

Arugula Spinach Salad with Shaved Parmesan

Prep time: 10 minutes | Cook time: 2 minutes | Serves 3

- 3 tablespoons raw pine nuts
- 3 cups arugula
- 3 cups baby leaf spinach
- 5 dried figs, pitted and chopped
- 2½ ounces (71 g) shaved Parmesan cheese
- For the Dressing:
- 4 teaspoons balsamic vinegar
- 1 teaspoon Dijon mustard
- 1 teaspoon honey
- 5 tablespoons extra virgin olive oil

1. In a small pan over low heat, toast the pine nuts for 2 minutes or until they begin to brown. Promptly remove them from the heat and transfer to a small bowl. 2. Make the dressing by combining the balsamic vinegar, Dijon mustard, and honey in a small bowl. Using a fork to whisk, gradually add the olive oil while continuously mixing. 3. In a large bowl, toss the arugula and baby spinach and then top with the figs, Parmesan cheese, and toasted pine nuts. Drizzle the dressing over the top and toss until the ingredients are thoroughly coated with the dressing. Serve promptly. (This salad is best served fresh.)

Per Serving:

calories: 416 | fat: 35g | protein: 10g | carbs: 18g | fiber: 3g | sodium: 478mg

Chapter 12 Pizzas, Wraps, and Sandwiches

Turkish Pizza

Prep time: 20 minutes | Cook time: 10 minutes | Serves 4

- 4 ounces (113 g) ground lamb or 85% lean ground beef
- ¼ cup finely chopped green bell pepper
- ¼ cup chopped fresh parsley
- 1 small plum tomato, seeded and finely chopped
- 2 tablespoons finely chopped yellow onion
- 1 garlic clove, minced
- 2 teaspoons tomato paste
- ¼ teaspoon sweet paprika
- ¼ teaspoon ground cumin
- ⅛ to ¼ teaspoon red pepper flakes
- ⅛ teaspoon ground allspice
- ⅛ teaspoon kosher salt
- ⅛ teaspoon black pepper
- 4 (6-inch) flour tortillas
- For Serving:
- Chopped fresh mint
- Extra-virgin olive oil
- Lemon wedges

1. In a medium bowl, gently mix the ground lamb, bell pepper, parsley, chopped tomato, onion, garlic, tomato paste, paprika, cumin, red pepper flakes, allspice, salt, and black pepper until well combined. 2. Divide the meat mixture evenly among the tortillas, spreading it all the way to the edge of each tortilla. 3. Place 1 tortilla in the air fryer basket. Set the air fryer to 400ºF (204ºC) for 10 minutes, or until the meat topping has browned and the edge of the tortilla is golden. Transfer to a plate and repeat to cook the remaining tortillas. 4. Serve the pizzas warm, topped with chopped fresh mint and a drizzle of extra-virgin olive oil and with lemon wedges alongside.

Per Serving:

calories: 172 | fat: 8g | protein: 8g | carbs: 18g | fiber: 2g | sodium: 318mg

Vegetable Pita Sandwiches

Prep time: 15 minutes | Cook time: 9 to 12 minutes | Serves 4

- 1 baby eggplant, peeled and chopped
- 1 red bell pepper, sliced
- ½ cup diced red onion
- ½ cup shredded carrot
- 1 teaspoon olive oil
- ⅓ cup low-fat Greek yogurt
- ½ teaspoon dried tarragon
- 2 low-sodium whole-wheat pita breads, halved crosswise

1. In a baking pan, stir together the eggplant, red bell pepper, red onion, carrot, and olive oil. Put the vegetable mixture into the air fryer basket and roast at 390ºF (199ºC) for 7 to 9 minutes, stirring once, until the vegetables are tender. Drain if necessary. 2. In a small bowl, thoroughly mix the yogurt and tarragon until well combined. 3. Stir the yogurt mixture into the vegetables. Stuff one-fourth of this mixture into each pita pocket. 4. Place the sandwiches in the air fryer and cook for 2 to 3 minutes, or until the bread is toasted. Serve immediately.

Per Serving:

calories: 115 | fat: 2g | protein: 4g | carbs: 22g | fiber: 6g | sodium: 90mg

Classic Margherita Pizza

Prep time: 10 minutes | Cook time: 10 minutes | Serves 4

- All-purpose flour, for dusting
- 1 pound (454 g) premade pizza dough
- 1 (15-ounce / 425-g) can crushed San Marzano tomatoes, with their juices
- 2 garlic cloves
- 1 teaspoon Italian seasoning
- Pinch sea salt, plus more as needed
- 1½ teaspoons olive oil, for drizzling
- 10 slices mozzarella cheese
- 12 to 15 fresh basil leaves

1. Preheat the oven to 475ºF (245ºC). 2. On a floured surface, roll out the dough to a 12-inch round and place it on a lightly floured pizza pan or baking sheet. 3. In a food processor, combine the tomatoes with their juices, garlic, Italian seasoning, and salt and process until smooth. Taste and adjust the seasoning. 4. Drizzle the olive oil over the pizza dough, then spoon the pizza sauce over the dough and spread it out evenly with the back of the spoon, leaving a 1-inch border. Evenly distribute the mozzarella over the pizza. 5. Bake until the crust is cooked through and golden, 8 to 10 minutes. Remove from the oven and let sit for 1 to 2 minutes. Top with the basil right before serving.

Per Serving:

calories: 570 | fat: 21g | protein: 28g | carbs: 66g | fiber: 4g | sodium: 570mg

Cucumber Basil Sandwiches

Prep time: 10 minutes | Cook time: 0 minutes | Serves 2

- 4 slices whole-grain bread
- ¼ cup hummus
- 1 large cucumber, thinly
- sliced
- 4 whole basil leaves

1. Spread the hummus on 2 slices of bread, and layer the cucumbers onto it. Top with the basil leaves and close the sandwiches. 2. Press down lightly and serve immediately.

Per Serving:

calories: 209 | fat: 5g | protein: 9g | carbs: 32g | fiber: 6g | sodium: 275mg

Dill Salmon Salad Wraps

Prep time: 10 minutes |Cook time: 10 minutes| Serves:6

- 1 pound (454 g) salmon filet, cooked and flaked, or 3 (5-ounce / 142-g) cans salmon
- ½ cup diced carrots (about 1 carrot)
- ½ cup diced celery (about 1 celery stalk)
- 3 tablespoons chopped fresh dill
- 3 tablespoons diced red onion (a little less than ⅛ onion)
- 2 tablespoons capers
- 1½ tablespoons extra-virgin olive oil
- 1 tablespoon aged balsamic vinegar
- ½ teaspoon freshly ground black pepper
- ¼ teaspoon kosher or sea salt
- 4 whole-wheat flatbread wraps or soft whole-wheat tortillas

1. In a large bowl, mix together the salmon, carrots, celery, dill, red onion, capers, oil, vinegar, pepper, and salt. 2. Divide the salmon salad among the flatbreads. Fold up the bottom of the flatbread, then roll up the wrap and serve.

Per Serving:

calories: 185 | fat: 8g | protein: 17g | carbs: 12g | fiber: 2g | sodium: 237mg

Mediterranean Tuna Salad Sandwiches

Prep time: 10 minutes | Cook time: 5 minutes | Serves 2

- 1 can white tuna, packed in water or olive oil, drained
- 1 roasted red pepper, diced
- ½ small red onion, diced
- 10 low-salt olives, pitted and finely chopped
- ¼ cup plain Greek yogurt
- 1 tablespoon flat-leaf parsley, chopped
- Juice of 1 lemon
- Sea salt and freshly ground pepper, to taste
- 4 whole-grain pieces of bread

1. In a small bowl, combine all of the ingredients except the bread, and mix well. 2. Season with sea salt and freshly ground pepper to taste. Toast the bread or warm in a pan. 3. Make the sandwich and serve immediately.

Per Serving:

calories: 307 | fat: 7g | protein: 30g | carbs: 31g | fiber: 5g | sodium: 564mg

Mediterranean-Pita Wraps

Prep time: 5 minutes | Cook time: 14 minutes | Serves 4

- 1 pound (454 g) mackerel fish fillets
- 2 tablespoons olive oil
- 1 tablespoon Mediterranean seasoning mix
- ½ teaspoon chili powder
- Sea salt and freshly ground black pepper, to taste
- 2 ounces (57 g) feta cheese, crumbled
- 4 tortillas

1. Toss the fish fillets with the olive oil; place them in the lightly oiled air fryer basket. 2. Air fry the fish fillets at 400ºF (204ºC) for about 14 minutes, turning them over halfway through the cooking time. 3. Assemble your pitas with the chopped fish and remaining ingredients and serve warm.

Per Serving:

calories: 275 | fat: 13g | protein: 27g | carbs: 13g | fiber: 2g | sodium: 322mg

Roasted Vegetable Bocadillo with Romesco Sauce

Prep time: 10 minutes | Cook time: 20 minutes | Serves 4

- 2 small yellow squash, sliced lengthwise
- 2 small zucchini, sliced lengthwise
- 1 medium red onion, thinly sliced
- 4 large button mushrooms, sliced
- 2 tablespoons olive oil
- 1 teaspoon salt, divided
- ½ teaspoon freshly ground black pepper, divided
- 2 roasted red peppers from a jar, drained
- 2 tablespoons blanched almonds
- 1 tablespoon sherry vinegar
- 1 small clove garlic
- 4 crusty multigrain rolls
- 4 ounces (113 g) goat cheese, at room temperature
- 1 tablespoon chopped fresh basil

1. Preheat the oven to 400°F(205ºC). 2. In a medium bowl, toss the yellow squash, zucchini, onion, and mushrooms with the olive oil, ½ teaspoon salt, and ¼ teaspoon pepper. Spread on a large baking sheet. Roast the vegetables in the oven for about 20 minutes, until softened. 3. Meanwhile, in a food processor, combine the roasted peppers, almonds, vinegar, garlic, the remaining ½ teaspoon salt, and the remaining ¼ teaspoon pepper and process until smooth. 4. Split the rolls and spread ¼ of the goat cheese on the bottom of each. Place the roasted vegetables on top of the cheese, dividing equally. Top with chopped basil. Spread the top halves of the rolls with the roasted red pepper sauce and serve immediately.

Per Serving:

calories: 379 | fat: 21g | protein: 17g | carbs: 32g | fiber: 4g | sodium: 592mg

Za'atar Pizza

Prep time: 10 minutes | Cook time: 15 minutes | Serves 4 to 6

- 1 sheet puff pastry
- ¼ cup extra-virgin olive oil
- ⅓ cup za'atar seasoning

1. Preheat the oven to 350°F(180ºC). 2. Put the puff pastry on a parchment-lined baking sheet. Cut the pastry into desired slices. 3. Brush the pastry with olive oil. Sprinkle with the za'atar. 4. Put the pastry in the oven and bake for 10 to 12 minutes or until edges are lightly browned and puffed up. Serve warm or at room temperature.

Per Serving:

calories: 374 | fat: 30g | protein: 3g | carbs: 20g | fiber: 1g | sodium: 166mg

Turkey Burgers with Feta and Dill

Prep time: 5 minutes | Cook time: 15 minutes | Serves 4

- 1 pound (454 g) ground turkey breast
- 1 small red onion, ½ finely chopped, ½ sliced
- ½ cup crumbled feta cheese
- ¼ cup chopped fresh dill
- 1 clove garlic, minced
- ½ teaspoon kosher salt
- ¼ teaspoon ground black pepper
- 4 whole grain hamburger rolls
- 4 thick slices tomato
- 4 leaves lettuce

1. Coat a grill rack or grill pan with olive oil and prepare to medium-high heat. 2. In a large bowl, use your hands to combine the turkey, chopped onion, cheese, dill, garlic, salt, and pepper. Do not overmix. Divide into 4 patties, 4' in diameter. 3. Grill the patties, covered, until a thermometer inserted in the center registers 165°F(74°C), 5 to 6 minutes per side. 4. Serve each patty on a roll with the sliced onion, 1 slice of the tomato, and 1 leaf of the lettuce.

Per Serving:

calories: 305 | fat: 7g | protein: 35g | carbs: 26g | fiber: 3g | sodium: 708mg

Moroccan Lamb Wrap with Harissa

Prep time: 10 minutes | Cook time: 10 minutes | Serves 4

- 1 clove garlic, minced
- 2 teaspoons ground cumin
- 2 teaspoons chopped fresh thyme
- ¼ cup olive oil, divided
- 1 lamb leg steak, about 12 ounces (340 g)
- 4 (8-inch) pocketless pita rounds or naan, preferably whole-wheat
- 1 medium eggplant, sliced
- ½-inch thick
- 1 medium zucchini, sliced lengthwise into 4 slices
- 1 bell pepper (any color), roasted and skinned
- 6 to 8 Kalamata olives, sliced
- Juice of 1 lemon
- 2 to 4 tablespoons harissa
- 2 cups arugula

1. In a large bowl, combine the garlic, cumin, thyme, and 1 tablespoon of the olive oil. Add the lamb, turn to coat, cover, refrigerate, and marinate for at least an hour. 2. Preheat the oven to 400°F(205°C). 3. Heat a grill or grill pan to high heat. Remove the lamb from the marinade and grill for about 4 minutes per side, until medium-rare. Transfer to a plate and let rest for about 10 minutes before slicing thinly across the grain. 4. While the meat is resting, wrap the bread rounds in aluminum foil and heat in the oven for about 10 minutes. 5. Meanwhile, brush the eggplant and zucchini slices with the remaining olive oil and grill until tender, about 3 minutes. Dice them and the bell pepper. Toss in a large bowl with the olives and lemon juice. 6. Spread some of the harissa onto each warm flatbread round and top each evenly with roasted vegetables, a few slices of lamb, and a handful of the arugula. 7. Roll up the wraps, cut each in half crosswise, and serve immediately.

Per Serving:

calories: 553 | fat: 24g | protein: 33g | carbs: 53g | fiber: 11g | sodium: 531mg

Greek Salad Wraps

Prep time: 15 minutes |Cook time: 0 minutes| Serves: 4

- 1½ cups seedless cucumber, peeled and chopped (about 1 large cucumber)
- 1 cup chopped tomato (about 1 large tomato)
- ½ cup finely chopped fresh mint
- 1 (2¼-ounce / 64-g) can sliced black olives (about ½ cup), drained
- ¼ cup diced red onion (about ¼ onion)
- 2 tablespoons extra-virgin
- olive oil
- 1 tablespoon red wine vinegar
- ¼ teaspoon freshly ground black pepper
- ¼ teaspoon kosher or sea salt
- ½ cup crumbled goat cheese (about 2 ounces / 57 g)
- 4 whole-wheat flatbread wraps or soft whole-wheat tortillas

1. In a large bowl, mix together the cucumber, tomato, mint, olives, and onion until well combined. 2. In a small bowl, whisk together the oil, vinegar, pepper, and salt. Drizzle the dressing over the salad, and mix gently. 3. With a knife, spread the goat cheese evenly over the four wraps. Spoon a quarter of the salad filling down the middle of each wrap. 4. Fold up each wrap: Start by folding up the bottom, then fold one side over and fold the other side over the top. Repeat with the remaining wraps and serve.

Per Serving:

calories: 217 | fat: 14g | protein: 7g | carbs: 17g | fiber: 3g | sodium: 329mg

Flatbread Pizza with Roasted Cherry Tomatoes, Artichokes, and Feta

Prep time: 5 minutes | Cook time: 20 minutes | Serves 4

- 1½ pounds (680 g) cherry or grape tomatoes, halved
- 3 tablespoons olive oil, divided
- ½ teaspoon salt
- ½ teaspoon freshly ground black pepper
- 4 Middle Eastern–style
- flatbread rounds
- 1 can artichoke hearts, rinsed, well drained, and cut into thin wedges
- 8 ounces (227 g) crumbled feta cheese
- ¼ cup chopped fresh Greek oregano

1. Preheat the oven to 500°F(260°C). 2. In a medium bowl, toss the tomatoes with 1 tablespoon olive oil, the salt, and the pepper. Spread out on a large baking sheet. Roast in the preheated oven until the tomato skins begin to blister and crack, about 10 to 12 minutes. Remove the tomatoes from the oven and reduce the heat to 450°F(235°C). 3. Place the flatbreads on a large baking sheet (or two baking sheets if necessary) and brush the tops with the remaining 2 tablespoons of olive oil. Top with the artichoke hearts, roasted tomatoes, and cheese, dividing equally. 4. Bake the flatbreads in the oven for about 8 to 10 minutes, until the edges are lightly browned and the cheese is melted. Sprinkle the oregano over the top and serve immediately.

Per Serving:

calories: 436 | fat: 27g | protein: 16g | carbs: 34g | fiber: 6g | sodium: 649mg

Sautéed Mushroom, Onion, and Pecorino Romano Panini

Prep time: 10 minutes | Cook time: 20 minutes | Serves 4

- 3 tablespoons olive oil, divided
- 1 small onion, diced
- 10 ounces (283 g) button or cremini mushrooms, sliced
- ½ teaspoon salt
- ¼ teaspoon freshly ground black pepper
- 4 crusty Italian sandwich rolls
- 4 ounces (113 g) freshly grated Pecorino Romano

1. Heat 1 tablespoon of the olive oil in a skillet over medium-high heat. Add the onion and cook, stirring, until it begins to soften, about 3 minutes. Add the mushrooms, season with salt and pepper, and cook, stirring, until they soften and the liquid they release evaporates, about 7 minutes. 2. To make the panini, heat a skillet or grill pan over high heat and brush with 1 tablespoon olive oil. Brush the inside of the rolls with the remaining 1 tablespoon olive oil. Divide the mushroom mixture evenly among the rolls and top each with ¼ of the grated cheese. 3. Place the sandwiches in the hot pan and place another heavy pan, such as a cast-iron skillet, on top to weigh them down. Cook for about 3 to 4 minutes, until crisp and golden on the bottom, and then flip over and repeat on the second side, cooking for an additional 3 to 4 minutes until golden and crisp. Slice each sandwich in half and serve hot.

Per Serving:

calories: 348 | fat: 20g | protein: 14g | carbs: 30g | fiber: 2g | sodium: 506mg

Herbed Focaccia Panini with Anchovies and Burrata

Prep time: 5 minutes | Cook time: 8 minutes | Serves 4

- 8 ounces (227 g) burrata cheese, chilled and sliced
- 1 pound (454 g) whole-wheat herbed focaccia, cut crosswise into 4 rectangles and split horizontally
- 1 can anchovy fillets packed in oil, drained
- 8 slices tomato, sliced
- 2 cups arugula
- 1 tablespoon olive oil

1. Divide the cheese evenly among the bottom halves of the focaccia rectangles. Top each with 3 or 4 anchovy fillets, 2 slices of tomato, and ½ cup arugula. Place the top halves of the focaccia on top of the sandwiches. 2. To make the panini, heat a skillet or grill pan over high heat and brush with the olive oil. 3. Place the sandwiches in the hot pan and place another heavy pan, such as a cast-iron skillet, on top to weigh them down. Cook for about 3 to 4 minutes, until crisp and golden on the bottom, and then flip over and repeat on the second side, cooking for an additional 3 to 4 minutes until golden and crisp. Slice each sandwich in half and serve hot.

Per Serving:

calories: 596 | fat: 30g | protein: 27g | carbs: 58g | fiber: 5g | sodium: 626mg

Moroccan Lamb Flatbread with Pine Nuts, Mint, and Ras Al Hanout

Prep time: 10 minutes | Cook time: 20 minutes | Serves 4

- 1⅓ cups plain Greek yogurt
- Juice of 1½ lemons, divided
- 1¼ teaspoons salt, divided
- 1 pound (454 g) ground lamb
- 1 medium red onion, diced
- 1 clove garlic, minced
- 1 tablespoon ras al hanout
- ¼ cup chopped fresh mint
- leaves
- Freshly ground black pepper
- 4 Middle Eastern-style flatbread rounds
- 2 tablespoons toasted pine nuts
- 16 cherry tomatoes, halved
- 2 tablespoons chopped cilantro

1. Preheat the oven to 450°F (235°C). 2. In a small bowl, stir together the yogurt, the juice of ½ lemon, and ¼ teaspoon salt. 3. Heat a large skillet over medium-high heat. Add the lamb and cook, stirring frequently, until browned, about 5 minutes. Drain any excess rendered fat from the pan and then stir in the onion and garlic and cook, stirring, until softened, about 3 minutes more. Stir in the ras al hanout, mint, the remaining teaspoon of salt, and pepper. 4. Place the flatbread rounds on a baking sheet (or two if necessary) and top with the lamb mixture, pine nuts, and tomatoes, dividing equally. Bake in the preheated oven until the crust is golden brown and the tomatoes have softened, about 10 minutes. Scatter the cilantro over the flatbreads and squeeze the remaining lemon juice over them. Cut into wedges and serve dolloped with the yogurt sauce.

Per Serving:

calories: 463 | fat: 22g | protein: 34g | carbs: 34g | fiber: 3g | sodium: 859mg

Mexican Pizza

Prep time: 10 minutes | Cook time: 7 to 9 minutes | Serves 4

- ¾ cup refried beans (from a 16-ounce / 454-g can)
- ½ cup salsa
- 10 frozen precooked beef meatballs, thawed and sliced
- 1 jalapeño pepper, sliced
- 4 whole-wheat pita breads
- 1 cup shredded pepper Jack cheese
- ½ cup shredded Colby cheese
- ⅓ cup sour cream

1. In a medium bowl, combine the refried beans, salsa, meatballs, and jalapeño pepper. 2. Preheat the air fryer for 3 to 4 minutes or until hot. 3. Top the pitas with the refried bean mixture and sprinkle with the cheeses. 4. Bake at 370°F (188°C) for 7 to 9 minutes or until the pizza is crisp and the cheese is melted and starts to brown. 5. Top each pizza with a dollop of sour cream and serve warm.

Per Serving:

calories: 484 | fat: 30g | protein: 24g | carbs: 32g | fiber: 7g | sodium: 612mg

Greek Salad Pita

Prep time: 15 minutes | Cook time: 0 minutes | Serves 4

- 1 cup chopped romaine lettuce
- 1 tomato, chopped and seeded
- ½ cup baby spinach leaves
- ½ small red onion, thinly sliced
- ½ small cucumber, chopped and deseeded
- 2 tablespoons olive oil
- 1 tablespoon crumbled feta cheese
- ½ tablespoon red wine vinegar
- 1 teaspoon Dijon mustard
- Sea salt and freshly ground pepper, to taste
- 1 whole-wheat pita

1. Combine everything except the sea salt, freshly ground pepper, and pita bread in a medium bowl. 2. Toss until the salad is well combined. 3. Season with sea salt and freshly ground pepper to taste. Fill the pita with the salad mixture, serve, and enjoy!

Per Serving:

calories: 123 | fat: 8g | protein: 3g | carbs: 12g | fiber: 2g | sodium: 125mg

Turkey and Provolone Panini with Roasted Peppers and Onions

Prep time: 15 minutes | Cook time: 1 hour 5 minutes | Serves 4

For the peppers and onions
- 2 red bell pepper, seeded and quartered
- 2 red onions, peeled and quartered
For the panini
- 2 tablespoons olive oil
- 8 slices whole-wheat bread
- 8 ounces (227 g) thinly sliced provolone cheese
- 2 tablespoons olive oil
- ½ teaspoon salt
- ½ teaspoon freshly ground black pepper
- 8 ounces (227 g) sliced roasted turkey or chicken breast

1. Preheat the oven to 375°F(190ºC). 2. To roast the peppers and onions, toss them together with the olive oil, salt, and pepper on a large, rimmed baking sheet. Spread them out in a single layer and then bake in the preheated oven for 45 to 60 minutes, turning occasionally, until they are tender and beginning to brown. Remove the peppers and onions from the oven and let them cool for a few minutes until they are cool enough to handle. Skin the peppers and thinly slice them. Thinly slice the onions. 3. Preheat a skillet or grill pan over medium-high heat. Make the panini: 4. brush one side of each of the 8 slices of bread with olive oil. Place 4 of the bread slices, oiled side down, on your work surface. Top each with ¼ of the cheese and ¼ of the turkey, and top with some of the roasted peppers and onions. Place the remaining 4 bread slices on top of the sandwiches, oiled side up. 5. Place the sandwiches in the skillet or grill pan (you may have to cook them in two batches), cover the pan, and cook until the bottoms have golden brown grill marks and the cheese is beginning to melt, about 2 minutes. Turn the sandwiches over and cook, covered, until the second side is golden brown and the cheese is melted, another 2 minutes or so. Cut each sandwich in half and serve immediately.

Per Serving:

calories: 603 | fat: 32g | protein: 41g | carbs: 37g | fiber: 6g | sodium: 792mg

Margherita Open-Face Sandwiches

Prep time: 10 minutes |Cook time: 5 minutes| Serves: 4

- 2 (6- to 7-inch) whole-wheat submarine or hoagie rolls, sliced open horizontally
- 1 tablespoon extra-virgin olive oil
- 1 garlic clove, halved
- 1 large ripe tomato, cut into 8 slices
- ¼ teaspoon dried oregano
- 1 cup fresh mozzarella (about 4 ounces / 113 g), patted dry and sliced
- ¼ cup lightly packed fresh basil leaves, torn into small pieces
- ¼ teaspoon freshly ground black pepper

1. Preheat the broiler to high with the rack 4 inches under the heating element. 2. Place the sliced bread on a large, rimmed baking sheet. Place under the broiler for 1 minute, until the bread is just lightly toasted. Remove from the oven. 3. Brush each piece of the toasted bread with the oil, and rub a garlic half over each piece. 4. Place the toasted bread back on the baking sheet. Evenly distribute the tomato slices on each piece, sprinkle with the oregano, and layer the cheese on top. 5. Place the baking sheet under the broiler. Set the timer for 1½ minutes, but check after 1 minute. When the cheese is melted and the edges are just starting to get dark brown, remove the sandwiches from the oven (this can take anywhere from 1½ to 2 minutes). 6. Top each sandwich with the fresh basil and pepper.

Per Serving:

calories: 176 | fat: 9g | protein: 10g | carbs: 14g | fiber: 2g | sodium: 119mg

Chapter 13 Pasta

Shrimp with Angel Hair Pasta

Prep time: 10 minutes | Cook time: 5 minutes | Serves 4

- 1 pound (454 g) dried angel hair pasta
- 2 tablespoons olive oil
- 3 garlic cloves, minced
- 1 pound (454 g) large shrimp, peeled and deveined
- Zest of ½ lemon
- ¼ cup chopped fresh Italian parsley
- ¼ teaspoon red pepper flakes (optional)

1. Fill a large stockpot three-quarters full with water and bring to a boil over high heat. Add the pasta and cook according to the package instructions until al dente, about 5 minutes. Drain the pasta and set aside. 2. In the same pot, heat the olive oil over medium heat. Add the garlic and sauté until fragrant, about 3 minutes. Add the shrimp and cook for about 2 minutes on each side, until pink and fully cooked. 3. Turn off the heat and return the pasta to the pot. Add the lemon zest and mix well. 4. Serve garnished with the parsley and red pepper flakes, if desired.

Per Serving:

calories: 567 | fat: 10g | protein: 31g | carbs: 87g | fiber: 4g | sodium: 651mg

Couscous with Crab and Lemon

Prep time: 10 minutes | Cook time: 7 minutes | Serves 4

- 1 cup couscous
- 1 clove garlic, peeled and minced
- 2 cups water
- 3 tablespoons extra-virgin olive oil, divided
- ¼ cup minced fresh flat-leaf parsley
- 1 tablespoon minced fresh
- dill
- 8 ounces (227 g) jumbo lump crabmeat
- 3 tablespoons lemon juice
- ½ teaspoon ground black pepper
- ¼ cup grated Parmesan cheese

1. Place couscous, garlic, water, and 1 tablespoon oil in the Instant Pot® and stir well. Close lid, set steam release to Sealing, press the Manual button, and set time to 7 minutes. When the timer beeps, let pressure release naturally for 10 minutes, then quick-release the remaining pressure and open lid. 2. Fluff couscous with a fork. Add parsley, dill, crabmeat, lemon juice, pepper, and remaining 2 tablespoons oil, and stir until combined. Top with cheese and serve immediately.

Per Serving:

calories: 360 | fat: 15g | protein: 22g | carbs: 34g | fiber: 2g | sodium: 388mg

Rotini with Red Wine Marinara

Prep time: 10 minutes | Cook time: 25 minutes | Serves 6

- 1 pound (454 g) rotini
- 4 cups water
- 1 tablespoon olive oil
- ½ medium yellow onion, peeled and diced
- 3 cloves garlic, peeled and minced
- 1 (15-ounce / 425-g) can
- crushed tomatoes
- ½ cup red wine
- 1 teaspoon sugar
- 2 tablespoons chopped fresh basil
- ½ teaspoon salt
- ¼ teaspoon ground black pepper

1. Add pasta and water to the Instant Pot®. Close lid, set steam release to Sealing, press the Manual button, and set time to 4 minutes. When the timer beeps, quick-release the pressure until the float valve drops and open the lid. Press the Cancel button. Drain pasta and set aside. 2. Clean pot and return to machine. Press the Sauté button and heat oil. Add onion and cook until it begins to caramelize, about 10 minutes. Add garlic and cook 30 seconds. Add tomatoes, red wine, and sugar, and simmer for 10 minutes. Add basil, salt, pepper, and pasta. Serve immediately.

Per Serving:

calories: 320 | fat: 4g | protein: 10g | carbs: 59g | fiber: 4g | sodium: 215mg

Tahini Soup

Prep time: 5 minutes | Cook time: 4 minutes | Serves 6

- 2 cups orzo
- 8 cups water
- 1 tablespoon olive oil
- 1 teaspoon salt
- ½ teaspoon ground black pepper
- ½ cup tahini
- ¼ cup lemon juice

1. Add pasta, water, oil, salt, and pepper to the Instant Pot®. Close lid, set steam release to Sealing, press the Manual button, and set time to 4 minutes. When the timer beeps, quick-release the pressure until the float valve drops, and open lid. Set aside. 2. Add tahini to a small mixing bowl and slowly add lemon juice while whisking constantly. Once lemon juice has been incorporated, take about ½ cup hot broth from the pot and slowly add to tahini mixture while whisking, until creamy smooth. 3. Pour mixture into the soup and mix well. Serve immediately.

Per Serving:

calories: 338 | fat: 13g | protein: 12g | carbs: 49g | fiber: 5g | sodium: 389mg

Creamy Spring Vegetable Linguine

Prep time: 10 minutes | Cook time: 10 minutes | Serves 4 to 6

- 1 pound (454 g) linguine
- 5 cups water, plus extra as needed
- 1 tablespoon extra-virgin olive oil
- 1 teaspoon table salt
- 1 cup jarred whole baby artichokes packed in water, quartered
- 1 cup frozen peas, thawed
- 4 ounces (113 g) finely grated Pecorino Romano (2 cups), plus extra for serving
- ½ teaspoon pepper
- 2 teaspoons grated lemon zest
- 2 tablespoons chopped fresh tarragon

1. Loosely wrap half of pasta in dish towel, then press bundle against corner of counter to break noodles into 6-inch lengths; repeat with remaining pasta. 2. Add pasta, water, oil, and salt to Instant Pot, making sure pasta is completely submerged. Lock lid in place and close pressure release valve. Select high pressure cook function and cook for 4 minutes. Turn off Instant Pot and quick-release pressure. Carefully remove lid, allowing steam to escape away from you. 3. Stir artichokes and peas into pasta, cover, and let sit until heated through, about 3 minutes. Gently stir in Pecorino and pepper until cheese is melted and fully combined, 1 to 2 minutes. Adjust consistency with extra hot water as needed. Stir in lemon zest and tarragon, and season with salt and pepper to taste. Serve, passing extra Pecorino separately.

Per Serving:

calories: 390 | fat: 8g | protein: 17g | carbs: 59g | fiber: 4g | sodium: 680mg

Pasta Salad with Tomato, Arugula, and Feta

Prep time: 10 minutes | Cook time: 4 minutes | Serves 8

- 1 pound (454 g) rotini
- 4 cups water
- 3 tablespoons extra-virgin olive oil, divided
- 2 medium Roma tomatoes, diced
- 2 cloves garlic, peeled and minced
- 1 medium red bell pepper,
- seeded and diced
- 2 tablespoons white wine vinegar
- 5 ounces (142 g) baby arugula
- 1 cup crumbled feta cheese
- ½ teaspoon salt
- ½ teaspoon ground black pepper

1. Add pasta, water, and 1 tablespoon oil to the Instant Pot®. Close lid, set steam release to Sealing, press the Manual button, and set time to 4 minutes. When the timer beeps, quick-release the pressure until the float valve drops, open lid, drain pasta, then rinse with cold water. Set aside. 2. In a large bowl, mix remaining 2 tablespoons oil, tomatoes, garlic, bell pepper, vinegar, arugula, and cheese. Stir in pasta and season with salt and pepper. Cover and refrigerate for 2 hours before serving.

Per Serving:

calories: 332 | fat: 12g | protein: 12g | carbs: 44g | fiber: 3g | sodium: 480mg

Couscous with Tomatoes and Olives

Prep time: 5 minutes | Cook time: 3 minutes | Serves 4

- 1 tablespoon tomato paste
- 2 cups vegetable broth
- 1 cup couscous
- 1 cup halved cherry tomatoes
- ½ cup halved mixed olives
- ¼ cup minced fresh flat-leaf parsley
- 2 tablespoons minced fresh
- oregano
- 2 tablespoons minced fresh chives
- 1 tablespoon extra-virgin olive oil
- 1 tablespoon red wine vinegar
- ½ teaspoon ground black pepper

1. Pour tomato paste and broth into the Instant Pot® and stir until completely dissolved. Stir in couscous. Close lid, set steam release to Sealing, press the Manual button, and set time to 3 minutes. When the timer beeps, let pressure release naturally for 10 minutes, then quick-release the remaining pressure and open lid. 2. Fluff couscous with a fork. Add tomatoes, olives, parsley, oregano, chives, oil, vinegar, and pepper, and stir until combined. Serve warm or at room temperature.

Per Serving:

calories: 232 | fat: 5g | protein: 7g | carbs: 37g | fiber: 2g | sodium: 513mg

Rotini with Spinach, Cherry Tomatoes, and Feta

Prep time: 5 minutes | Cook time: 30 minutes | Serves 2

- 6 ounces (170 g) uncooked rotini pasta (penne pasta will also work)
- 1 garlic clove, minced
- 3 tablespoons extra virgin olive oil, divided
- 1½ cups cherry tomatoes, halved and divided
- 9 ounces (255 g) baby leaf spinach, washed and chopped
- 1½ ounces (43 g) crumbled feta, divided
- Kosher salt, to taste
- Freshly ground black pepper, to taste

1. Cook the pasta according to the package instructions, reserving ½ cup of the cooking water. Drain and set aside. 2. While the pasta is cooking, combine the garlic with 2 tablespoons of the olive oil in a small bowl. Set aside. 3. Add the remaining tablespoon of olive oil to a medium pan placed over medium heat and then add 1 cup of the tomatoes. Cook for 2 to 3 minutes, then use a fork to mash lightly. 4. Add the spinach to the pan and continue cooking, stirring occasionally, until the spinach is wilted and the liquid is absorbed, about 4 to 5 minutes. 5. Transfer the cooked pasta to the pan with the spinach and tomatoes. Add 3 tablespoons of the pasta water, the garlic and olive oil mixture, and 1 ounce (28 g) of the crumbled feta. Increase the heat to high and cook for 1 minute. 6. Top with the remaining cherry tomatoes and feta, and season to taste with kosher salt and black pepper. Store covered in the refrigerator for up to 2 days.

Per Serving:

calories: 602 | fat: 27g | protein: 19g | carbs: 74g | fiber: 7g | sodium: 307mg

Creamy Chicken Pasta

Prep time: 10 minutes | Cook time: 4 to 6 hours | Serves 4

- ¼ cup water
- 2 tablespoons arrowroot flour
- 2 pounds (907 g) boneless, skinless chicken breasts or thighs
- 1 (28-ounce / 794-g) can no-salt-added diced tomatoes, plus more as needed
- 1 green or red bell pepper, seeded and diced
- 1 small red onion, diced
- 2 garlic cloves, minced
- 1 teaspoon dried oregano
- 1 teaspoon dried parsley
- 1 teaspoon sea salt
- ½ teaspoon freshly ground black pepper
- 8 ounces (227 g) dried pasta
- 1 cup low-sodium chicken broth (optional)

1. In a small bowl, whisk together the water and arrowroot flour until the flour dissolves. 2. In a slow cooker, combine the chicken, tomatoes, bell pepper, onion, garlic, oregano, parsley, salt, black pepper, and arrowroot mixture. Stir to mix well. 3. Cover the cooker and cook for 4 to 6 hours on Low heat. 4. Stir in the pasta, making sure it is completely submerged. If it is not, add an additional 1 cup of diced tomatoes or 1 cup of chicken broth. Replace the cover on the cooker and cook for 15 to 30 minutes on Low heat, or until the pasta is tender.

Per Serving:

calories: 555 | fat: 12g | protein: 52g | carbs: 61g | fiber: 11g | sodium: 623mg

Fresh Tomato Pasta Bowl

Prep time: 10 minutes | Cook time: 15 minutes | Serves 4

- 8 ounces (227 g) whole-grain linguine
- 1 tablespoon extra-virgin olive oil
- 2 garlic cloves, minced
- ¼ cup chopped yellow onion
- 1 teaspoon chopped fresh oregano
- ½ teaspoon salt
- ¼ teaspoon freshly ground black pepper
- 1 teaspoon tomato paste
- 8 ounces (227 g) cherry tomatoes, halved
- ½ cup grated Parmesan cheese
- 1 tablespoon chopped fresh parsley

1. Bring a large saucepan of water to a boil over high heat and cook the linguine according to the package instructions until al dente (still slightly firm). Drain, reserving ½ cup of the pasta water. Do not rinse the pasta. 2. In a large, heavy skillet, heat the olive oil over medium-high heat. Sauté the garlic, onion, and oregano until the onion is just translucent, about 5 minutes. 3. Add the salt, pepper, tomato paste, and ¼ cup of the reserved pasta water. Stir well and allow it to cook for 1 minute. 4. Stir in the tomatoes and cooked pasta, tossing everything well to coat. Add more pasta water if needed. 5. To serve, mound the pasta in shallow bowls and top with Parmesan cheese and parsley.

Per Serving:

calories: 310 | fat: 9g | protein: 10g | carbs: 49g | fiber: 7g | sodium: 305mg

Pasta with Marinated Artichokes and Spinach

Prep time: 10 minutes | Cook time: 5 minutes | Serves 6

- 1 pound (454 g) whole-wheat spaghetti, broken in half
- 3½ cups water
- 4 tablespoons extra-virgin olive oil, divided
- ¼ teaspoon salt
- 2 cups baby spinach
- 1 cup drained marinated
- artichoke hearts
- 2 tablespoons chopped fresh oregano
- 2 tablespoons chopped fresh flat-leaf parsley
- 1 teaspoon ground black pepper
- ½ cup grated Parmesan cheese

1. Add pasta, water, 2 tablespoons oil, and salt to the Instant Pot®. Close lid, set steam release to Sealing, press the Manual button, and set time to 5 minutes. 2. When the timer beeps, quick-release the pressure until the float valve drops and open lid. Drain off any excess liquid. Stir in remaining 2 tablespoons oil and spinach. Toss until spinach is wilted. Stir in artichokes, oregano, and parsley until well mixed. Sprinkle with pepper and cheese, and serve immediately.

Per Serving:

calories: 414 | fat: 16g | protein: 16g | carbs: 56g | fiber: 9g | sodium: 467mg

Pasta with Chickpeas and Cabbage

Prep time: 20 minutes | Cook time: 30 minutes | Serves 8

- 1 pound (454 g) rotini pasta
- 8 cups water, divided
- 2 tablespoons olive oil, divided
- 1 stalk celery, thinly sliced
- 1 medium red onion, peeled and sliced
- 1 small head savoy cabbage, cored and shredded
- ⅔ cup dried chickpeas,
- soaked overnight and drained
- 8 ounces (227 g) button mushrooms, sliced
- ½ teaspoon salt
- ¾ teaspoon ground black pepper
- ½ cup grated Pecorino Romano cheese

1. Add pasta, 4 cups water, and 1 tablespoon oil to the Instant Pot®. Close lid, set steam release to Sealing, press the Manual button, and set time to 4 minutes. When the timer beeps, quick-release the pressure until the float valve drops, open lid, and drain pasta. Press the Cancel button. Set aside. 2. Press the Sauté button and heat remaining 1 tablespoon oil. Add celery and onion, and cook until just tender, about 4 minutes. Stir in cabbage and cook until wilted, about 2 minutes. Add chickpeas, mushrooms, and remaining 4 cups water. Stir well, then press the Cancel button. 3. Close lid, set steam release to Sealing, press the Manual button, and set time to 20 minutes. When the timer beeps, let pressure release naturally, about 25 minutes. 4. Open lid and stir well. Season with salt and pepper. Use a fork to mash some of the chickpeas to thicken sauce. Pour sauce over pasta and top with cheese. Serve hot.

Per Serving:

calories: 301 | fat: 5g | protein: 9g | carbs: 49g | fiber: 3g | sodium: 207mg

Simple Pesto Pasta

Prep time: 10 minutes | Cook time: 10 minutes | Serves 4 to 6

◀ 1 pound (454 g) spaghetti
◀ 4 cups fresh basil leaves, stems removed
◀ 3 cloves garlic
◀ 1 teaspoon salt
◀ ½ teaspoon freshly ground
◀ black pepper
◀ ¼ cup lemon juice
◀ ½ cup pine nuts, toasted
◀ ½ cup grated Parmesan cheese
◀ 1 cup extra-virgin olive oil

1. Bring a large pot of salted water to a boil. Add the spaghetti to the pot and cook for 8 minutes. 2. Put basil, garlic, salt, pepper, lemon juice, pine nuts, and Parmesan cheese in a food processor bowl with chopping blade and purée. 3. While the processor is running, slowly drizzle the olive oil through the top opening. Process until all the olive oil has been added. 4. Reserve ½ cup of the pasta water. Drain the pasta and put it into a bowl. Immediately add the pesto and pasta water to the pasta and toss everything together. Serve warm.

Per Serving:

calories: 1067 | fat: 72g | protein: 23g | carbs: 91g | fiber: 6g | sodium: 817mg

Puglia-Style Pasta with Broccoli Sauce

Prep time: 15 minutes | Cook time: 25 minutes | Serves 3

◀ 1 pound (454 g) fresh broccoli, washed and cut into small florets
◀ 7 ounces (198 g) uncooked rigatoni pasta
◀ 2 tablespoons extra virgin olive oil, plus 1½ tablespoons for serving
◀ 3 garlic cloves, thinly sliced
◀ 2 tablespoons pine nuts
◀ 4 canned packed-in-oil anchovies
◀ ½ teaspoon kosher salt
◀ 3 teaspoons fresh lemon juice
◀ 3 ounces (85 g) grated or shaved Parmesan cheese, divided
◀ ½ teaspoon freshly ground black pepper

1. Place the broccoli in a large pot filled with enough water to cover the broccoli. Bring the pot to a boil and cook for 12 minutes or until the stems can be easily pierced with a fork. Use a slotted spoon to transfer the broccoli to a plate, but do not discard the cooking water. Set the broccoli aside. 2. Add the pasta to the pot with the broccoli water and cook according to package instructions. 3. About 3 minutes before the pasta is ready, place a large, deep pan over medium heat and add 2 tablespoons of the olive oil. When the olive oil is shimmering, add the garlic and sauté for 1 minute, stirring continuously, until the garlic is golden, then add the pine nuts and continue sautéing for 1 more minute. 4. Stir in the anchovies, using a wooden spoon to break them into smaller pieces, then add the broccoli. Continue cooking for 1 additional minute, stirring continuously and using the spoon to break the broccoli into smaller pieces. 5. When the pasta is ready, remove the pot from the heat and drain, reserving ¼ cup of the cooking water. 6. Add the pasta and 2 tablespoons of the cooking water to the pan, stirring until all the ingredients are well combined. Cook for 1 minute, then remove the pan from the heat. 7. Promptly divide the pasta among three plates. Top each serving with a pinch of kosher salt, 1 teaspoon of the lemon juice, 1 ounce (28 g) of the Parmesan, 1½ teaspoons of the remaining olive oil, and a pinch of fresh ground pepper. Store covered in the refrigerator for up to 3 days.

Per Serving:

calories: 610 | fat: 31g | protein: 24g | carbs: 66g | fiber: 12g | sodium: 654mg

Meaty Baked Penne

Prep time: 10 minutes | Cook time: 40 minutes | Serves 8

◀ 1 pound (454 g) penne pasta
◀ 1 pound (454 g) ground beef
◀ 1 teaspoon salt
◀ 1 (25-ounce / 709-g) jar marinara sauce
◀ 1 (1-pound / 454-g) bag baby spinach, washed
◀ 3 cups shredded mozzarella cheese, divided

1. Bring a large pot of salted water to a boil, add the penne, and cook for 7 minutes. Reserve 2 cups of the pasta water and drain the pasta. 2. Preheat the oven to 350°F(180ºC). 3. In a large saucepan over medium heat, cook the ground beef and salt. Brown the ground beef for about 5 minutes. 4. Stir in marinara sauce, and 2 cups of pasta water. Let simmer for 5 minutes. 5. Add a handful of spinach at a time into the sauce, and cook for another 3 minutes. 6. To assemble, in a 9-by-13-inch baking dish, add the pasta and pour the pasta sauce over it. Stir in 1½ cups of the mozzarella cheese. Cover the dish with foil and bake for 20 minutes. 7. After 20 minutes, remove the foil, top with the rest of the mozzarella, and bake for another 10 minutes. Serve warm.

Per Serving:

calories: 454 | fat: 13g | protein: 31g | carbs: 55g | fiber: 9g | sodium: 408mg

Avgolemono

Prep time: 10 minutes | Cook time: 3 minutes | Serves 6

◀ 6 cups chicken stock
◀ ½ cup orzo
◀ 1 tablespoon olive oil
◀ 12 ounces (340 g) cooked chicken breast, shredded
◀ ½ teaspoon salt
◀ ½ teaspoon ground black
◀ pepper
◀ ¼ cup lemon juice
◀ 2 large eggs
◀ 2 tablespoons chopped fresh dill
◀ 1 tablespoon chopped fresh flat-leaf parsley

1. Add stock, orzo, and olive oil to the Instant Pot®. Close lid, set steam release to Sealing, press the Manual button, and set time to 3 minutes. When the timer beeps, quick-release the pressure until the float valve drops. Open lid and stir in chicken, salt, and pepper. 2. In a medium bowl, combine lemon juice and eggs, then slowly whisk in hot cooking liquid from the pot, ¼ cup at a time, until 1 cup of liquid has been added. Immediately add egg mixture to soup and stir well. Let stand on the Keep Warm setting, stirring occasionally, for 10 minutes. Add dill and parsley. Serve immediately.

Per Serving:

calories: 193 | fat: 5g | protein: 21g | carbs: 15g | fiber: 1g | sodium: 552mg

Toasted Orzo Salad

Prep time: 15 minutes | Cook time: 8 minutes | Serves 6

- 2 tablespoons light olive oil
- 1 clove garlic, peeled and crushed
- 2 cups orzo
- 3 cups vegetable broth
- ½ cup sliced black olives
- 3 scallions, thinly sliced
- 1 medium Roma tomato, seeded and diced
- 1 medium red bell pepper,
- seeded and diced
- ¼ cup crumbled feta cheese
- 1 tablespoon extra-virgin olive oil
- 1 tablespoon red wine vinegar
- ½ teaspoon ground black pepper
- ¼ teaspoon salt

1. Press the Sauté button on the Instant Pot® and heat light olive oil. Add garlic and orzo and cook, stirring frequently, until orzo is light golden brown, about 5 minutes. Press the Cancel button. 2. Add broth and stir. Close lid, set steam release to Sealing, press the Manual button, and set time to 3 minutes. When the timer beeps, let pressure release naturally for 5 minutes, then quick-release the remaining pressure until the float valve drops and open lid. 3. Transfer orzo to a medium bowl, then set aside to cool to room temperature, about 30 minutes. Add olives, scallions, tomato, bell pepper, feta, extra-virgin olive oil, vinegar, black pepper, and salt, and stir until combined. Serve at room temperature or refrigerate for at least 2 hours.

Per Serving:

calories: 120 | fat: 4g | protein: 4g | carbs: 17g | fiber: 1g | sodium: 586mg

Whole-Wheat Capellini with Sardines, Olives, and Manchego

Prep time: 5 minutes | Cook time: 15 minutes | Serves 4

- 1 (7-ounce / 198-g) jar Spanish sardines in olive oil, chopped (reserve the oil)
- 1 medium onion, diced
- 4 cloves garlic, minced
- 2 medium tomatoes, sliced
- 1 pound (454 g) whole-
- wheat capellini pasta, cooked according to package instructions
- 1 cup pitted, chopped cured black olives, such as Kalamata
- 3 ounces (85 g) freshly grated manchego cheese

1. Heat the olive oil from the sardines in a large skillet over medium-high heat. Add the onion and garlic and cook, stirring frequently, until softened, about 5 minutes. Add the tomatoes and sardines and cook, stirring, 2 minutes more. 2. Add the cooked and drained pasta to the skillet with the sauce and toss to combine. 3. Stir in the olives and serve immediately, topped with the grated cheese.

Per Serving:

calories: 307 | fat: 11g | protein: 8g | carbs: 38g | fiber: 6g | sodium: 433mg

Quick Shrimp Fettuccine

Prep time: 10 minutes | Cook time: 10 minutes | Serves 4 to 6

- 8 ounces (227 g) fettuccine pasta
- ¼ cup extra-virgin olive oil
- 3 tablespoons garlic, minced
- 1 pound (454 g) large shrimp (21-25), peeled and
- deveined
- ⅓ cup lemon juice
- 1 tablespoon lemon zest
- ½ teaspoon salt
- ½ teaspoon freshly ground black pepper

1. Bring a large pot of salted water to a boil. Add the fettuccine and cook for 8 minutes. 2. In a large saucepan over medium heat, cook the olive oil and garlic for 1 minute. 3. Add the shrimp to the saucepan and cook for 3 minutes on each side. Remove the shrimp from the pan and set aside. 4. Add the lemon juice and lemon zest to the saucepan, along with the salt and pepper. 5. Reserve ½ cup of the pasta water and drain the pasta. 6. Add the pasta water to the saucepan with the lemon juice and zest and stir everything together. Add the pasta and toss together to evenly coat the pasta. Transfer the pasta to a serving dish and top with the cooked shrimp. Serve warm.

Per Serving:

calories: 615 | fat: 17g | protein: 33g | carbs: 89g | fiber: 4g | sodium: 407mg

Fettuccine with Tomatoes and Pesto

Prep time: 15 minutes | Cook time: 10 minutes | Serves 4

- 1 pound (454 g) whole-grain fettuccine
- 4 Roma tomatoes, diced
- 2 teaspoons tomato paste
- 1 cup vegetable broth
- 2 garlic cloves, minced
- 1 tablespoon chopped fresh oregano
- ½ teaspoon salt
- 1 packed cup fresh basil leaves
- ¼ cup extra-virgin olive oil
- ¼ cup grated Parmesan cheese
- ¼ cup pine nuts

1. Bring a large stockpot of water to a boil over high heat, and cook the fettuccine according to the package instructions until al dente (still slightly firm). Drain but do not rinse. 2. Meanwhile, in a large, heavy skillet, combine the tomatoes, tomato paste, broth, garlic, oregano, and salt and stir well. Cook over medium heat for 10 minutes. 3. In a blender or food processor, combine the basil, olive oil, Parmesan cheese, and pine nuts and blend until smooth. 4. Stir the pesto into the tomato mixture. Add the pasta and cook, stirring frequently, just until the pasta is well coated and heated through. 5. Serve immediately.

Per Serving:

calories: 636 | fat: 22g | protein: 11g | carbs: 96g | fiber: 3g | sodium: 741mg

Chapter 14 Staples, Sauces, Dips, and Dressings

Tahini Dressing

Prep time: 5 minutes | Cook time: 0 minutes | Serves 8 to 10

◄ ½ cup tahini
◄ ¼ cup freshly squeezed lemon juice (about 2 to 3 lemons)

◄ ¼ cup extra-virgin olive oil
◄ 1 garlic clove, finely minced or ½ teaspoon garlic powder
◄ 2 teaspoons salt

1. In a glass mason jar with a lid, combine the tahini, lemon juice, olive oil, garlic, and salt. Cover and shake well until combined and creamy. Store in the refrigerator for up to 2 weeks.

Per Serving:

calories: 121 | fat: 12g | protein: 2g | carbs: 3g | fiber: 1g | sodium: 479mg

Skinny Cider Dressing

Prep time: 5 minutes | Cook time: 0 minutes | Serves 2

◄ 2 tablespoons apple cider vinegar
◄ ⅓ lemon, juiced

◄ ⅓ lemon, zested
◄ Salt
◄ Freshly ground black pepper

1. In a jar, combine the vinegar, lemon juice, and zest. Season with salt and pepper, cover, and shake well.

Per Serving:

calories: 2 | fat: 0g | protein: 0g | carbs: 1g | fiber: 0g | sodium: 0mg

Kidney Bean Dip with Cilantro, Cumin, and Lime

Prep time: 10 minutes | Cook time: 30 minutes | Serves 16

◄ 1 cup dried kidney beans, soaked overnight and drained
◄ 4 cups water
◄ 3 cloves garlic, peeled and crushed
◄ ¼ cup roughly chopped

cilantro, divided
◄ ¼ cup extra-virgin olive oil
◄ 1 tablespoon lime juice
◄ 2 teaspoons grated lime zest
◄ 1 teaspoon ground cumin
◄ ½ teaspoon salt

1. Place beans, water, garlic, and 2 tablespoons cilantro in the

Instant Pot®. Close the lid, set steam release to Sealing, press the Bean button, and cook for the default time of 30 minutes. 2. When the timer beeps, let pressure release naturally, about 20 minutes. Press the Cancel button, open lid, and check that beans are tender. Drain off excess water and transfer beans to a medium bowl. Gently mash beans with potato masher or fork until beans are mashed but chunky. Add oil, lime juice, lime zest, cumin, salt, and remaining 2 tablespoons cilantro and stir to combine. Serve warm or at room temperature.

Per Serving:

calories: 65 | fat: 3g | protein: 2g | carbs: 7g | fiber: 2g | sodium: 75mg

Apple Cider Dressing

Prep time: 5 minutes | Cook time: 0 minutes | Serves 2

◄ 2 tablespoons apple cider vinegar
◄ ⅓ lemon, juiced

◄ ⅓ lemon, zested
◄ Salt and freshly ground black pepper, to taste

1. In a jar, combine the vinegar, lemon juice, and zest. Season with salt and pepper, cover, and shake well.

Per Serving:

calories: 7 | fat: 0g | protein: 0g | carbs: 1g | fiber: 0g | sodium: 1mg

Yogurt Tahini Dressing

Prep time: 5 minutes | Cook time: 0 minutes | Makes 1 cup

◄ ½ cup plain Greek yogurt
◄ ⅓ cup tahini
◄ ¼ cup freshly squeezed

orange juice
◄ ½ teaspoon kosher salt

1. In a medium bowl, whisk together the yogurt, tahini, orange juice, and salt until smooth. Place in the refrigerator until ready to serve. Store leftovers in an airtight container in the refrigerator for up to 5 days.

Per Serving:

2 tablespoons: calories: 70 | fat: 2g | protein: 4g | carbs: 4g | fiber: 1g | sodium: 80mg

Crunchy Yogurt Dip

Prep time: 5 minutes | Cook time: 0 minutes | Serves 2 to 3

- 1 cup plain, unsweetened, full-fat Greek yogurt
- ½ cup cucumber, peeled, seeded, and diced
- 1 tablespoon freshly squeezed lemon juice
- 1 tablespoon chopped fresh mint
- 1 small garlic clove, minced
- Salt
- Freshly ground black pepper

1. In a food processor, combine the yogurt, cucumber, lemon juice, mint, and garlic. Pulse several times to combine, leaving noticeable cucumber chunks. 2. Taste and season with salt and pepper.

Per Serving:

calories: 128 | fat: 6g | protein: 11g | carbs: 7g | fiber: 0g | sodium: 47mg

Piri Piri Sauce

Prep time: 5 minutes | Cook time: 0 minutes | Makes about 1 cup

- 4 to 8 fresh hot, red chiles, stemmed and coarsely chopped
- 2 cloves garlic, minced
- Juice of 1 lemon
- Pinch of salt
- ½ to 1 cup olive oil

1. In a food processor, combine the chiles (with their seeds), garlic, lemon juice, salt, and ½ cup of olive oil. Process to a smooth purée. Add additional oil as needed to reach the desired consistency. 2. Pour the mixture into a glass jar or non-reactive bowl, cover, and refrigerate for at least 3 days before using. Store in the refrigerator for up to a month.

Per Serving:

calories:84 | fat: 10g | protein: 0g | carbs: 0g | fiber: 0g | sodium: 13mg

Sherry Vinaigrette

Prep time: 5 minutes | Cook time: 0 minutes | Makes about ¾ cup

- ⅓ cup sherry vinegar
- 1 clove garlic
- 2 teaspoons dried oregano
- 1 teaspoon salt
- ½ teaspoon freshly ground black pepper
- ½ cup olive oil

1. In a food processor or blender, combine the vinegar, garlic, oregano, salt, and pepper and process until the garlic is minced and the ingredients are well combined. With the food processor running, add the olive oil in a thin stream until it is well incorporated. Serve immediately or store, covered, in the refrigerator for up to a week.

Per Serving:

calories: 74 | fat: 8g | protein: 0g | carbs: 0g | fiber: 0g | sodium: 194mg

Tomatillo Salsa

Prep time: 5 minutes | Cook time: 15 minutes | Serves 4

- 12 tomatillos
- 2 fresh serrano chiles
- 1 tablespoon minced garlic
- 1 cup chopped fresh cilantro
- leaves
- 1 tablespoon vegetable oil
- 1 teaspoon kosher salt

1. Remove and discard the papery husks from the tomatillos and rinse them under warm running water to remove the sticky coating. 2. Place the tomatillos and peppers in a baking pan. Place the pan in the air fryer basket. Air fry at 350ºF (177ºC) for 15 minutes. 3. Transfer the tomatillos and peppers to a blender, add the garlic, cilantro, vegetable oil, and salt, and blend until almost smooth. (If not using immediately, omit the salt and add it just before serving.) 4. Serve or store in an airtight container in the refrigerator for up to 10 days.

Per Serving:

calories: 68 | fat: 4g | protein: 1g | carbs: 7g | fiber: 2g | sodium: 585mg

Parsley-Mint Sauce

Prep time: 5 minutes | Cook time: 0 minutes | Serves 6

- ½ cup fresh flat-leaf parsley
- 1 cup fresh mint leaves
- 2 garlic cloves, minced
- 2 scallions (green onions), chopped
- 2 tablespoons pomegranate molasses
- ¼ cup olive oil
- 1 tablespoon fresh lemon juice

1. Combine all the ingredients in a blender and blend until smooth. Transfer to an airtight container and refrigerate until ready to use. Can be refrigerated for 1 day.

Per Serving:

calories: 90 | fat: 9g | protein: 1g | carbs: 2g | fiber: 0g | sodium: 5mg

Lemon Tahini Dressing

Prep time: 5 minutes | Cook time: 0 minutes | Makes ½ cup

- ¼ cup tahini
- 3 tablespoons lemon juice
- 3 tablespoons warm water
- ¼ teaspoon kosher salt
- ¼ teaspoon pure maple syrup
- ¼ teaspoon ground cumin
- ⅛ teaspoon cayenne pepper

1. In a medium bowl, whisk together the tahini, lemon juice, water, salt, maple syrup, cumin, and cayenne pepper until smooth. Place in the refrigerator until ready to serve. Store any leftovers in the refrigerator in an airtight container up to 5 days.

Per Serving:

2 tablespoons: calories: 90 | fat: 7g | protein: 3g | carbs: 5g | fiber: 1g | sodium: 80mg

Zucchini Noodles

Prep time: 5 minutes | Cook time: 0 minutes | Serves 4

◄ 2 medium to large zucchini

1. Cut off and discard the ends of each zucchini and, using a spiralizer set to the smallest setting, spiralize the zucchini to create zoodles.
2. To serve, simply place a ½ cup or so of spiralized zucchini into the bottom of each bowl and spoon a hot sauce over top to "cook" the zoodles to al dente consistency. Use with any of your favorite sauces, or just toss with warmed pesto for a simple and quick meal.

Per Serving:

calories: 27 | fat: 1g | protein: 2g | carbs: 5g | fiber: 2g | sodium: 13mg

Olive Tapenade

Prep time: 10 minutes | Cook time: 0 minutes | Makes about 1 cup

◄ ¾ cup pitted brine-cured green or black olives, chopped fine
◄ 1 small shallot, minced
◄ 2 tablespoons extra-virgin olive oil

◄ 1 tablespoon capers, rinsed and minced
◄ 1½ teaspoons red wine vinegar
◄ 1 teaspoon minced fresh oregano

1. Combine all ingredients in bowl. (Tapenade can be refrigerated for up to 1 week.)

Per Serving:

¼ cup: calories: 92 | fat: 9g | protein: 0g | carbs: 2g | fiber: 1g | sodium: 236mg

Arugula and Walnut Pesto

Prep time: 5 minutes | Cook time: 0 minutes | Serves 8 to 10

◄ 6 cups packed arugula
◄ 1 cup chopped walnuts
◄ ½ cup shredded Parmesan cheese

◄ 2 garlic cloves, peeled
◄ ½ teaspoon salt
◄ 1 cup extra-virgin olive oil

1. In a food processor, combine the arugula, walnuts, cheese, and garlic and process until very finely chopped. Add the salt. With the processor running, stream in the olive oil until well blended. 2. If the mixture seems too thick, add warm water, 1 tablespoon at a time, until smooth and creamy. Store in a sealed container in the refrigerator.

Per Serving:

calories: 292 | fat: 31g | protein: 4g | carbs: 3g | fiber: 1g | sodium: 210mg

Peanut Sauce

Prep time: 5 minutes | Cook time: 0 minutes | Serves 4

◄ ⅓ cup peanut butter
◄ ¼ cup hot water
◄ 2 tablespoons soy sauce
◄ 2 tablespoons rice vinegar

◄ Juice of 1 lime
◄ 1 teaspoon minced fresh ginger
◄ 1 teaspoon minced garlic
◄ 1 teaspoon black pepper

1. In a blender container, combine the peanut butter, hot water, soy sauce, vinegar, lime juice, ginger, garlic, and pepper. Blend until smooth. 2. Use immediately or store in an airtight container in the refrigerator for a week or more.

Per Serving:

calories: 408 | fat: 33g | protein: 16g | carbs: 18g | fiber: 5g | sodium: 2525mg

Appendix 1: Measurement Conversion Chart

VOLUME EQUIVALENTS(DRY)

US STANDARD	METRIC (APPROXIMATE)
1/8 teaspoon	0.5 mL
1/4 teaspoon	1 mL
1/2 teaspoon	2 mL
3/4 teaspoon	4 mL
1 teaspoon	5 mL
1 tablespoon	15 mL
1/4 cup	59 mL
1/2 cup	118 mL
3/4 cup	177 mL
1 cup	235 mL
2 cups	475 mL
3 cups	700 mL
4 cups	1 L

VOLUME EQUIVALENTS(LIQUID)

US STANDARD	US STANDARD (OUNCES)	METRIC (APPROXIMATE)
2 tablespoons	1 fl.oz.	30 mL
1/4 cup	2 fl.oz.	60 mL
1/2 cup	4 fl.oz.	120 mL
1 cup	8 fl.oz.	240 mL
1 1/2 cup	12 fl.oz.	355 mL
2 cups or 1 pint	16 fl.oz.	475 mL
4 cups or 1 quart	32 fl.oz.	1 L
1 gallon	128 fl.oz.	4 L

TEMPERATURES EQUIVALENTS

FAHRENHEIT(F)	CELSIUS(C) (APPROXIMATE)
225 °F	107 °C
250 °F	120 °C
275 °F	135 °C
300 °F	150 °C
325 °F	160 °C
350 °F	180 °C
375 °F	190 °C
400 °F	205 °C
425 °F	220 °C
450 °F	235 °C
475 °F	245 °C
500 °F	260 °C

WEIGHT EQUIVALENTS

US STANDARD	METRIC (APPROXIMATE)
1 ounce	28 g
2 ounces	57 g
5 ounces	142 g
10 ounces	284 g
15 ounces	425 g
16 ounces (1 pound)	455 g
1.5 pounds	680 g
2 pounds	907 g

Appendix 2: The Dirty Dozen and Clean Fifteen

The Environmental Working Group (EWG) is a nonprofit, nonpartisan organization dedicated to protecting human health and the environment Its mission is to empower people to live healthier lives in a healthier environment. This organization publishes an annual list of the twelve kinds of produce, in sequence, that have the highest amount of pesticide residue-the Dirty Dozen-as well as a list of the fifteen kinds ofproduce that have the least amount of pesticide residue-the Clean Fifteen.

THE DIRTY DOZEN	THE CLEAN FIFTEEN
• The 2016 Dirty Dozen includes the following produce. These are considered among the year's most important produce to buy organic:	• The least critical to buy organically are the Clean Fifteen list. The following are on the 2016 list:

THE DIRTY DOZEN		THE CLEAN FIFTEEN	
Strawberries	Spinach	Avocados	Papayas
Apples	Tomatoes	Corn	Kiw
Nectarines	Bell peppers	Pineapples	Eggplant
Peaches	Cherry tomatoes	Cabbage	Honeydew
Celery	Cucumbers	Sweet peas	Grapefruit
Grapes	Kale/collard greens	Onions	Cantaloupe
Cherries	Hot peppers	Asparagus	Cauliflower
		Mangos	

• *The Dirty Dozen list contains two additional itemskale/collard greens and hot peppers-because they tend to contain trace levels of highly hazardous pesticides.*	• *Some of the sweet corn sold in the United States are made from genetically engineered (GE) seedstock. Buy organic varieties of these crops to avoid GE produce.*

Made in the USA
Las Vegas, NV
20 January 2025